No Way Back

No Way Back

A Personal History of Charismatic Renewal in the
New Zealand Anglican Church

Don Battley

No Way Back
Published by Don Battley
New Zealand

© 2019 Don Battley

ISBN 978-0-473-48791-1 (Softcover)
ISBN 978-0-473-48792-8 (ePUB)
ISBN 978-0-473-48793-5 (Kindle)

Production & Typesetting:
Andrew Killick
Castle Publishing Services
www.castlepublishing.co.nz

Cover design:
Paul Smith

Scriptures taken from
the Holy Bible, New International Version®, NIV®.
Copyright © 1973, 1978, 1984, 2011 by Biblica, Inc.™
Used by permission of Zondervan.
All rights reserved worldwide.

ALL RIGHTS RESERVED

No part of this publication may be reproduced,
stored in a retrieval system, or transmitted
in any form or by any means, electronic, mechanical,
photocopying, recording or otherwise,
without prior written permission from the author.

*In grateful thanks to God the Holy Spirit
who breathes Faith, Hope and Love
upon the Church in all generations
and to those brothers and sisters
who shared this exciting journey with me
over the last fifty years.*

Foreword

Don Battley has written a compelling story of his life and ministry within the wider context of the growth and development of the charismatic movement in the Anglican Church in New Zealand. This is a book which I predict you, like me, will want to read in one sitting. (I didn't quite succeed, but I tried!)

It is in every respect a partisan book. Don is deeply identified with the charismatic movement within the Anglican Church. In his story, we can see how deeply he invested in the spirituality and community that made up this evolving movement. Inevitably readers may find themselves on different sides in some of the issues that he explores.

And yet this is not just the story of one person's life and commitments. Don knows that he became part of a movement that was under way when he was baptised in the Spirit, and he recognises that the movement continues today after he has largely retired from it. Working from careful research into the wider story, and drawing carefully on the research of Allen Neil and Dale Williamson, he provides at last a published account, and one that synthesises earlier research while correcting and extending it. Don is a careful writer; I know from his earlier research that he wants to get details correct, and the manuscript of this autobiography was held up as he clarified broader aspects of the story he was part of. He has an eye for a clear narrative, and this book will be an invaluable starting point, that carefully conveys the story of a movement vastly greater in impact than some may care to acknowledge. Looking through the names of people mentioned, we can see that many significant leaders of the church were shaped by the Anglican charismatic movement.

It is a personal history, however, and people from out of Auckland are bound to notice that vigorous movements in other parts of the country are covered more briefly. This is Don's story, and he is most interesting when he tells his story and gives his perspective. At times I feel inclined to protest. At some points in the story I think he is too generous or too loyal when criticism seems called for. The Anglican Church surely was inexcusably discouraging to a movement within its own borders. Above all, the story seems hopeful and optimistic to the end, although surely the great age of the charismatic movement is gone and almost forgotten.

Yet in its essence this is a story of faith and experience. Don shines through as a person who with genuine uncertainty and longing, turns corners and finds faith and experience in God. He is not the classic Pentecostal; he is an accountant, a secretary, an organiser, but he along with his beloved wife Eleanor became people who saw a living and vibrant life that is bigger and richer than the confines of any organisation or denomination.

For all these reasons, I warmly commend this book.

Peter Lineham
Emeritus Professor of History
Massey University, Auckland

Contents

Introduction	11
1. Baptismal Waters *Personal Beginnings*	15
2. Faithful Springs *Training and First Parishes*	27
3. Rain in High Places *Dennis Bennett, Ken Prebble, Bishop Gowing*	37
4. Streams & Mountain Tarns *The First Auckland Renewal Parishes*	53
5. Fresh from the Fountain *Ray Muller and Christian Advance Ministries*	67
6. Rushing Streams *The Parish Renewal Movement*	77
7. Under the Waterfall *The Spirit Falls at Pakuranga*	89
8. No Way Back *Living in the Consequences*	111
9. Spreading Waters *Renewal Floods Auckland Diocese*	127
10. Joining the Streams *Developing Anglican Renewal Ministries*	145
11. Shooting the Rapids *Travelling the Country*	167

12. Running the River *Whanganui to the Vineyard*	181
13. Riding the Wave *The Growth of ARMNZ*	195
14. Uniting the Rivers *Affirming Orthodox Faith*	217
15. Beside the Lake *The Birth of Summer Wine*	239
16. Cascades from Toronto *The 'Toronto Blessing'*	245
17. Spreading Waters *Beside Two Lakes*	261
18. Where the Rivers Divide *Millennium Transitions*	271
19. The Ebbing Tide?	291
An Epilogue	303
Glossary of Abbreviations	305
Index of Topics	307
Index of Names	312

Introduction

'It's all your fault!' the Archdeacon said with a winsome smile. My fault? What was she thinking of? We had just been chatting about the challenges of her role as vicar to a new mission district in the Diocese of Auckland and now suddenly it was all *my* fault?

'Don't you remember,' she continued, 'how my husband and I came to you at Pakuranga in 1976 to ask about the spiritual experience that had so changed my sister's life? We came to ask if we could join your next Life in the Spirit Seminar and you said, "You don't need that. You look ready for it right now!" And you and Kerry took us into the church and prayed for us immediately. All this started back then.'[1]

Yes, I could just remember it. Another couple of enquirers, excited by a wave of spiritual renewal, bright-eyed and hungry, wanting the gift of the Holy Spirit in their lives. How many had there been? And strikingly, how many of them had grown into ministry? Here was yet another of those who found their confidence in God at that time and were now ministers and leaders in Christ's church.

This is one priest's story of how that movement of spiritual

---

1. The Archdeacon was the Venerable Marilyn Welch, Archdeacon of Manukau 1994-98, Missioner, Turanga Mission District 1991-98, Bishop's Chaplain for Pastoral Support, 1998-2011, Archdeacon of Hunua 2001-2011, and her husband Allan.

renewal, known generally as the charismatic movement, revitalised many New Zealanders in the 1960s and 1970s and still does today. It explores why it happened and what the results have been in the years that followed. It is not simply a story of highs and triumphs. There has been pain and even despair along this journey. There have been casualties as well as survivors. This is one survivor's story.

When the history of Christianity in the twentieth century is written one development that will stand out will be the consistent increase of Pentecostal or charismatic spirituality. In 2001 researcher David Barrett reported that around the world about 520 million believers could be classified as Pentecostal or charismatic Christians.[2] It is part of Pentecostal mythology that the baptism of the Spirit and the gift of tongues were restored to the church on the first of January 1900, thus marking the twentieth century as a particular period of restoration of the Pentecostal powers to Christianity. That belief ignores, however, the experiences of charismatic gifts in previous centuries amongst the Catholic Apostolics, the Quakers, some aspects of the Wesleyan revivals as well as the many reports of the charismata occurring amongst the Catholic saints. It also ignores the restoration of the ministry of healing amongst Anglicans in the nineteenth century.

Nevertheless the twentieth century has seen a remarkable development of Pentecostal spirituality, not just in the Pentecostal churches but also in the historic churches. In the first half of the

---

2. For convenience 'Pentecostal' will be used to refer to the Pentecostal denominations and 'charismatic' will usually refer to charismatics in the mainline or older denominations. The words are in fact interchangeable: Pentecostals consider themselves to be charismatic Christians while charismatics in the older churches can be called Pentecostals, e.g. see John Gunstone's book *Pentecostal Anglicans*. For statistics see *Global statistics for all religions: 2001 AD*. David Barrett et. al., World Christian Encyclopedia, 3rd ed.

twentieth century many who believed they had received a baptism of spiritual power and were experiencing charismatic gifts were caused to leave their churches or chose to do so. A common Pentecostal message of 'Come ye out from among them'[3] led to the formation of a number of Pentecostal churches. Starting with meagre resources other than their faith they raised up substantial new denominations throughout the world.

Since 1940 this pattern changed as increasing numbers of 'spirit-filled' people chose to remain in the older churches, often hearing the Lord tell them to do so. This change of attitude gave rise to what has been called the charismatic movement in those churches. The charismatic movement caused much joy and many tensions in those churches. Slowly but steadily, despite various forms of opposition and discouragement, the charismatic movements in the Anglican, Catholic, Presbyterian, Lutheran, Methodist, Baptist and other churches won a credible place for themselves and have wrought lasting changes in those churches.

This is the story of one couple's experience of that journey and of the learnings and decisions which reshaped the lives and ministries of many New Zealand Christians at that time.

---

3. Derived from Isaiah 52:11: 'Depart, depart, go out from there! Touch no unclean thing! Come out from it and be pure, you who carry the vessels of the Lord.'

– 1 –

Baptismal Waters
Personal Beginnings

I was born in February 1939, the long-awaited first child of Jack and Joyce Battley and was baptised a few months later in St Aidan's Remuera where my father had been raised and my parents had married. In the baptismal service of the Book of Common Prayer the priest asked God 'that this child may be baptised with the Holy Ghost'. According to my Anglican sacramental theology, that's where it all began.

My parents' first home was on the Winstone estate in Mt Roskill, a raw new 1930s suburb in west Auckland. They had built a pretty little house set further back from the road than most of the other houses – my parents aspired to better things even then. Apparently my maternal grandmother lived with us, most likely after the birth of my sister in 1942.

My two earliest memories are of my father driving my mother and sister home from the maternity home, the old 1924 Fiat coming down the descent of Winstone Road towards our home, and of going out with my mother in pouring rain to help pump out the wartime dugout in our back garden. While the Second World War never got anywhere near our Auckland suburb, in my childhood imagination it was as close as that cramped little dugout. Many years later my mother said to me, of the birth of my sister, 'You will never be able to imagine what it felt like to bring a child into the world at that time.'

Singapore had fallen in December 1941 and Darwin was bombed only a few days before she gave birth to my sister. At that time the Japanese drive into the South Pacific looked unstoppable. In 1943 my father was called into the army to train for coastal defence but after just seventy-seven days' service he was man-powered back to the company he worked for as accountant. The Japanese were by then in retreat and the accountant of margarine manufacturer Abels Ltd was more use ensuring the supply of food for the American forces. I have no recall of VE or VJ Day – perhaps we were not the celebratory kind – but the war and its aftermath, the nuclear threat, were to shape my life.

My parents were communicant Anglicans – neither ardent believers nor nominal ones. My father had been raised in a dedicated Anglican household to which his widowed mother had returned with her two young sons after my grandfather died accidentally in 1910. This was a classic late-Victorian Christian household, led by a redoubtable matriarch, a vicar's daughter known to us as 'Little Granny,' who lived surrounded by her unmarried adult children, her widowed daughter and her two grandsons in a nine-bedroom villa in Remuera. It must have been an unusual upbringing for the boys with a number of mother figures and two unmarried uncles as male role models. They worshipped regularly at St Aidan's Church though one of them, Aunt Dolly, I discovered much later, also attended a Pentecostal church. Dad had been quite committed to his church when young and was personal friends with young clergy like Martin Sullivan (who married them) and 'Jumbo' Rushworth who occasionally stayed with us when he visited Auckland.

My mother had been raised in the Congregational Church although her mother, Clara (Donna) Joslin, had been raised an Anglican. At Easter 1923 my mother and grandmother visited her family at Te Aroha where they attended the Anglican Easter service.

That was it for my mother – the music, the artistry, the dignity drew her and she became an Anglican by her own choice.

In 1944 we moved to a quite large house in Entrican Avenue in Remuera where my sister and I were raised. It was a secure and in some ways privileged upbringing. My life consisted of home, school, scouts and Sunday school, the latter two both at St Aidan's. I owe both of them a great deal. I was a compliant sort of boy and Sunday school, though crowded, was interesting with the hymns and stories. I had a short spell in the junior (pre-school) Sunday school behind the parish hall where one of the teachers was Maureen, daughter of the vicar, Canon Connelly. Such are the circles of grace that, forty years later, I found myself taking home communion to her and her invalid husband in Whanganui.

The main Sunday school was a boisterous affair with many classes jammed in between divider curtains around the hall and some on the stage and in its wings. It was led by Mr and Mrs Barnes, a vigorous evangelical couple. He was a big-built builder; she was a tiny, bright sparrow beside his imposing build. I have a vivid memory of one Sunday when they asked all of the children to raise a hand if we were sure we would go to heaven when we died. Few of us did, but they raised their hands firmly. I was horrified. How could these people be so sure they were living a good life, pleasing to God? My child's theology of rewards and punishments could not comprehend the truth of blessed assurance – that they knew in whom they believed and had faith in the completed work of the cross. That understanding lay many years in the future. I recall also a rather weary looking Baptist pastor teaching our Bible in School class the parable of the shepherd and the one lost sheep. Something of the heart of God and the promise and urgency of rescue became real to me that day.

At age fourteen we were told we were to be confirmed by the

bishop and a class of about seventy of us were assigned to confirmation classes about which I remember little except the image of a three-leaf clover for the Trinity, an image I have never found helpful in understanding such a complex truth. But I became aware that confirmation was a serious decision, on reflection probably the most significant decision I had had to make for myself. I recall puzzling about whether I really believed it or not and came to a two-fold conclusion, both of which I hold to still. First, that if these competent people around me sincerely believed it, I should trust it, and that if Jesus had not risen from the dead then Christianity was the greatest con ever worked on humankind. Not too bad a starting base for a fourteen-year-old.

So the big night came and it held a special threat for me. Around the age of seven I had started to stammer, despite having had excellent diction as a child – or maybe because of that. The starting cause has never been identified – school-ground bullying? tensions in the home? post-war stress? – who knows? My mother had a slight stutter so inheritance is a likely factor. At the confirmation, when my name was called I had to answer 'With the help of God I will.' Would it even come out? And it did! Loud and clear. Something was born in me that scary night – a hope that I could be normal and free with the implication that it could be in and through the church and its faith.

At the end of the service Bishop Simkin asked that all the boys meet him at the back of the church. We sat in the gallery at the back and he gave us a short talk about the need of the church for clergy (no women's ordination in those days!) and he concluded by saying in his curiously sonorous voice, 'And I am sure there is at least one young man sitting here who is called of God to the Sacred Ministry.' My young heart gave a distinct flip within me but I had no idea what it meant. There was no talk about 'witnesses of the Holy Spirit' in those days. Indeed, we had been specifically told not to expect anything to happen to us when the bishop laid his hands on us! Such low expectation surrounded us.

While many of those confirmed with me soon drifted away, I responded seriously and went, often by myself, to the 8.00am Communion service and walked home for breakfast – my parents forbad us to ride our bicycles on Sundays. Then after a year or two I was asked to teach a Sunday school class, for which I was totally unprepared, but having to swot the lesson up on Saturday night got me started in reading scripture and retelling what it said. Teaching Sunday school was quite an ordeal but I kept at it.

St Aidan's Scouts were also good for me. They taught me skills I used for many years – map-reading, first aid, camping, cooking and above all team work. It was an introduction to outdoor activities and self-confidence. My first experiences of leadership were as a patrol leader in scouts. And I took and passed the public speaking badge and proved again that I was actually a fluent speaker if I was not being subjected to anxiety. Church and scouts were introductions to a world wider than home and school. The learning aspects of school I always enjoyed.

But the spiritual development at church was quite slow mainly because that was how the leaders there, often young clergy, seemed to think it had to be done. Soft sell was the approach: 'Let's not be too religious or they will go away!' A youth group was formed where Bruce Gilberd (subsequently bishop of Auckland from 1985 to 1994) was chairman and I, typically, wound up as secretary. We had short studies or discussions at youth group at 5.00pm and some social time followed by evensong at 7.00pm.

The best part of it all was the sermons of our vicar Canon Austin Clelland Flowerday Charles. 'Uncle' Austin as we nicknamed him had been raised in the Brethren church before he became an Anglican and in retrospect I recall him as combining the best of both. He had a dynamic way of presenting the biblical stories and material – I still recall the impact of his telling of St Paul's ministry and ending with Paul's execution in Rome. Combined with this he offered the Prayer Book services in a way that reflected his background in amateur theatre.

I had discovered amateur theatricals, first through the Boy Scout Gang Show and then through the Auckland Grammar School Drama Club and ended up playing the lead role in a fast-moving Moliere comedy. I then directed some Christian plays which the youth group presented at St Aidan's including the Passion section of Dorothy Sayers' *Man Born to be King*. I received warm support from Austin Charles who was himself a recovered stammerer. He was an important role model for me though I also remember Auckland Grammar School speech and drama teacher Alan McSkimming with much gratitude. I was getting the victory on the speech front but had a long way to go spiritually.

Near the end of my sixth form year (Year 12) my father surprised me by telling me that they could only support me for one more year and I could choose between having a seventh form year at Grammar or having one year at university. I was flabbergasted. We had never discussed the future or what I might want to do in life. It seemed better to get the year at university but what to study? What career path was I interested in? With no one else to guide me I opted to do what my father did – accountancy.

So I wound up doing a Bachelor of Commerce degree with no clear idea of what I really wanted to do with my life. I did well enough at it – the family has a penchant for figures with accountants in the last four generations – grandfather Frederick Battley who ended his career as General Manager of the ill-fated NZ Loan and Mercantile Agency Company; his son Frank Battley who founded chartered accountants Battley and Johnston, and his daughter Ella Battley; and my father and his brother Cecil Battley. Cecil and Jack's mother Leila had also earned her living as a bookkeeper.

I had one full-time year at university doing stage one papers, then went to work with Robinson Sons and Strickett for a year where auditing bored me rigid, then a year with Howell and Walker doing tax accounting and then two years with paint manufacturer BALM Dulux as their costing clerk. By age twenty-one I had completed all papers for the B. Com and was admitted as a registered accountant (A.R.A.N.Z. as it was then). I was earning £1000 a year – the equivalent of at least $50,000 in today's money. Business was desperate for qualified staff and the world was my oyster. For a time I looked at doing an MBA at Harvard but the costs were far beyond me.

But deeper issues had been arising. Our dynamic assistant curate John Powell had impressed me and given me another view of a clergyman's role – that one could be enthusiastic, approachable and excited about ministry in the church. A number of students from St John's theological college used to drop into St Aidan's on Sunday nights and their lively behaviour surprised me. Only later did I realise their high spirits were a reaction to the cloistered world of the college. I particularly remember Cyril Cooze, Derek Grinder and Denis Mellsop impressing me.

To cap it off, Bruce Gilberd announced that he was going to train for ordination at St John's College. So this was where priests came from! They weren't old men who just appeared; they were young people who the church trained nearby. But I didn't like the idea that much. We knew they were poorly paid and seemed to work all hours of the week, and as for the funny costumes and collar – no thank you!

When Billy Graham came to the country for his 1959 series of crusades, Canon Charles was, as I recall, an Anglican representative on the inter-church committee that planned the Auckland crusade. Knowing what was to come, he arranged for the Anglican Church Army to send an evangelist to St Aidan's some weeks before the crusade to present the gospel to the youth group and to invite our response. I recall Captain Bert Sutcliffe very clearly and my fascination with his direct presentation of the gospel. Then he challenged us to respond to it by coming forward to the altar rail. A few of us went forward and I battled with myself in the pew. After a short while, with my young heart pounding, I went forward feeling quite uncertain really, prayed whatever prayer we were given and returned to my seat with the sense that I had done something important but I wasn't too sure quite what.

When we all went to Billy Graham's crusade meeting a few weeks later and people streamed forward in response to his invitation I remained sitting on the slope at Carlaw Park saying to myself, 'I don't need to do that. I have already done it in my parish church.' I wasn't avoiding the call. I was affirming that what I had done was real. My commitment to the gospel has grown steadily ever since 1959. I have had a soft spot for the Church Army and an active interest in primary evangelism ever since.

What clinched my change of vocation, however, was something quite different. The late 1950s were a time of vivid fear of the nuclear threat. In those days the Cold War kept threatening to become hot and the possibility of an actual exchange of nuclear weapons was widely feared. We have since become used to living with the dangers of nuclear weapons and nuclear power and have adjusted to the threats and possibly have become complacent about them. But back then it was a serious issue.

One night I went to see the film of Neville Shute's prescient book *On the Beach*. I exited the movie shocked to my core. The movie portrayed the likely effect upon Australia and, by implication New Zealand, of a radiation cloud from a nuclear exchange in the northern hemisphere. It was a portrayal of panic, catastrophe and hopelessness. My conclusion was that I couldn't spend my life counting other people's money when this sort of danger threatened us all. I had to find a way to help create a safer world. Concluding that this was above all an international political problem I first investigated service with the Department of External Affairs as I think it was called at the time. They were recruiting graduates to expand New Zealand's diplomatic service.

Then I began to see that the problem was even deeper than politics. It was the basic human problem of destructive attitudes – of fear and rivalry and guilt and competition and, above all, of ideology. It was a spiritual problem which needed a spiritual solution. By then Canon Charles had left the parish to work in Christian broadcasting and our new vicar was the Rev. Lionel Beere, a well-educated Irishman of gentle speech – usually delivered past a cloud of pipe smoke. He had been vicar of Ponsonby for many years during which time the award-winning All Saints Church, designed by Professor Toy, had been constructed. Lionel Beere had been an Anglican missionary in North Korea and had only just escaped from there when the Japanese invaded Korea. I still have the red silk chasuble that he brought out with him which he gave to me for my ordination as a priest.

So one night I asked to see him in his study and, trying to be very oblique, I asked him, 'How would a young man know if God was calling him to the sacred ministry?' No doubt he saw right through that one.

He quietly replied, 'I think God would do something special to convince him.' And the phone rang. 'Yes, my Lord,' he said; 'No, my Lord.' And then, 'There's a young man here who needs to speak with you' and he thrust the phone at me saying, 'It's the bishop. Make an appointment to see him.'

A few weeks later I had an interview with Bishop Eric Gowing and in about twenty minutes I was accepted for ordination training and had lost control of my life. Bishop Gowing attracted a wave of young men to the ordained ministry and most of them have given sound and lasting service.

Bishop Gowing made it plain to me that I would not be able to marry for four years – the three years in St John's Theological College and then one year as a deacon that would follow. That didn't seem to be a problem. My latest girlfriend had dropped me when she saw the way I was heading and I had no marriage plans. Then I had to tell my parents what I had done. Lionel Beere thought they would be okay with it.

My mother said she was not surprised at all. Apparently when she was having difficulty conceiving she made a Hannah bargain with God that if she conceived a boy she would give him back to God. Talk about being set up!

My father was more cautious and, probably concerned about the career prospects I was giving away, asked if I really wanted to spend all my life 'selling something people didn't want'. That never seems to have been a problem – there have always been more people wanting my services than I have had enough time for. When that did not deter me he made an excellent suggestion that, as I would never again have the money to travel overseas (in which he was totally mistaken), I should defer entry to college for a year and travel overseas. These days we would call it 'taking a gap year' but then it was known as 'doing one's OE' – the overseas experience. That I did like the sound of so I deferred my entry to St John's College and booked a trip to Europe starting the next May after my graduation.

Then the youth group were encouraged to attend an Ecumenical Youth Conference being held in Lower Hutt over New Year 1960/61 and I decided that, if I was to be ordained, I should attend that conference rather go tramping in the South Island with the University Tramping Club. By then I had acquired a Morris Minor car and I gave Denis Mellsop a lift down with me. Then it happened.

In the mess queue one day Denis introduced me to a stunning young woman he had known in the Student Christian Movement at Auckland, one Eleanor Nelson. Unknown to either of them, I had fallen in love with this aquiline beauty four years before in the Auckland University library and, shy lad that I was, had done nothing about it. And here she was! Right in front of me! Then she and her sister opened a letter telling them their cat had died and they burst into tears. I was smitten.

Our friendship grew quickly amid the stimulating environment of Philip Potter's dynamic bible teachings and the vision of a church modernised and re-united to make a safer world.

At the end of the conference Eleanor was heading off for a trip around the South Island. When she asked me to take some books back to Auckland for her I recognised a promising sign. She had to give me her address! Things were looking good.

After she got back she gave a report on the conference to the St Columba's youth group. She stood up in St Columba's hall, straight and confident, and delivered a very competent address. 'Wow!' I thought. 'What a vicar's wife she will make!' And she did – when we were allowed to get there. The practical problem was I was going overseas for the rest of the year; she was bonded to teach for two more years (so couldn't come with me even if it had been allowed), and then I would be on a four-year marriage ban. So we faced a long courtship which worried Eleanor less than it came to worry me.

A few months later I set off on an overseas trip by myself and managed to start it on a honeymoon island off the coast of Australia just to rub salt into the wound of having left Eleanor behind. The rest was a great trip most of which I did solo. After six weeks on an Italian immigrant ship I bought an Italian scooter in Milan and drove 8,000 miles around Europe and Britain exploring heritage as varied as Venice, the Dachau concentration camp, the Dunkirk beaches and the Berlin Wall (which I watched being built). By sleeping outdoors under a fly-sheet I was living for about £1 a day – roughly $50 in today's money.

No Way Back

By some homing instinct on arriving in England I drove straight to Canterbury Cathedral, arriving for the 7.00am Communion service. Forty years later I discovered that an ancestor had been the historian of the cathedral – one Rev. Nicholas Batteley – and his brother Dr John Batteley, Archdeacon of Canterbury, was memorialised by a plaque on the wall. Both were recognised English antiquarians in the early 1700s. I had driven straight to my roots. I returned to New Zealand in January 1962 after visiting twenty countries and having sent a stream of letters home to Eleanor. We were undoubtedly in love, and I still have all the letters. But we had a long wait ahead of us.

– 2 –

Faithful Springs
Training and First Parishes

Discovering Ancient Wells

Entry into St John's College in February 1962 was a sudden change from freedom to confinement although it was a pleasant collegial life with much interesting information being taught. As we were taught the mysteries of biblical studies and the richness of church history I used to think, 'Why don't they teach all this stuff to the people in the parishes?' and resolved to do so when my time came.

My courtship with Eleanor continued, without the help of the Morris Minor which had been sold. One day she rang to say, 'Wait for me by the kerb-side.' As I stood there a bit perplexed it dawned on me – this time she had bought the car! She arrived in a cute old Hillman. We had wheels! From then on we joined the small cluster of courting couples in cars that parked behind the water reservoir on College Road before compline service began.

The college operated a firm curfew on the two evenings we were allowed out. We managed to negotiate that the girlfriends and fiancées could attend the service of compline on those nights. In 1962 the married men had to live apart from their wives and families during term time as there was no housing for them, though this was rectified by 1963 when the first of the flats were built. At the end of 1962 Eleanor and I became engaged and then she set off for her year-long OE while I lived a monastic life at St John's.

I missed her terribly but there was a lot of interest happening at the college under the new warden, Canon Raymond Foster, and his warm-hearted and outgoing wife Muriel.

College life was built around a sequence of daily prayer; of matins, meditation and Holy Communion at 7.00am; the monastic office of sext at twelve; evensong at 5.30pm and compline at 9.00pm virtually every day. It was a pseudo-monastic sort of life reflecting the fading anglo-catholicism of much New Zealand Anglicanism of the time. It had some positive benefits. We certainly got to hear a lot of scripture read and gained confidence in presenting the prayer book services. But I did find the life-style frustrating. Every day was constantly interrupted by chapel, lectures and meals – when could we ever really study? And something important was lacking. The prayer life was formal and ritualised, just as Anglicanism likes things to be. But where was the adventure of knowing a real God?

Early in my second year an evangelical student from Christchurch named David Harper gathered a few of us together and proposed that we meet weekly to try to get closer to God. He claimed there were ways that God wanted to speak with believers and that if we asked the Holy Spirit to come amongst us He would do so.

We went to tell Canon Foster what we wanted to do. He introduced us to a booklet written by a fellowship known as 'The Servants of Christ the King'.[1] During the Second World War this British group had formed cells of people who developed a practice of group prayer to sustain themselves under the stresses of war. Their approach was to gather quietly without conversation, to pray a simple prayer together and then go into silence for at least twenty minutes. The prayer was:

---

1. Olive Parker, *The New Commandment: Servants of Christ the King*, Darton, Longman and Todd: London, 1962.

Spirit of the Living God, fall afresh on us.
Take us, break us, recreate us;
Spirit of the Living God, fall afresh on us.

With that simple but risky prayer, offered by seven students in St John's College in 1963, my experience of the charismatic movement began. And it happened under the oversight of the warden of the college. The group included David Harper, Bob Cooper, Bill Bennett, Barrie Allom, Neil Fuge, Arthur Mead and myself.

When we came out of the silence, by simply waiting till everyone had opened their eyes, we would share what we had been thinking. Despite the challenging nature of the prayer ('Take us, break us' always makes me anxious!) nothing remarkable happened except that time and again we found that we had been meditating on the same subject despite there being no prior conversation about possible topics.

We were starting to experience the revelation of the mind of the Spirit to a community – a form of knowing that is an integral part of the Holy Spirit's ministry to the church. We were also learning that group praying does not have to be ritualised in order to work. We called the group GUTS and if asked why would say, jokingly, that it meant General Union of Theological Students. In fact it meant Guidance Under The Spirit.

Later that year the Pentecostal dimension began to enter the student body. One of the less conformist of the students, Bill Smith from Ruawai, nicknamed 'the Ruawai Kid',[2] had attended a Pentecostal church and came back claiming he had been 'baptised

---

2. Bill was the type of daring student who would climb the steep roof of the chapel at night to tie a sock around the bell-clapper, to embarrass the bell-ringer of the week (me!). When the bell failed to sound I approached the Sub-Warden, Dr Catley, to say, 'The bell won't ring, Sub-Warden.' Dryly he replied, 'I noticed. Get the hand-bell, Battley.'

in the Spirit'. Bill began to share his experience with some of the students and invited me to meet with him, testified to me and offered to lay hands on me and pray that the Holy Spirit would 'baptise' me. I didn't really know what to make of this but let him try. It all seemed a bit awkward until he began to speak in an unknown language. A flow of the most beautiful sounds issued forth from the mouth of this rather rough-hewn fellow-student. This certainly wasn't something alarming. It was mysteriously beautiful, aesthetically pleasing and deeply peaceful. Whatever had happened to Bill was something holy and not to be shunned.

I was quite impressed but wasn't aware of anything special happening to me and wasn't ready to pursue it further. I was leaving college to be ordained after only two year's training and the pressure was on to get ready for that. Just before exiting in November 1963 I was sitting in the student common room when the radio announced the assassination of US President John F. Kennedy in Dallas. The modernising Pope John XXIII had died of cancer not long before. It felt as if the hopes of a new dawn in church and international politics were fading rapidly.

Ordination and Training Curacies

I was ordained deacon in my favourite church – St Mary's pro-cathedral, Parnell – on St Andrew's Day 1963 and was assigned to the Takapuna parish for a training curacy with the Rev. Gordon King. I had little opportunity to explore spirituality further. I was the junior member of a five-person team and we did what we were told to do. With six centres of worship and about 1,700 parish families it was a full-on life and I was still commuting back to the college twice a week for some lectures. The staff team consisted of the vicar, Gordon King, 'Father' Bob Hattaway as senior assistant curate, Church Army Captain Barry Ingham as parish evangelist, retired former missionary Canon Henry Jackson and myself – a very diverse group. The staff's shared prayer life was the offering of the daily offices of Morning and Evening Prayer.

Once a month Eleanor and I would meet with a few others in the home of parishioners Len and Celia Tinsley and we followed the prayer style of the Servants of Christ the King and shared a bible study. At the end of 1964 Eleanor and I were able to marry and we found the spiritual life and hospitality of the Tinsleys a quiet inspiration. I recall another parishioner trying to have conversations with me about what she had experienced when she visited a nearby Assembly of God church. I tried to discourage her from getting involved in a group prone to dogmatism and extremism. I knew nothing about what I was being dogmatic about.

After two years I was transferred to Ponsonby parish and was followed at Takapuna by Bill Smith. I recall Gordon King saying that the bishop was sending Bill Smith to him to 'sort out the Pentecostal nonsense' Bill was involved in. To his credit Gordon dryly commented, 'How can I discipline a man for doing things St Paul did?'

Our first son Mark was born in 1965 and I was reassigned to All Saints, Ponsonby to train with the Rev. Lin Dawson, a kindly and wise priest who had been a much-loved military chaplain during the Second World War, but he promptly moved to Devonport parish. His replacement was the Rev. Harry Boyd-Bell, a crusty but hard-working priest who had also had wartime chaplaincy experience of the toughest kind – he had served on the New Zealand hospital ship for about three years. It had left him a changed man.[3]

I worked alongside Harry for three solid years and learned much

---

3. I once commented in his wife's presence on the women whose husbands had not come home from the war. Her eyes filled with tears and she said quietly, 'My husband never came back from the war.'

about faithfulness to the church's basic ministries: we celebrated Communion, preached, taught, baptised, married and buried the dead on a scale not seen today. In hindsight, we were witnessing the end of Christendom. At that time the Death of God controversy swept into our unsuspecting lives and challenged the confidence of many clergy. By 1967 we had a second son, Christopher – our Christ-bearer. And Eleanor was challenged by the local Plunket nurse to visit other lonely young mothers. In some trepidation she did her first visit, to be amazed by the desperate welcome she received. Her own pastoral ministry was beginning.

In 1968, in the fifth and final year of my two curacies, I was selected for a Rotary Group Study Exchange team to visit Indiana in the USA. While this had no charismatic connections, it introduced me to the more personalised approach to worship in some Episcopal (Anglican) American churches, which attracted me, and to the benefits of the interconnected church buildings Americans had created to cope with their harsh winters. I realised that the separated buildings of New Zealand would have to be changed to more interconnected buildings and I returned with new ideas for modernisation of Anglican buildings and ministry.

By the end of the 1960s ideas for modernising Anglican church life were spreading rapidly and I was amongst the fast adopters. A new eucharistic liturgy had been approved for trial in 1966, guitar-based songs were being introduced in some worship services and proposals for church union were being developed. They were promising days.

Beside the Wairoa River

In 1969 I was appointed to the country parish of Ruawai in Northland. It was standard practice in those days that the younger clergy were sent to the rural parishes. I had looked at some of them and felt most were too large and scattered for my liking but the Ruawai parish looked compact and manageable so I was pleased to be offered it. We arrived one day in February with two children under five only to discover that our furniture, which had been in storage, was not yet on the truck from Auckland. The firm had the delivery date wrong by a month! So we repainted the study while parishioners showed their rural practicality by bringing in essential furniture and food. Both parties impressed the other with their coping skills and we settled happily into life in an area of 3,500 people. Eleanor joined the Playcentre committee and I joined Jaycees and that about covered all the young families in the district.

The parish had five worship centres: the Ruawai St Michael's and All Angels, a compact timber building sitting on a mere one–eighth of an acre; the Matakohe Coates Memorial Church – a memorial to Gordon Coates the Prime Minister of the depression era; the tiny Hukatere Church, an original Selwyn church which had been brought from Hakaru near Kaiwaka; the attractive All Saints at Mititai which featured curved kauri roof beams and had originally been at the timber milling settlement of Aratapu before it was floated across the Wairoa River and hauled up the Mititai hill – they are very adept at moving timber buildings in the Northern Wairoa – and, at the Maori settlement of Naumai, eight kilometres north of Ruawai, worship was offered in a corrugated-iron kumara shed where the congregation froze in winter and roasted in summer.

The parish had $1500 in the bank to build them a church. I set about solving the problem with the conviction that the North already had too many churches sitting around barely used – surely one of them could be got for little cost? I surveyed a variety of surplus parish buildings and found the right one at the former fishing village of Batley of all places, just south of Maungaturoto. Not only was there only one house left at Batley but the church was beside the Kaipara Harbour so transportation by water was possible.

Paparoa parish agreed to sell us the building for the price of a picket fence around the graves – a generous response. So one afternoon I set off on the towing launch to go to Batley and collect St Andrew's church. With a hiss and a roar the engine blew a frost plug and we wallowed in the rapidly outgoing tide. This was no problem to the old hands on the launch who shaped a length of timber, hammered it into the frost plug hole and restarted the engine. The whole contract was done with a piece of timber sticking out the side of the engine.

The next day a bulldozer towed the church down to the barge and away she sailed and was beached for the night on the sand-flats at Tinopai. A charming photograph appeared soon after in the *New Zealand Herald* of the church on its barge sitting on a sandbank at Tinopai. A day later the church was hauled over the stop-bank at Naumai, across the borrowpit drain, through a kumara field and over the highway to come to rest on new foundations. Some working bees later, we had a refurbished church ready for re-consecration for a total cost of $2500. The Te Paa family of Naumai and others rejoiced to see their dream fulfilled.

I enjoyed a close working relationship with the minister of the Union parish, Fred Cook, and when a paddock came on the market beside the Methodist church hall I knew we had to buy it. With a bit of help from the diocese we secured it and some years later St Michael and All Angels was brought across to its new site and joined to the Methodist hall to provide a centre for what is now the Co-operating Parish of Ruawai.

Being on my own, I was faced with a spiritual challenge. It was part of the duties of an Anglican priest to say the morning and evening prayers of the prayer book daily not only for themselves but also for their community. Research at the time by the warden of St John's College had revealed that only about half the clergy actually did this, and I was amongst the half for whom it wasn't working. It was just possible to do it with others (if compelled) but alone it seemed tiresome.[4] So finally I said to the Lord, 'This just isn't working for me, so I'm going to drop it. If this puts me into the wilderness, you will just have to come and find me there!' and I stopped it. Five years later I was dry enough to seek what God was offering.

The only occurrence at that time relating to charismatic renewal was that two men not of the parish came to see me to ask if I would provide 'covering' for a prayer meeting they were holding as I seemed to be 'a man of the Spirit'. I had no idea what they were on about and fobbed them off. I simply lacked the insight to recognise that a small cell of Pentecostals in the community needed a minister to support them. It was a missed opportunity which I regret.

Our third son Philip arrived in May 1970 and towards the end of that year Ted Buckle, the Bishop's Ecumenical Development Officer, visited us and I took him to see St Andrew's at Naumai. Sitting in his car outside the church I said to him, 'I'm really enjoying this country experience. I just hope we can get back to a new suburb soon enough to be a young family ministering amongst other young families.' I had no idea the diocese was about to appoint the first vicar to Pakuranga and was surprised and thrilled to find an offer of that position in my mail soon after. I accepted not in order to leave the rural experience, but because I knew my heart and calling was in suburban ministry. So began the most exciting twelve years of our lives. Unknown to us, God's timing was coming closer.

---

4. Years later, through the Myers Briggs study I discovered an explanation. For my ENFP personality type (= extroverted, intuitive, feelings, processor) set routines bore us rigid. We thrive on change and challenge. Even later I heard world-renowned Canon Michael Green, an able and talented extrovert, tell a huge conference, 'This prayer thing just doesn't work for me, unless I'm in a group,' and I thought, 'Bingo – that's me too!'

– 3 –

Rain in High Places
Dennis Bennett, Ken Prebble, Bishop Gowing

During my first year at Ponsonby I had been invited – I know not why – I guess Bill Smith put me up to it[1] – to join a small group that was planning a visit to Auckland of an American Episcopalian priest by the name of Father Dennis Bennett. Dennis Bennett had been on the front cover of TIME magazine in 1960[2] after he had been forced out by his Los Angeles congregation for advocating speaking in tongues and teaching about a 'baptism in the Spirit'.[3] Father Kenneth Prebble of St Paul's Symonds Street was hosting the group which met in St Paul's vicarage. I had little contribution to make as the others seemed to know what they wanted. Bennett's visit was to change church life in New Zealand extensively.

Cloudburst – Ken Prebble and Dennis Bennett

Father Prebble as he was widely known (though the clergy usually referred to him as Ken Prebble) was the leading anglo-catholic

---

1. Ray Muller confirms that Bill Smith contacted Fr Prebble for Ray. Email RM to DHB, 14 June 2014.
2. *TIME,* August 15, 1960, 55.
3. See Bennett, Dennis, *Nine O'clock in the Morning,* Logos International/Kingsway, Eastbourne, 1970. 77ff. He resigned on 3 April 1960.

priest in Auckland diocese. He was a well-educated man; unlike most New Zealand clergy he had an Oxford M.A. and under his leadership St Paul's had become an influential centre for 'high' Anglicanism. A committed man of prayer, Ken Prebble had been on a search for something more.[4] The story of his introduction to charismatic renewal is told in Harcourt Merritt's book *To God be the Glory* which records the first ten years of renewal at St Paul's,[5] in Ken Prebble's own words in *Logos Magazine*[6] and in Denis Bennett's influential book *Nine O'clock in the Morning*.[7]

One day Father Prebble struck up a conversation with a young Baptist man who came to St Paul's Church on weekdays to pray. When he learned that this man – Derek Batts – spoke in tongues, Father Prebble was intrigued. Derek Batts had clear memories of the encounter forty-five years later: 'We got talking. He said, "So you are a Baptist are you?" and I said, "I'm not really a total Baptist. I'm really a Pentecostal Baptist." And he said, "Oh, do you speak in tongues?" And I said, "Yes," and he said, "Come to my study, I want to talk to you."'[8] The result was that Father Prebble and his wife Mary began attending a prayer-meeting held in the home of Baptist leader Wyn Fountain. Here began an unlikely partnership that had lasting implications. The prayer meeting had begun with six people in the Fountains' home in Kohimarama in February

---

4. Barbara Thatcher, an early participant in the St Paul's renewal, says that they had been meeting in prayer cells following 'The Servants of Christ the King' prior to the events of 1966. Interview, Barbara Thatcher, 25 August 2010, 1.

5. Merritt, N.F.H., *To God Be The Glory: The first 10 ½ years of the charismatic renewal in St Paul's*, St Paul's Outreach Trust, Auckland, 1981, 20-25.

6. *Logos*, 1:3 (February 1967), 8.

7. Bennett, *Nine O'clock*, op. cit., 191-199.

8. Interview, Derek Batts, 21 July 2009.

1966[9] and rapidly grew until it was crowded with people from many churches including some from St Paul's. Father Prebble was struck by the quality of spiritual love and expectation in the meeting and returned a number of times, learning and observing the operation of the spiritual gifts and the anointing of the Holy Spirit.

Despite the differences in Wyn Fountain and Ken Prebble's backgrounds, trust grew between them and Father Prebble, Mary and a few other St Paul's people learned the core charismatic ideas in that meeting. As a result Father Prebble was asked to chair the committee to plan the visit to Auckland of Father Dennis Bennett[10] who had been invited to New Zealand by a renewal group in Palmerston North at the initiative of the Massey University Chaplain, the Rev. Ray Muller.[11] Father Prebble had decided to await Dennis Bennett's visit before he asked God for the gift of renewal and of tongues as, in Merritt's words,

> Father Bennett ... was a man of his own kind, a priest in the Catholic tradition, the vicar of a parish and one who apparently combined an ordinary parish ministry with the exercise of the charismatic gifts. He wanted to be assured by

9. Merritt, 22.

10. Dennis Bennett records that Father Prebble was approached by 'two very junior clergy of this area' who advised him that Dennis Bennett would be visiting – the likely candidates are Bill Smith and Gerry Hadlow as Bennett meetings were held in the parishes they were curates in, Takapuna and St Matthew's respectively. See Bennett, *Nine O'clock,* 193. Merritt records that Prebble acted 'with the permission of his Bishop' (Bishop Gowing) who Bennett says was initially 'not too pleased' but gave consent when he received a favourable letter from Bennett's bishop. Merritt, 25, Bennett, 194.

11. Email Ray Muller to DHB, 14 April 2014, 'Yes. I was the instigator and organiser of the visit. On re-reading Dennis' diary notes, I see he stayed with my friends around the country. Arnold and Janet Kimberley and Cecil Marshall would have been part of my discussions and planning.'

meeting him personally and making his own assessment of him as a man.[12]

Bennett's three-week[13] New Zealand tour began with five days in Auckland where he was met by Archdeacon Prebble[14] and taken in pouring rain to St Paul's vicarage. Bennett does not tell what discussion or prayer ministry ensued, but in a subsequent testimony for Dale Williamson Prebble said Bennett prayed for him that evening. In his morning prayers in St Paul's, while Denis Bennett was still asleep,[15] Archdeacon Prebble began to speak in tongues. Merritt, undoubtedly quoting Prebble, says:

> His prayer was rewarded by the wonderful gift of a tongue, a language of great beauty, which formed itself on his lips 'as the Spirit gave him utterance'… At first there was a great flood of words, as though they had been dammed up for a long time somewhere within him, waiting to be spoken. They flowed easily and without emotion and continued to do so.[16]

That day (a Wednesday[17]) Bennett was flown to Gisborne to address a meeting and was due to arrive back in Auckland to address

---

12. Merritt, 24-25.
13. Bennett, *Nine O'clock*, 190, 198.
14. Fr Prebble had been appointed Archdeacon of Hauraki (Auckland's North Shore area) in early 1966.
15. Bennett, 195. Testimony Prebble for D. Williamson, email Rob Yule to DHB, 7 September 2019.
16. Merritt, 25.
17. Hugh Cromwell recalled in 2011 that it was a Wednesday night (21 September). Interview, H. Cromwell, 17 February 2011.

his first Auckland meeting in St Matthew's Church. Around 200 people gathered that evening and waited in expectation and I was amongst them. Unknown to us the weather had intervened and Dennis's plane was unable to leave Gisborne. Merritt describes what followed:

> Just before the meeting was due to open Wyn Fountain entered the church. It contained about 200 people but he saw Father Prebble walking around looking very agitated. 'I have a problem,' Father Prebble greeted him in his quiet English manner. 'Dennis Bennett is held up on the plane from Gisborne and is not going to be here for the meeting. What on earth are we going to do about that?' He hesitated: 'Do you know what the Lord is telling me? He is saying, "Take the meeting yourself. Tell them your story."'
>
> Wyn Fountain felt his eyes grow large with anticipation. He did not know what Father Prebble would do. But before his eyes the vicar walked into the pulpit and began to explain Father Dennis Bennett's absence. And instead of hearing Father Bennett the unsuspecting assembly listened to a radiant Father Prebble give his testimony… He described his spiritual experience at confirmation and said that when he began his theological training he had possessed a great faith but had lost it. Ever since that time he had been looking for it. 'I want to tell you that during this week I have refound it' he told everyone and he described his experiences with Father Bennett and how he had come to speak in tongues.[18]

Harvey Smith, who was a student at St John's College in 1966, confirms that as a protegé of Ray Muller's ministry at Palmerston

---

18. Merritt, 25.

North, he had been invited to arrange Bennett's ministry at St John's College:

> I saw the Warden of St John's who kindly invited Dennis to speak at Evensong which was an unusual invitation. Dennis spoke so well in giving his testimony that it was agreed he would remain after dinner to speak again to those who wished to hear. Most did.

Harvey also confirms the episode when Ken Prebble gave his testimony at St Matthew's Church:

> Prior to the evening meeting at St Matthew's I was in the vestry with Father Prebble, Bill Smith and Tony Ross. Dennis was late in arriving back from Gisborne. Following prayer Father Prebble said, 'Leave it to me,' which we did.[19]

The effect on the meeting was electrifying. A senior cleric of the Anglican Church was now declaring a full-scale charismatic experience with the expected sign and was relating it to his previous experience of early faith and its association with the Anglican rite of confirmation. Dennis Bennett arrived at the meeting around 9.30pm expecting to find a dejected crowd only to find 'a tremendously enthusiastic group of people'.[20] According to the Rev. Paul Gravelle about forty of them had stayed on and were prayed for by Bennett:

> A group of us stayed on in the church and (Dennis) said, 'Well, I'd better pray for you guys' and he invited us up to

---

19. Email Harvey Smith to DHB, 21 June 2019.
20. Bennett, *Nine O'clock*, 195.

the altar rail and I was second in line – I seem to remember that Wyn Fountain was on my left. He prayed for him and Dennis Bennett came to me and said, 'How shall I pray for you?' and I just said, 'I want to receive the Holy Spirit.' And I didn't remember what happened after that. I didn't feel his hands on my head. I knew that my eyes were shut and Jesus was standing in front of me and suddenly I was, as many other people experienced, I was just filled up with warm oil. My wife said I made a real fool of myself – I was obviously speaking in tongues in great volume. But I have never been the same since then – never been the same again.[21]

On the next two nights Dennis Bennett ministered at St Matthew's Church and on Sunday morning at St Paul's. John Boniface recalls being taken as a sixteen-year-old by his father, Herbert Boniface, the vicar of Hillsborough, to the Saturday night event where he witnessed Dennis Bennett and Ken Prebble releasing a troubled woman from an evil spirit. From that night on his father was 'sold hook, line and sinker' on the renewal as being of God.[22]

During that week Dennis Bennett also spoke to a meeting attended by Bishop Gowing and many clergy who, hearing of the Archdeacon's experience, had come out in force.[23] Murray Spackman recalls the day (Thursday, 22nd) vividly:

And then Bill [Smith] invited me to a meeting in the crypt at St Paul's when Dennis Bennett was speaking … and he spoke about the Baptism in the Holy Spirit, and I'm thinking,

21. Interview, Paul Gravelle, 24 July 2009, 1.
22. Interview, John Boniface, 24 July 2008, 1.
23. Bennett, 195.

'This is what I'm missing – and this is what I don't have' … only three months ordained as deacon – and I'm thinking, 'What really do I have to share, and what really is the good news and is there reality in all of this?' And Dennis Bennett spoke about the Baptism in the Spirit and so on and said, 'This is what you can do. God desires that we be filled with the Spirit and this is how we can be filled with the Spirit, and we be available; we be surrendered; we claim the promises; we ask and God will fulfil the promise,' and sort of basically saying it is as easy as that.

And I thought, 'That sounds pretty good. Gee, like that?' and … I felt a need to leave and head back home and on my way to where I was living at the time I went past little St Michael and All Angels at Bayswater. I remember going into the church on my own and thinking, 'That's what I need from God – to carry on in ministry – this is what it's all about.'

So I went into the church and I remember kneeling down and just sort of thinking, 'What was it Dennis had said?' and just going through those steps and, okay, well ask, and then he spoke about just freeing your tongue up and being willing to speak in tongues and began to do that and suddenly there was kind of a release, if you like, which they often talk about, but there a sense of the freedom and I began to speak in tongues. And there was an awareness I think for me of the Holy Spirit and the presence of God in a way that I don't think I had experienced before. And I quickly looked around – I sort of stopped talking in tongues and looked around and under the pews to make sure no-one was hiding there! – and so just enjoyed that sense of God's presence and that infilling.[24]

24. Interview, Murray Spackman, 13 October 2010.

On the Sunday evening Eleanor and I attended a meeting where Dennis spoke at St Peter's, Takapuna. He taught from scripture about the person and work of the Holy Spirit using the New Testament passages about being baptised in the Holy Spirit and the evidence of the relationship between the filling of the Spirit and the reception of spiritual gifts, especially the gift of tongues. He then invited any who wanted to be prayed with to come to the front pews where he would pray for them. Eleanor and I went forward, knelt like good Anglicans, and Dennis prayed briefly over us laying a hand on us and then moved on.[25] Nothing seemed to happen. No surge of power; no rush of a strange language; perhaps a sense of peace. We went home convinced we had failed the course and I concluded that this was something for extremists and not for reasonable people like us.

After almost a week in Auckland which included a meeting at St John's theological college, Dennis Bennett travelled through much of New Zealand speaking to bishops and clergy in Christchurch, Dunedin, Wellington and Waikato dioceses, to students and staff in a second theological college[26] and to a large gathering of students at Massey University in Palmerston North where about five percent of the student body had already received baptism in the Holy Spirit.[27] Bennett writes that he spoke on at least fifty-seven occasions.[28]

Bennett's tour of New Zealand had been initiated by a young priest in Palmerston North who was to have life-long impact on the

---

25. Murray Spackman who was there as an assistant curate tells that he was conscripted in to assist in the laying on of hands as Dennis had no ministry team to help him minister to so many people. Murray 'had no idea what he was meant to do'.
26. College House, Christchurch.
27. Bennett, *Nine O'clock*, 196.
28. Bennett, 190. New Zealanders have a reputation for working their overseas speakers very hard.

charismatic movement in New Zealand. The Rev. Ray Muller was jointly assistant curate at All Saints Palmerston North and part-time Anglican chaplain at Massey University. He had been baptised in the Spirit at his ordination in 1962 and later again by Baptist student Murray Robertson.[29] He attended a prayer meeting held in the home of Pentecostal pastor Ken Wright in Palmerston North and then commenced one in his own home which soon had to transfer to a larger home where seventy to eighty students attended.[30] Ray had assisted Ken Wright and his church in organising a tour of New Zealand by David du Plessis in February 1966 and initiated and conducted the subsequent visit of Dennis Bennett[31] with help from fellow Anglicans Arnold and Jane Kimberley and Cecil Marshall and the Rev. Bill Smith, Harvey Smith and Tony Ross in Auckland.[32]

In organising this as an assistant curate without reference to any bishop, Ray had stepped well beyond normal Anglican deference to episcopal authority. Bennett records in his book *Nine O'clock in the Morning* Father Prebble's surprise that 'it was a clear case of the tail wagging the dog'.[33] Unconsciously perhaps, the early charismatics were claiming the freedom to learn from whom they chose and to make use of the opportunities offered by international air travel.

29. Interview R. J. Muller, 1 June 2010, 5.

30. Williamson, Dale, *An Uncomfortable Engagement: The Charismatic Movement in the New Zealand Anglican Church 1965-85*, Ph D thesis, University of Otago, December 2007, 39.

31. Williamson, Thesis, footnote 50. Muller is clear that he initiated the visits by Bennett and Michael and Jeanne Harper, but not the du Plessis tour. Ray Muller interview with Dale Williamson, Wellington, 19 March 1996, 1.

32. Email RJM to DHB, 11 April 2014. 'Yes, I was the instigator and organiser of the visit,' and letters Dennis Bennett to RJM 8 February 1966 and 22 May 1966. Also Email from Harvey Smith, 21 June 2019.

33. Bennett, *Nine O'clock*, 158.

For a while after Bennett's visit, I and a boarder we had staying with us attended the Wednesday night prayer meetings at St Paul's which I found challenging and a bit overwhelming. I recall asking Father Prebble to pray with me one night for baptism in the Spirit but again nothing seemed to happen. The claims of life with two young children worked against regular attendance and I gave up going and accepted my vicar's warning that 'that sort of thing is for the spiritually insecure'.

The one identifiable fruit from that time was that I commenced a bible study group of young parishioners who had been visiting St Paul's. I found it far easier to understand and interpret the New Testament. We studied Colossians verse by verse. Its high christology was now very real. From that small group one became a missionary teacher; another became a churchwarden; another and her husband became long-term members at St Paul's and another became a music and worship leader and finally a priest. Just one became a member of a Pentecostal church. Exposition of scripture became my leading spiritual gift and I soon began to preach from notes rather than a full text. Apart from that, I kept on with the basic duties of an assistant curate in Ponsonby and drew back from the charismatic journey.

Bishop Gowing and 'Renewal'

While the term 'renewal' was promptly claimed by the early charismatic movement[34] it was not the only use of the term in the mid-1960s. Earlier in February 1966 Bishop Gowing had raised

---

34. Charismatics in general preferred the term 'charismatic renewal' to 'charismatic movement'. See Williamson, 4-7; and Battley, 'What is Genuine and What is Ephemeral in the Charismatic Wind?' in *Towards an Authentic New Zealand Theology*, ed. Ker and Sharpe, (Auckland: University of Auckland Chaplaincy Trust, 1984), 39.

the matter of spiritual renewal in the diocese by issuing a Call to Renewal at a Diocesan Service of Thanksgiving. He had called upon the diocese to pray, 'Renew thy church, O Lord, beginning with me.' While it is unlikely that he was seeking what became the charismatic movement, there is little doubt that as a deeply spiritual man, with both an evangelical and catholic background, he was sincere in saying to his 1967 Synod,

> This is an extremely important prayer, for if the Church in this Diocese is to be renewed there must be renewal on the individual level – I must be renewed. There must be renewed love for our Lord, a new understanding of Him and His Mission, a new devotion to Him. I must be honest before God about myself. In what ways is my Christianity a formal, lifeless thing? How are my priorities – where do they depart from those of our Lord? What part has mission in my life? I ask that these questions be pondered not only in private but that they be considered in groups – clergy together, clergy and lay people in groups.[35]

He desired that these questions be dealt with over some time and proposed an examination of aspects of the diocese's corporate life in the following year. He stated that in his view 'there is nothing so essential as to give those responsible for spiritual leadership the opportunity to be renewed' and spoke of a 'consequent hope of renewal'.[36]

The visit of Dennis Bennett to the diocese later that year stirred up the issue of renewal and charismatic gifts and the Rev. John Mullane, then vicar of Clevedon and probably the most intelli-

---

35. Bishop's Address to Synod, 1967 Year Book of the Diocese of Auckland, 25.
36. Ibid.

gent priest in the diocese, challenged the emphasis on speaking in tongues with a critical article in the Anglican newspaper *Church and People*. In its November 1966 issue he asked, 'Just What is Speaking in Tongues?'[37] and questioned what the slight scriptural evidence actually witnesses to and whether there was any evidence that what was being currently claimed in any way matched what the disciples might have experienced. His key question was, 'Can it be true that a man [sic] must go beyond the rational and reasonable in order to experience God and his power?'

Ken Prebble, by then a convinced renewalist, responded in January with a well-argued article. He claimed that Luke's Acts is more historical than Mullane allowed; that Paul's evidence was by no means confused; that there can never be 'proof', as Mullane demanded it, that a current spiritual experience was identical to those in the apostolic period; and vigorously defended Michael Harper's scriptural analysis (which Mullane had judged harshly). Prebble appealed for a patient and fair attitude to this movement.[38] This published debate staked out positions between the liberal and charismatic theological streams that lasted for a long time.

Herbert Boniface followed up in September 1967 with publication of a provocative address he had given to the Auckland Clerical Association entitled 'Dangerous but Vital?' In this he claimed that 'our neo-pentecostal members, of whom he was now one, represent the greatest threat in centuries to our Anglican way of life and worship (and that) … the "Baptism in the Spirit" is either a dreadful, desperately dangerous delusion, or the most important movement

---

37. *Church and People*, 25 Nov, 1966, 8.

38. *Church and People*, 27 Jan, 1967, 8, 9, 12. In the same issue American William Stringfellow was reported as having warned youth at an Anglican youth conference that tongues could be evidence of the demonic, as in voodooism, and warned that it should not be coerced. He had affirmed the role of spiritual gifts in the life of the church. Ibid, 5.

in the Church in sixteen hundred years'. He also alleged that, if the claims of Pentecostalism were correct, then 'our bishops, theologians and teachers have been leading us astray for a very long time'. He challenged his colleagues to take the movement seriously and to study it carefully before rejecting it.[39] The article was accompanied by an advertisement for the visit of Michael Harper to New Zealand that month.

The next month, the Rev. Lionel Beere of St Aidan's Remuera responded with a critique of Herbert Boniface's overstatements and affirmed, 'I do not doubt that (the Anglican Church) will cope with this movement; … if pentecostalism has anything of permanent value it, too, can be woven into the rope.' Again, both writers staked out the shape of a dynamic that has continued ever since – radical change or patient absorption?

The following year, having attended the 1968 Lambeth Conference which he considered would prove to be one of the outstanding Lambeth conferences, Bishop Gowing spoke at length to his synod on renewal in the three sections adopted by the Lambeth Conference: Renewal in Faith, Renewal in Ministry and Renewal in Unity.[40]

On Renewal in Faith he reported that the conference had called us to 'a faith in the living God which is adventurous, expectant, calm and confident'. He referred to the 'current controversy' (the Death of God controversy) as one we could not ignore but called for adventurous faith to manifest itself, as a faith which entails radical change which could entail reform of our structures which 'are unlikely to be effective unless men and women are themselves renewed in faith and life'.

39. *Church and People*, 11 Aug 1967, 5.
40. *The Lambeth Conference 1968, Resolutions and Reports*, SPCK and Seabury, London and New York, 1968, 63-148.

It is not clear what kind of renewal in faith Bishop Gowing was seeking, though, by then he would have been aware of the charismatic movement. His address proceeded to identify issues of war, racism, hunger and aid as matters where a renewed faith must be lived out, thus signaling the increasing emphasis on social issues that the Lambeth Conference had addressed. These would become major emphases of the latter part of his episcopate.

Under Renewal in Ministry the bishop called for 'adaptability and daring' to implement necessary changes and identified a need to explore the theology of baptism and confirmation in relation to the need to commission the laity for their task in the world; to promote involvement of young people in decision-making; to open the diaconate to people remaining in secular occupations; the ordination of men to the 'supplementary ministry'; and to address the ordination of women to the priesthood.[41] These issues of ministry all became significant to those in charismatic renewal.

We were not sure what Bishop Gowing's appreciation of charismatic renewal was at this time but he certainly put the concept of renewal into the diocese's consciousness. It was in the dual context of early charismatic experiences and Bishop Gowing's calls for renewal in the life of the church that the first vicars to experience charismatic renewal had to work out the implications of what they had encountered.

While these debates were unfolding, a renewal was occurring amongst students in St John's College. David Guthrie recalled that he was introduced to charismatic renewal in his last year at St John's College in 1966. He had been impacted by David Wilkersons' book *The Cross and the Switchblade* and 'the whole theological world was convulsed and changed at that time … with a shift from reliance on

---

41. Ibid, 25.

No Way Back

the past as the authority to the immediacy of spiritual experience'.[42] The student body experienced some tensions between the students, and the warden at the time, Dr Raymond Foster, was threatened by it and the extreme claims of some of the students.[43] A tension had been inadvertently created which would affect the church for many years. Renewal students from those early days had troubling memories of judgemental academics, and the academics of dogmatic charismatics.

The recurring experiences of some students of academic non-acceptance of charismatic experience and theology may underlie the continuing anti-intellectualism that still exists amongst older charismatic clergy. But those early young charismatics who survived the college experience moved out into parish ministry and achieved substantial changes in Anglican life over the next forty years. And it began with the first renewal parishes.

---

42. Notes of a telephone interview with the Rev. David Guthrie on 18 February 2001, Battley Interviews folder.

43. Derek Lightbourne reported many years later, 'The emphasis on speaking in tongues … had been quite scary early on in St John's College where in those very early days there developed almost an A and B team and there was quite a division of where you stood'. Interview Derek Lightbourne, 31 May 2010, Battley Interviews file.

– 4 –

Streams & Mountain Tarns
The First Auckland Renewal Parishes

St Paul's Symonds Street

Following Dennis Bennett's ministry in Auckland, St Paul's became a rallying point for the emerging charismatic renewal although some expressions of it commenced elsewhere notably at Hillsborough and also in individual ministers' lives. While Dennis Bennett had led many people into a personal pentecost and some experience of the spiritual gifts, no local models existed as to how this could be expressed in an Anglican church. The only available model was the renewal-style prayer meeting and this became the main model for the rest of the 1960s.

Bennett advised Prebble not to change anything in his public worship but to introduce a parish prayer meeting in the charismatic style. Following Bennett's ministry at St Paul's, Father Prebble announced that a prayer meeting would be held in the parish hall to which anyone was welcome. Around forty people attended the first meeting, about half being charismatic non-parishioners.[1] These Wednesday evening prayer meetings began to attract people

---

1. Neil, Allen G., *The Institutional Churches and the Charismatic Renewal*, S.Th. Diploma Thesis, Joint Board of Theological Studies, Christchurch, 1974, 193.

from all around Auckland and beyond[2], some of them university students.[3]

To avoid division in the parish, Father Prebble initially sought to confine charismatic activity to the prayer meeting, yet some tensions did appear in the parish about the new emphasis. Despite these tensions, between 1966 to 1973 only five families left the parish over the renewal.[4] Prior to 1972 music played little part in the prayer meeting reflecting the leadership's inexperience in the possibilities of music in worship and evangelism.[5] Yet the singing gradually improved and was reflected in the Sunday worship although the separation of the 'renewed' people into the prayer meeting hindered the overall renewal of the parish and some charismatics moved on to the nearby Assembly of God.

Merritt described the situation by the end of 1967 as, 'we were almost divided into two congregations – upstairs and downstairs. The upstairs group [Sunday worshippers] never went downstairs but the downstairs worshippers [the Wednesday prayer meeting] also celebrated upstairs.'[6] Merritt says that by late 1968 following a teaching visit of the English Anglican Michael Harper[7] the prayer meeting dwindled to a small group of about fifteen and then grew back to about twenty-five. 'The meetings were still difficult at times and not always helpful to participants … because we really did not

---

2. Barbara Thatcher said that one couple drove from Rotorua each week to attend. Interview, Barbara Thatcher, 25 August 2010, 2.
3. Merritt describes the early months of the prayer meeting and the impact of Barbara Thatcher's healing in *To God be the Glory*, 28-29.
4. Neil, op. cit., 195.
5. Neil, 197.
6. Merritt, 33.
7. The Rev. (later Canon) Michael Harper was an early leader in the renewal and published a number of influential books on charismatic renewal.

know where we were going or what the Holy Spirit was doing with us.'[8] In Merritt's assessment, since Dennis Bennett's visit to New Zealand in 1966 St Paul's was in turmoil and there were few signs of progress: 'there seemed to be a division into two irreconcilable groups'.[9] By 1969 both the prayer meeting and the Sunday congregation had reached an impasse.[10]

Late in 1969 Father Prebble took leave to visit the Soviet Union for a return visit to the archbishop of Karkov and to visit his ailing mother in the UK.[11] On his return journey Mary Prebble joined him in the USA where they visited Dennis Bennett's church, St Luke's in Seattle, and Graham Pulkingham's Church of the Redeemer in Houston.[12] There they experienced practical ways of melding charismatic and liturgical worship. At St Luke's Dennis Bennett had introduced spontaneous prayers of praise, thanksgiving and intercession which Father Prebble determined to follow.

At the Church of the Redeemer he was impressed by the use of the Kiss of Peace; music which blended Anglican worship with simple rhythmic choruses and expressed sound theology and a revitalised spirituality. He was also impressed with the concept of community living with an emphasis on households as a base for ministry especially the way that supported a staff of fourteen people most of whom were unpaid.[13]

Ken and Mary Prebble returned in February 1970 from their visits to St Luke's Seattle and the Church of the Redeemer Houston with

---

8. Merritt, 30, 39, 43; Neil, 198.

9. Merritt, 35.

10. Neil, 198.

11. The leave was from September 1969 to February 1970. Merritt, 42.

12. Merritt reports only the visit to Redeemer but Neil reports a visit also to Seattle. Neil, 199.

13. Neil, 199-201, Merritt, 45-6.

new vision of how renewal could be expressed in the local church. Many St Paul's parishioners knew of the Church of the Redeemer and had read accounts of the renewal there and were keen to hear what they had experienced. Prebble shared what had impressed him at the two churches and during 1970-71 the fruits were seen in the institution of spontaneous prayers in the Eucharist, the 'passing of the Peace', a monthly healing service and shared leadership.[14]

In May 1970 Canon Jim Glennon of Sydney Cathedral conducted a healing ministry in St Paul's which led to a decision to commence a healing service.[15] St John's College student David McGregor introduced guitar music in July-August 1970[16] and in April 1971 Graham Pulkingham and Bill Farra conducted a ministry which promoted hugs and introduced new music.[17] Bill Farra returned in September 1971 to live in the vicarage as a non-paid lay worker. In mid-1971 an American Assembly of God pastor, John Childers with his Kiwi wife Yvonne, joined the growing ministry team bringing valuable charismatic experience[18] and a young brother and sister, John and Sue Smith, joined bringing further musical gifts. The presence of Bill Farra, John Childers and John and Sue Smith transformed the Wednesday night prayer meeting which increased rapidly. At the end of 1971 the Rev. Terry Molloy was appointed to St Paul's as assistant curate[19] so by end of 1971 Father Prebble had a diversely talented team around him. Merritt observes that the 1966-70 drift away from St Paul's to Pentecostal churches was reversed from this time.[20]

14. Neil, 201-212.
15. Merritt, 49-50.
16. Ibid, 59.
17. Ibid, 61. The mission was held 1-11 April 1971.
18. Ibid, 62, 65.
19. Ibid 66-67.
20. Ibid, 69-70.

As a result the years 1972-73 became harvest years for St Paul's. In March 1972 Graham Pulkingham returned and taught on total commitment to the life of 'the Body'.[21] Young people began attending in numbers and a singing group of mainly younger people developed using guitars, flutes and other instruments and the Sunday evening Testimony Service grew to around 200.[22] As repeated attempts to form a choir had failed, the singers were then brought upstairs to lead the music at the Sunday morning eucharist and by the end of 1972 they were named 'The St Paul's Singers'.[23] From then on St Paul's was a parish in renewal, not just a parish with a renewal 'downstairs'.

St Margaret's Hillsborough

Another parish impacted by Dennis Bennett's visit was St Margaret's Hillsborough where Herbert Boniface ('Boni' to all) was vicar. Boni had been a Fleet Air Arm pilot in the Second World War and had the support of many returned servicemen. He had been vicar of the extensive parish of Mt Roskill and effected its division into three separate parishes becoming the first vicar of the Hillsborough area. He thus had the advantage of being the 'founding vicar' but this did not protect him from costly conflict about parish renewal.

The early years of renewal at Hillsborough were surveyed in Allen Neil's 1974 thesis *Institutional Churches and the Charismatic Renewal*.[24] Neil observed that Boni had a ministry in counselling and had been a founder of the Auckland Marriage Guidance Service. This could explain why the parish seemed to have had an unusual

21. Ibid, 74.
22. Ibid, 73-74. Williamson, 113-114.
23. Ibid, 77-78.
24. Neil, 230f.

number of neurotic women some of whom quickly became a destabilising influence in the parish. Neil describes the contrast between the early years in St Paul's and St Margaret's as 'between tranquil existence'[25] and explosive disturbance' (which) reflected different theological and liturgical interests and the diverse sociological, psychological and religious temperament of parishioners.[26]

Boni was baptised in the Spirit at the Wednesday night at St Matthew's and spoke in tongues a few weeks later.[27] His ministry immediately took a new direction. John Boniface states that his father's personality was dramatically changed from being a 'cold fish' to being outgoing and warm.[28] Hugh Cromwell, one of Boni's healing ministry elders, also testified to the radical change:

> What hit me between the eyes was the change in Boni. Within a week his preaching changed – he used to sound a bit sarcastic at times about Baptists, etc. until the change. Then he changed completely. In a week. Spoke confidently about the Bible and it was all on![29]

Boni found the spiritual gifts operated in counselling situations with positive results but within a few months unwise actions by a few unstable women were creating difficulties and a complaint was made by a parish couple to the bishop who instructed the vicar not

---

25. Clearly Merritt and Neil had different perceptions of life at St Paul's – Merritt had lived it on the inside.
26. Neil, 230.
27. Neil, 231, based upon his interview with Herbert Boniface, 24 May 1973.
28. Interview, Rev. John Boniface, 24 July 2008, 1.
29. Interview, Hugh Cromwell, 17 February 2011, 1.

to allow charismatic meetings in houses.³⁰ Boni obeyed this direction and the ecumenical prayer meetings in the parish, which were a common manifestation for the fellowship of charismatic Christians throughout New Zealand in 1967,³¹ were disbanded, altering the shape of renewal in the parish. Instead some charismatic parishioners met early each morning in the church for prayer, and traditional evensong was progressively transformed by introduction of testimonies, choruses and spontaneous prayers.

The restrictions caused Boni to use a liturgical context as a setting for the renewed life amongst his parishioners. But the bishop's ban unnerved renewed parishioners for quite a time and there were no charismatic prayer meetings in the parish until 1972 when a Tuesday night bible study developed as a branch of the healing ministry.³² Allen Neil comments that:

> Bishop Gowing, in dealing with this crisis, became one of a number of the Anglican hierarchy in New Zealand who were confronted with problems directly related to the charismatic renewal. These encounters initially caused grave concern and doubts as to the authenticity of the renewal. The emerging maturity and evident responsibility of participants over the [late 1960s to 1973] … dispelled these misgivings to some extent.³³

Tension within the parish was further generated by the boldness of renewed parishioners in sharing their faith in ways not usually seen amongst Anglicans. The renewal had moved amongst the

---

30. Neil, 234, based on interview with H. Boniface.
31. Neil, ibid.
32. Neil, 235.
33. Neil, 236.

young people of the parish and their enthusiasm and inexperience caused difficulties. When the vicar moved to control this situation the youth work moved into a long dry spell and did not recover until 1973. These difficulties caused Boni to question whether youth were psychologically mature enough to be introduced to charismatic experience.

Underlying all these difficulties was the basic problem of marrying Pentecostal beliefs and practices with traditional Anglicanism. Non-charismatic parishioners felt that the children's and youth ministries were being taken over by a foreign culture. Spontaneous prayers, spiritual gifts and the emphasis on praise and healing contributed to the anxiety of some parishioners who thought these features encouraged a revivalist Christianity alien to the spirit and ethos of Anglicanism. Neil observed that the combination of emotionally unstable people, episcopal intervention, undiluted enthusiasm, problems with the young people, and the presence of revivalist cultural baggage slowly caused a polarisation in the parish.[34]

This culminated in a confrontation at a special general meeting in about 1970 called ostensibly to discuss recent renovations to the church but in fact intended to drive the vicar and the charismatics out. Neil, who based his observations on an interview with the vicar, stated that out of 190 people attending only six spoke of their dissatisfaction with the charismatic activity.[35]

John Boniface, who was a teenager at the time, remembering forty years later, claimed that the charismatics had met and prayed before the meeting and had been told by the Holy Spirit to keep silent and that in the event no-one spoke against the vicar. Both reports say that the opposition collapsed through confusion

34. Neil, 241.
35. Ibid.

amongst them. This was a turning point for the charismatics and restored their confidence especially as the majority of the parishioners were clearly supportive. Neil commented in 1974 that:

> in the charismatic renewal in New Zealand such a small but vocal number of dissidents in Anglican parishes have caused similar confrontations. Even though such events have often proved painful, nevertheless they appear to have been a catalyst to increase interest in the renewal.[36]

Boni also found himself being pressured by charismatics who considered things were not moving strongly enough. Feeling a sense of responsibility to the renewal overall, in which only St Paul's and St Margaret's were attempting parish renewal, he tried to pace the process of change and so avoided division and eventually achieved a climate of acceptance and tolerance.

Despite the problems, there were beneficial and lasting results. The principal one was the development of a weekly Sunday evening healing service. Seeking an approach acceptable to Anglicans and the bishop, Boni utilised the Anglican Guild of St Raphael, becoming in time its national vice-president and chairman of the Auckland committee, and modelled his service on that used by Canon Jim Glennon at Sydney Anglican Cathedral. Five lay people were appointed by vestry to be elders for laying on of hands (possibly the first use of the term 'elder' in an Anglican church in New Zealand). This approach to the healing ministry had the approval of Bishop Gowing and, being Anglican in origin, was not seen in the parish as explicitly charismatic.

The healing ministry challenged them with the issue of exorcism. Neil noted that Maori priests appeared to have knowledge

---

36. Neil, 242.

of this area and that in the early 1970s Pakeha priests at times sought help from Maori priests to seek their advice on exorcisms. Murray Spackman, for instance, specifically described the coaching and support he received from the Rev. Maori Marsden[37] who was chaplain at the Devonport naval base at the time and how Maori would take him out for house-cleansings and other ministries. He recalled,

> I had the benefit of Maori's support and encouragement. And just his whole conversation (was) that this is the norm … this is not something that is way out … there is the Holy Spirit and also the other side – the dark side – and demonic forces and powers and so on. It was actually in some of those things that Maori was very influential.[38]

The healing ministry at St Margaret's gave rise to a telephone-based prayer-support system, a transport system and a weekly evening Bible study group. To reduce the tensions in the first five years, at no time did all the charismatics meet together at one time and, in retrospect, Boni considered this was a mistake. By 1970 the open and vocal hostility of a minority had given way to cautious acceptance of the renewal and the parish was moving to a more proclamatory phase.[39]

Allen Neil reported that by 1970 only two Auckland parishes (St Paul's and St Margaret's) could be considered to be moving in renewal and each of them had had to work their way past difficulties and misunderstandings. In the Auckland area by 1970 Dennis

---

37. The Rev. Maori Marsden was a priest from a prominent North Auckland family who bridged the Maori-Pakeha world boldly and was a leader in Maori and charismatic spirituality.
38. Interview, Murray Spackman, 2.
39. Neil, 249-250.

Bennett's visit seemed to have produced little beyond a prayer meeting at St Paul's Symonds Street and an evening healing service at St Margaret's Hillsborough, a few curates wondering what to do with the spiritual experiences they had encountered and some enthusiastic laity looking for ministry opportunities, some of whom had drifted to Pentecostal churches.

The expansion lay in the future and awaited the development of workable concepts of charismatic parish renewal. A few of the younger clergy who were not vicars found ways to use what they had received. While Murray Spackman was unable to express his renewal in Takapuna parish, when he moved to a second curacy at Manurewa in late 1969 he worked with the youth group where renewal began to occur.[40] Green shoots of charismatic renewal were starting to spring up but something major was required to give it form. These developments occurred in the early 1970s and were models for parish renewal, the formation of Christian Advance Ministries and the arrival of the Life in the Spirit Seminars. And an anointed signs-following lay evangelistic couple.

Harry Greenwood and Bill and Pat Subritzky

In 1972 St Margaret's hosted the ministry of British healing-evangelist Harry Greenwood. The Rev. Harry Greenwood was described as 'an evangelist with an international outreach. In the last six months, he has been a leading figure wherever he goes. This fame comes not from his evangelistic preaching ... but from the healing work that is the most striking feature of his ministry.' His ministry in Mt Roskill was over February 9-12 and March 1-5.[41] Although

---

40. Interview, Murray Spackman, 13 October 2010. 4.
41. Leaflet 'Introducing Harry Greenwood', AADA S10 P44 Box 11/1 Vestry Correspondence 1972-74, Kohimarama Parish.

this in some ways re-emphasised the fundamentalist nature of such ministry[42] its impact on one family was to be far reaching. Bill and Pat Subritzky and their four children had been active members of St Martin's Anglican Church in Mt Roskill for some years. Bill seeking, he says, prominence and contacts, had over twenty years filled some significant lay roles in the life of the diocese but, as they both openly declare in their respective books and in their public testimonies, their marriage was in dire straits. Pat and her daughter Maria began attending the evening services at St Margaret's where the whole service was 'alive and vibrant'. As Pat describes it:

> The highlight of the service for me was the singing in the Spirit, or singing in tongues. When I closed my eyes and listened I felt as if I was hearing a heavenly orchestra. It was an introduction to a dimension of the Christian life I had never experienced or imagined.[43]

There they heard an American businessman from Full Gospel Business Men's Fellowship International (FGBMFI) speaking of being 'born again'. Maria was fascinated, bought a book, prayed as it instructed and was born again and baptised in the Spirit. Pat was impressed but hesitant.

When Harry Greenwood, who in Pat's words had been 'a drunken sailor in the British Navy and had had a conversion testimony of coming from out of the pit of hell to the glorious

---

42. Neil, 240. In 1973 Brian Jenkins view of Harry Greenwood was 'his preaching was terrible and his use of the bible lamentable, nevertheless his open and joyous approach to the Christian life was non-threatening to people'. Interview Allen Neil with Brian Jenkins, May 1973, quoted in Neil, 270.

43. Subritzky, Pat/Vic Francis, *Chosen Destiny: The Pat Subritzky Story*, Dove Ministries, Auckland, 1992, 33.

knowledge of salvation in Christ', ministered at the evening service at St Margaret's she felt she could relate to him and hung on every word. She watched in wonder as he prayed for the sick and healings took place before her eyes. She and Maria took Bill to the Saturday meeting and they both received healing for their injured knees.

Harry Greenwood moved on to minister in Hamilton and when Bill and Pat found themselves getting into their separate cars to go to hear him they decided to share one car. They returned the following night and there on 10 March 1971, Pat, Bill, Paul, John and Janne Subritzky gave their lives to the Lord and were baptised in the Spirit. Bill and Pat's marriage was instantly healed.[44] Only God knew how much ministry was in store for them but the miracle healings Bill had witnessed had changed his life and purpose for ever.

Barely three days later God told each of them they should start a prayer meeting in their home.[45] Six people attended the first evening; the ministry became hugely influential and continued in the public ministries they conducted for so many years.

---

44. See Pat Subritzky, *Chosen Destiny*, 33-37 and Bill Subritzky/Vic Francis, *On The Cutting Edge: The Bill Subritzky Story*, Sovereign, Tonbridge, 1993. 59-72. Also Bill Subritzky's Address at ARMNZ National Conference October 1992, 12, ARMNZ papers.
45. Bill Subritzky, *Cutting Edge*, 73.

– 5 –

Fresh from the Fountain
Ray Muller and Christian Advance Ministries

Ray Muller – The Pioneer

The impact of Dennis Bennett's visit was not confined to Auckland. In 1967 the Rev. Ray Muller, chaplain at Massey University where a charismatic move had developed,[1] and a group of Wellington-based clergy arranged a ministry tour by Rev. Michael and Jeanne Harper from the UK. Michael had been assistant curate at All Souls Langham Place in London when he was baptised in the Spirit. Although he experienced initial opposition from John Stott, the famed Rector of All Souls, Michael and others subsequently set up the Fountain Trust as an agency to promote charismatic theology and experience. Ray had been in contact with Michael Harper since 1965.[2]

Michael and Jeanne arrived on 9 August 1967 and departed on 9 September having ministered in Wellington, Palmerston North, Eltham, Auckland, Christchurch, Geraldine and at a conference at the Arahina Conference Centre at Marton. Twenty-four peo-

---

1. See Report of the Provincial Commission on Charismatic Renewal, 45-46. 'By September 1966 five percent of the total number of students at Massey University were participants in an emerging charismatic renewal. Over half of the students were Anglicans.' Battley papers.
2. Williamson, 109.

ple including ten clergy attended the conference which Ray Muller considered was 'the first conference for [Anglican] charismatic clergy ever held in New Zealand'.[3] The extent of this tour evidences that an effective network of leading charismatics had quickly come into existence. These included Ray Muller, Cecil Marshall, Ken Prebble, Martin Warren and David Balfour.

The ministry of Michael and Jeanne modelled something that became widespread in the charismatic movement – the shared ministry of a husband and wife working in harmony with mutual recognition of the spiritual gifts they had received.[4] It is notable how quickly all this developed – Ray had been introduced to baptism in the Spirit in 1965 and by 1967 networks existed across the country and had relationships with significant leadership in the USA and Britain. Most of the New Zealand initiators were young clergy.

Ray left Palmerston North in 1968 to be vicar of Patea. In 1971 he and his wife Elaine went to the UK to work with Michael Harper at the Fountain Trust where they experienced how a renewal ministry based on an independent charitable trust could be organised and run. They assisted at Fountain Trust renewal conferences and met many of the key speakers of the renewal from Britain and other countries and denominations. In addition to British leaders like David Watson and Merv and Merla Watson, these included Father Francis MacNutt, a Dominican Catholic and writer, Dr Kevin Rannaghan from the Catholic charismatic renewal in the USA, the Baptist Dr Robert Frost and others who Ray was able to invite to come to New Zealand as speakers.

Ray and Elaine returned to New Zealand via the Catholic Community of the Word of God in Ann Arbor, Michigan where they stayed with Ralph Martin the leader of the community. They

3. Williamson, 41, Muller interview.
4. Williamson, 111, Muller interview, 2.

attended a Catholic Charismatic Renewal weekend at Notre Dame University, South Bend, attended by about 11,000 people where they witnessed a huge number of Catholics worshipping in the Spirit and singing songs like 'I have decided to follow Jesus, no turning back'. Elaine Muller was astonished to see Catholic people worshipping in such a way and was convinced this was genuine Christianity. Ray was introduced to a teaching course the National Catholic Charismatic Renewal Committee had been trialling. The course was known as the 'Life in the Spirit Seminars' (LiSS) and Ray was given a copy of the final draft to bring back to New Zealand.

On their way back they stopped at Fiji to take part in an eleven-day renewal mission[5] in the Diocese of Polynesia that had been organised by Rev. Edward Subramani. They were joined by Ken Prebble, John Childers and John Smith from St Paul's. Ray recalls:

> The mission was held in the Cathedral in Suva and we stayed at St John's Theological College. The weather was memorably humid and damp ... and it was not a particularly comfortable time.
>
> Following a ceremonial welcome on 26 July, in subsequent days we visited and spoke at the Pacific Theological College, Bishop Kempthorne Memorial School, Holy Trinity School, St Christopher's Home, St John's School, [and] Holy Trinity School.
>
> Mission Services were held each evening at 7.30pm in the Cathedral and numbers grew as the week progressed. The Dean was an American and he was not very pleased with the mission and mostly absented himself. Fr Prebble was the main speaker but I spoke several times as did John Childers.

---

5. Ray Muller gives the dates as 26 July to 5 August, 1972. Email 14 June 2014.

The final night was an 'altar call' for people to receive the Holy Spirit. Hundreds came forward to the altar rails which surrounded a free-standing altar on four sides. We prayed for them all one by one including Anglican and Roman Catholic religious.

I have the lasting memory of praying with Catholic and Anglican nuns and have them receiving the Holy Spirit, swooning and draping themselves over the altar rails only coming around in time to move on as we approached to pray for others on the circuit. It was a significant time and marked the beginning of the charismatic renewal in both the Anglican and Roman Catholic churches in Fiji.[6]

On their landing at Auckland airport they were met by Bill and Pat Subritzky and taken to Brian and Trish Jenkin's vicarage at Mt Roskill for breakfast[7] where Ray told them about the Life in the Spirit Seminars.[8] This was probably the first introduction of the seminars to Anglicans.[9]

Ray and Elaine's trip to the centres of charismatic renewal had remarkable impact on the renewal in New Zealand. They brought back knowledge of how to set up and run a renewal agency; how to plan and present major renewal conferences; personal knowledge of some of the leading speakers; and the remarkable resource of the

---

6. Email Ray Muller to DHB, 12 April 2014, 2.

7. Interview Brian Jenkins, 5 Nov 2010, 4. 'I remember meeting Ray Muller – they came back from England and arrived in Auckland and Bill and Pat went and got them and brought them to our place for breakfast.'

8. See my essay 'The Use and Effect of "Life in the Spirit Seminars" in the Anglican Diocese of Auckland 1973 to 1993', Massey paper 148.799, 7-8.

9. Catholic charismatics in New Zealand may have been trialling an earlier version during 1972.

Life in the Spirit Seminars coupled with experience of an outreach in the South Pacific. The stage was set for major development of the renewal.

Christian Advance Ministries

When Ray and Elaine returned from their time with the Fountain Trust, Ray and some colleagues from Anglican, Presbyterian, Catholic and Baptist churches set up a ministry called Christian Advance Ministries (CAM). Their aim was to be an ecumenical agency similar to the Fountain Trust to promote charismatic renewal in the mainstream New Zealand churches.[10] Initiated in August 1972, CAM had extensive impact around the country for twenty years. The Anglican founders were Ray and Elaine Muller,[11] Cecil Marshall (chaplain at Hutt Hospitals at the time), David MacGregor, student Keven Hall[12] and Arnold, Janet and James Kimberley.[13] David MacGregor was at the time managing a bookshop in Palmerston North, which became a centre for charismatic resources. He was subsequently ordained, served a curacy at Whanganui and emigrated to South Africa. An able guitarist, he helped shape the blending of new music with liturgical worship.

---

10. A fuller description is in Williamson's thesis *Uncomfortable Engagement*, 150-205.
11. Dale Williamson observed, 'It was Ray Muller's experience of the success of the Fountain Trust that was responsible for the setting up of CAM in New Zealand in 1972, and without his leadership skills and personal networks CAM would have probably never been created.' Ibid, 159.
12. Keven Hall subsequently gained a Ph D in biology at Auckland where he led Professor John Morton into charismatic experience. Keven was ordained and served as Director of Christian Education in Auckland diocese before moving to the UK.
13. Williamson, 153.

Ray Muller was founding Director of CAM from 1972 to 1975 and Cecil Marshall was Director from 1975 to 1980.

The aims of CAM as stated in its founding Deed witness to the theological maturity and imagination of the founders. The aims included:

a. To present by all forms of modern communications the message, saving acts and power of Jesus Christ in the integrity of the Scriptural witness as relevant to contemporary society.
b. To encourage Christians to receive the power of the Holy Spirit as bestowed upon the first day of Pentecost and in that continuing reality to glorify Jesus Christ by manifesting in their lives the fruit, gifts and graces of the same Spirit…
c. To serve the various branches of the Christian Church by:-
   i. Presenting the challenge of the renewal of the Church through the power of the Holy Spirit.
   ii. Encouraging parishes and local churches to seek such renewal and recover and exercise charismatic gifts and ministries as an authentic and normal expression of the Body of Christ.
   iii. Maintaining in such renewal the Lordship of Jesus Christ consistent with the teaching and experience of the New Testament and the balance and weight of theological and historical wisdom of the Church since the New Testament era.
   iv. Providing such forms of ministries including conferences, teaching, seminars, meetings, speakers, tapes, cassettes, films, literature and other services…[14]

---

14. Sourced from Williamson, 154-156, quoting from the CAM Deed of Declaration of Trust, February 1975, Cecil Marshall Collection, folder E-3-1,1.

The Council subsequently resolved 'that CAM be a service organisation for the Catholic and Anglican churches specifically, but ready to serve other mainline churches in a similar way' and some Roman Catholics were added to the leadership. In a subsequent response the Executive stated, 'We believe we have a part to play in the liaison or dialogue between the "classical" Pentecostals and the "charismatic".'[15] In 1976 a publicity leaflet described CAM as a 'para-parochial organism' which (looked) forward to the time when the need for CAM ... will be absorbed into a renewed and united Church of God, in which the charismatic gifts and ministries are a normative and authentic expression.[16]

The vision was for the service of renewal in the Anglican and Catholic churches but also for wider dissemination, and for liaison with Pentecostal churches. CAM quickly established itself as the communication hub, especially for Anglican renewal clusters that functioned in different areas but lacked the ability to organise widely or to bring speakers from overseas. In December 1975 CAM invited a number of people to be a consultative council with membership drawn from around the country and including denominations beyond Anglican and Catholic. Although that council never met, they were visited and consulted by Cecil Marshall as he moved around the country.[17]

CAM's first and defining project was to organise its first Summer School which was held at Massey and Lincoln Universities in January 1973.[18] Researcher Allen Neil subsequently described the first CAM Summer School as the New Zealand charismatic

---

15. Williamson, 157, quoting Minutes of the Executive Meeting of CAM Trust, 13 October 1975.
16. Williamson, 158, quoting Cecil Marshall Collection, folder B 1-1.
17. Williamson, 161.
18. The history of the Summer Schools is described in Williamson, 164-178.

movement's 'coming of age'.[19] The Summer Schools were promoted as 'for invited church leaders to hear at firsthand about the "charismatic" or "Pentecostal" renewal of the Church'.[20] Speakers at the first Summer School included Michael Harper from the UK, Catholic layman Kevin Ranaghan and Baptist minister Robert Frost.[21]

New Zealand speakers were Cecil Marshall on pastoral care; Ken Prebble on parish renewal, Catholics Fr John McAlpine on sacramental theology and Fr Bruce McGill CSSR on the spiritual life and (then) layman Charles Waldegrave on social concern.[22] The selection of the speakers and their topics showed CAM's commitment to the renewal of the historic churches, and their breadth of vision.

The Rev. Cecil Marshall, an Anglican evangelical charismatic and gifted scripture teacher, was also secretary to CAM and he ensured that all clergy known to be moving into renewal were encouraged to attend the early summer schools. The CAM Summer Schools seemed to be designed for unmarried university students, a major sector of the early renewal, and local church leaders who could somehow leave their children behind. Nevertheless, the summer schools were high-impact events. They were principally attended by Anglicans and Catholics who comprised between 60 to 80 percent of attendees between 1974 and 1977.[23]

---

19. Neil, *Institutional Churches*, 131.
20. 1973 leaders' invitation, CAM records, Box 2, folder 4.
21. Williamson, 170.
22. Charles Waldegrave, QSO, was active in the renewal from its start at Massey University and into its CAM days. He was ordained in 1975 and has served as a researcher in issues of poverty and justice since 1979.
23. See Table 1 in Williamson, 168. 'From one hundred and seventy-five participants in 1973 there was an increase to over five hundred in 1975.'

As a result of the visits of the first speakers like Dennis Bennett and Michael Harper, the distribution of the LiSS and the Summer Schools, clergy around the country had been initiated into the renewal. These included evangelicals like John Meadowcroft, Wallace Marriott, Malcolm Welch and David Harper and anglo-catholics like David Balfour (who were all in the South Island) and a wide range of priests in the North Island, many relating closely to Ray Muller, Cecil Marshall or Ken Prebble.[24]

By the time I became actively involved in charismatic renewal, New Zealanders had a number of key support systems in place: a good number of priests and others who had been developing charismatic theology and practice since 1966; a few role-model parishes; the Life in the Spirit Seminars; local support groups for clergy in Auckland and Christchurch; and the CAM Summer Schools. The stage was set for an outburst of activity.

---

24. It needs to be noted that there were some clergy who had experienced Baptism in the Spirit long before the visit of Dennis Bennett. Those known to me included Cyrus Meharry (from the 1940s), Maori Marsden and Derek Eaton (later Bishop of Nelson).

– 6 –

Rushing Streams
The Parish Renewal Movement

Parish Renewal – St Paul's

In January 1973 around fifty parishioners from St Paul's attended the first Christian Advance Ministries Summer School at Palmerston North where the St Paul's Singers led the music.[1] Merritt describes this as an extraordinary time for St Paul's which created great enthusiasm and great stress; it was 'the dawning of the growing period at St Paul's.'[2] The St Paul's Singers established a new style of singing at the choral eucharist and grew to sixteen members and began writing their own songs. In February 1973 the parish commenced using the Life in the Spirit Seminars – probably the first use by a parish in New Zealand.[3] By June 1973 a ministry of dance was added following a ministry visit of the Reverend David Watson and Merv and Merla Watson from York in England.[4] Merritt summarised this period:

> The message of the importance of a strong church in the Body of Christ given to St Paul's by the Rev. Graham Pulkingham

1. Merritt, op.cit., 83.
2. Ibid, 83-85.
3. Ibid, 86.
4. Ibid, 91.

was largely heeded in the two years 1972-1973 ... As the church matured the congregation learned new forms or expressions of worship. New ministries emerged and became established parts of the church's worship.[5]

But despite a number of attempts, little progress was made with community living.

A striking feature of St Paul's was that it modeled both informal charismatic worship on Wednesday and Sunday evenings and a renewal-style anglo-catholic eucharistic worship on Sunday mornings. The morning eucharist blended charismatic songs and spiritual gifts with full Anglican liturgy with robes and incense. Each of the services balanced the other and inspired enquirers to appreciate both. The sung praise in particular attracted people from other parishes who visited and returned to their home churches with new vision for contemporary worship.

By 1973 the ripples of influence from St Paul's were spreading widely. The trail-blazing efforts of St Paul's and St Margaret's in the Auckland area – and of some other parishes elsewhere in the country – had prepared a way which others began to follow. Father Prebble resigned as vicar of St Paul's in 1974 after twenty years service in order to make way for a younger priest to lead the parish[6] and became vicar of Wellsford, and Rev. Fr David Balfour was appointed the next vicar. David brought current renewal experience from his time as vicar of Lyttelton.

By 1973 another three Auckland parishes were becoming established in charismatic renewal.

5. Ibid, 94.
6. Interview, Mary Prebble, 2014.

St Thomas New Lynn

The Rev. David Guthrie, who had been baptised in the Spirit while in St John's College, arrived at St Thomas New Lynn in 1972 and saw possibilities for renewal.[7] This began with a group of men who for some years had been meeting as the Full Gospel Businessmen's Fellowship International whose prayer support encouraged David to move towards parish renewal.

A week's visit by Ray Muller in 1972 showed that renewal did not have to be tied to a Pentecostal or FGBMFI culture and that a more Anglican interpretation was possible. Some families who had attended St Paul's or other churches decided to commit to St Thomas including Paul Gravelle who became an influential teacher. David introduced liturgical changes (which were being promoted in the diocese at the time) including the use of more contemporary songs – like many of the younger clergy David was a guitarist – and the passing of the Peace which quickly changed the feeling and character of the liturgy and caused some conflict.

The CAM Summer School of 1973 showed David the place of charismatic gifts in a liturgical setting and he adopted four principles for parish renewal: personal and corporate renewal of people's relationships with God; being corporately led by the Holy Spirit; rediscovery of Christian community; and renewal of individual and corporate responsibility for mission. A parish prayer group for parish renewal was commenced in the vicarage on Tuesday nights where the spiritual gifts were exercised. The prayer group included communion. Three other small prayer groups were started and care levels amongst members increased markedly.

Although the parish's style was anglo-catholic there was a marked

---

7. This section is based upon Allen Neil, *Institutional Churches*, 251-267 and on Neil's interview with David Guthrie, 17 May 1973.

increase in evangelism and mission. Some parishioners found the changes unsettling but by teaching the baptism of the Spirit as a 'release' of the gift received in baptism some tensions were reduced. There was little immaturity amongst the leading charismatics. But the process was very new when Neil reported on it. The parish's first use of the LiSS was in 1974 and by that time 'the place was fair humming with new life'.[8]

St Martin's Mt Roskill

The Reverend Brian Jenkins arrived at St Martin's Mt Roskill early in 1972 and was advised by the departing vicar, Father Fisher, that he should attend the prayer meeting Bill and Pat Subritzky were holding in their home as Bill regularly attended the early morning parish prayers.[9] Although Brian found the style of the meeting 'a foreign culture' he recognised that something of real value was happening.[10]

> We gathered around and we worshipped and people shared what was happening in their lives. It was really the first time I had experienced people sharing publicly in a church meeting like that… And the next thing I noticed was the way, as people shared, other people would say something that would often be fairly blunt but it was given and received in love. It didn't seem to cause offence and … they felt able to share them in this atmosphere and they often got very good, common sense, sound advice or counsel and it was all wrapped

8. Interview with Paul Gravelle, 16 July 2010, 2.
9. This section is based on Allen Neil, 267-281 and on Battley interview with Brian Jenkins, 5 November 2010.
10. Neil, 270.

up in turning to God and what we call 'prayer counselling'. And then there were testimonies to how people's lives were changed – there may be little testimonies – just ordinary things – just people's ordinary lives ... but they were very meaningful for the people sharing them.

I remember when they prayed one night for Trish [Brian's wife] at this prayer meeting. She just came into a beautiful tongue, just like that, and I thought to myself, 'She's off!' but not for me, so it was a much longer, harder road and it was months later when they were praying for somebody next to me and I was totally relaxed and I just opened my mouth and it flowed out – there was no pressure. So gradually I became more and more deeply involved in this prayer meeting which kept growing and growing.[11]

As the Subritzky's home meeting was attracting more and more people from all around Auckland, the parish commenced a parish prayer meeting on Sunday evenings for church members. The parish was also impacted by the healing mission of Harry Greenwood in 1972 and by ministry by John and Yvonne Childers from St Paul's.[12]

A parish planning meeting recommended more spontaneity in worship, extempore prayers at the intercession, introduction of contemporary songs and encouragement of prayer and bible study groups. A new spirit of freedom and joy infused the Sunday worship. The use of the laying on of hands for blessing and healing increased. The CAM Summer School of 1973 equipped Brian with wider understanding of charismatic ideas and practices and in 1973 they commenced using the LiSS. By 1973 renewal was develop-

11. Interview, Brian Jenkins, 5 November 2010, 2.
12. Neil, 271.

ing in the 'cautious yet open and responsible approach' that Brian adopted.[13]

Lynfield Community Church

The Rev. Canon Mangatitoki Cameron (known as Manga) became minister of the Anglican-Methodist Co-operating Parish of Lynfield in 1971. He had had previous encounter with the charismatic movement while vicar of Glen Innes but been put off by some of the enthusiasts and what he deemed to be simplistic beliefs. In 1971 he was struggling with the death of God theology and found himself moving rapidly away from it.

Towards the end of 1971 he came into 'the fullness of the Christ-experience'[14] and found that he now believed in miracles. The charismatic experience came to reinforce this recovery of faith and he found that freedom in worship and freedom from theological wrangling were two early results of Spirit baptism. As a Maori he began to appreciate Maori religious insights which he had previously considered to be superstitious ignorance and to realise that 'the evisceration of traditional Christianity has left many Maori bewildered and confused'.[15] Neil recorded in 1973, no doubt reflecting Cameron's views,

> Maoris who have embraced the charismatic spirituality have found a kinship with Pakeha charismatics, even beyond their own ecclesial boundaries. Generally both Maori and Pakeha charismatics firmly adhere to the fundamental Christian

---

13. Neil, 280.
14. Neil, 283, quoting his interview with Manga Cameron in June 1973. Neil does not describe what Cameron meant by this.
15. Ibid.

dogmas which have from the beginning been the framework and structure of Christian faith. This position is not necessarily fundamentalism or a rejection of scholarship, but simply an honest and realistic recognition that Christianity involves some definite doctrinal positions which cannot be set aside without abandoning Christianity itself.[16]

Cameron's conclusion on Lynfield Co-operating parish was that 'charismatic renewal has contributed almost nothing to the parish but a gradual growth towards inculcation of Christian spirituality shows signs of movement towards eventual renewal'.[17]

Neil observed in 1973 that 'the number of theologically literate Anglican charismatic clergy who are able to distinguish between scholarly interpretation and sophistic falsification in the Church is increasing'.[18] A scholar who made significant contributions to the acceptance of charismatic renewal was Professor John Morton, Professor of Zoology at Auckland University. A devout and erudite Christian, whose extempore speeches in synod were a delight to experience, Morton had been introduced to baptism in the Spirit by his student Keven Hall. Morton was soon engaged in vigorous debate in the pages of the Anglican newspaper *Church and People*.[19] In March 1973, following his attendance at the 1973 CAM Summer School, Morton wrote 'from now on I am fully committed and engaged'.[20] He remained a committed participant to his final days.[21]

16. Neil, 283-4.
17. Neil, 288.
18. Neil, 284.
19. Williamson, 247-248.
20. *Church and People*, 12 March 1973, 6.
21. Personal conversation with John Morton, 21 May 2010, Mss notes, Battley papers.

Synod Debates

In July 1970 the Auckland charismatics presented a motion to their synod on the renewal. Father Prebble moved 'that this Synod recognises the importance of the Pentecostal movement and commends it to all church people for their study'. Not helped by the unfortunate use of the word 'Pentecostal', the motion generated vigorous debate and some harsh criticisms which were defended by Ken Prebble, Herb Boniface, Bob Hansen and Gerry Hadlow. An oppositional amendment was then moved, 'That this Synod recognises the variety of the gifts of the Holy Spirit in the individual and corporate life of the church' and, despite Bishop Gowing describing this as 'a ridiculous motion as the church had always believed in these things', the amendment was carried. *Church and People* described it as 'an unsatisfactory and inconclusive end'.[22] The debate left the charismatics feeling somewhat disheartened but still determined.

In 1973 Bishop Gowing appointed Manga Cameron as his official liaison person with the charismatic renewal in Auckland[23] and Cameron presented a further motion to the 1973 Synod:

> That for the guidance of Anglicans, especially laymen, a Commission be appointed to study the theology of the Holy Spirit, particularly in relation to the Charismatic Movement which is affecting all denominations, and to report to the next synod.

The resulting commission consisted of Dr Anderson, Warden of St John's College, Archdeacon Ted Buckle, Canon Manga

---

22. *Church and People* 31 July 1970, 15.
23. Neil, 137.

Cameron, Professor John Morton, Rev. Michael Houghton, Dean John Rymer, Ph D student Keven Hall and Bill Subritzsky. Their report, which John Morton collated, was presented to the Synod in November 1974. It was a balanced analysis of the theology and early development of the charismatic movement in the diocese and observed that:

> The Church in New Zealand is very different today from five years ago; and of all the developments responsible for its present style and tempo, the charismatic movement – though still a minority – is probably the most influential.[24]

The report drew on sound and affirmative work from the Catholic Church in its evaluation of charismatic renewal but also drew from that source a list of possible faults such as illuminism, charismania, paraclericalism, overinflation, exclusivism, anti-intellectualism and social-political ambivalence. The generally open nature of the report set the tone for a responsible debate. The *Church and People* correspondent reported that:

> The discussion was marked by apparent goodwill and the cautionary statements were made without rancour, but rather in an entirely positive manner. The Commission's report was received without opposition.[25]

This synod response was helpful to those of us hovering on the edge of the movement as it signalled that it was acceptable to

---

24. Report of the Synod Commission on the Theology of the Holy Spirit and the Charismatic Movement presented to the Auckland Diocesan Synod in July, 1974, 14, Battley papers.
25. *Church and People*, December 1974, 1.

participate and to take the people into it. The change in tone from the 1970 synod debate to 1974 showed that understanding and acceptance had improved significantly.

Auckland members of General Synod, led by Professor Morton, then took the matter to the 1974 General Synod[26] which authorised a commission appointed by the archbishop to study the significance of the charismatic renewal and to 'consider the theological, pastoral, liturgical and evangelistic implications of the movement as it currently affects the Church of the Province'.[27] Renewal members of the commission included Wallace Marriott of Dunedin, Ray Muller of Wellington and Allen Neil. The report of the commission is well summarised in Dale Williamson's thesis.[28] The report concluded that:

> There are now Anglican charismatic Christians in almost every urban and rural centre in New Zealand. Many of these Christians receive fellowship and teaching outside their Church, in interdenominational charismatic fellowships… Many charismatic Anglicans have found difficulty in relating in a positive way to the institutional Church.[29]

Dale's summary of the situation by 1976 states:

> Because of the growth of the Charismatic Movement in the

---

26. Morton, 21 May 2010, 'The Report of the Provincial Commission on the CR came from the Aucklanders, stimulated by the Auckland Committee which brought the matter to the Auckland Diocesan Synod'. 'I was on the committee in Auckland and I spoke at the General Synod in 1978.' Mss notes, op. cit.
27. Williamson, 253.
28. Williamson, 253-8.
29. Report of the Provincial Commission, op. cit., 69.

1970s it was a time for the NZA[30] to assess its place. This 1976 General Synod report showed that the growth of the movement meant it had to be accepted as part of the NZA. Even though some dangers were acknowledged, this report saw that the Charismatic Movement provided a vehicle for spiritual renewal in the Church.[31]

By the mid-1970s Anglican charismatic renewal had developed the core resources to propagate widespread renewal: its basic theology and practice; experience in healing ministries; models for charismatic Sunday worship both liturgical and free-form; a vehicle for spreading baptism in the Spirit; new music and a nation-wide renewal agency in CAM. The first wave of renewal was completed and the second wave was about to surge.

---

30. NZA is Dale Williamson's abbreviation for the Anglican Church in Aotearoa, New Zealand and Polynesia.

31. Ibid, 258.

- 7 -

Under the Waterfall
The Spirit Falls at Pakuranga

Beside the Tamaki River – Pakuranga Parish

Eleanor and I were blithely unaware of these spiritual developments when we arrived in March 1971 at the newly-created parish of Pakuranga. Pakuranga had been a rural area situated between the colonial villages of Howick to the east and Panmure to the west. Worship had been provided by Howick Parish somewhere in the area in the 1880s when attendances ranged from thirty to eighty at a 7.00pm evening service. Sunday morning worship had commenced on Easter Day 1898 but it is not clear where the services were held.[1]

By the 1960s substantial suburban development was happening at the western side of Pakuranga which was serviced by the Panmure Parish where the Rev. Bruce Moore was vicar from 1964. That year the churches conducted an inter-church household survey which revealed more than 350 Anglican families were living in Pakuranga as well as 600 in Panmure.[2] Sunday schools were begun in Pakuranga Heights and Anchorage Park schools and it soon became apparent that a worship centre was needed in the new suburb. The Rev. Bruce Gilberd arrived in 1965 as assistant

---

1. Auckland Diocesan Archives (ADA) S10 P33 Box 5.
2. *150 Years of History, 1852-2002, St Matthias Church, Panmure,* Peter J Taylor, self-published, Panmure: Auckland, 2002, 62.

curate with mission responsibility for Pakuranga and worship was commenced in a classroom at the Pakuranga Heights School with Communion twice a month and a Family Service or Matins on the other Sundays.

The Reeves family were subdividing their Greenhill farm in the 1960s and they sold four sections to the church at favourable terms. The vicarage section in Reeves Road was paid for by selling a section the parish held in Tiraumea Drive. The three sections for the church site in Udys Road were purchased on a ten-year deferred purchase granted by Frank and Florence Reeves. Diocesan finance was granted to build a vicarage and hall[3] and by September 1966 the vestry had accepted tenders for £16,500 to build the vicarage and a hall with a small chapel, toilets and a kitchen. The buildings were dedicated by Bishop Gowing on Sunday 3 September 1967, the bishop optimistically stating, 'It will be five years before work is begun on the Anglican Church adjoining the hall.'[4]

When Bruce Gilberd became vicar of Avondale he was replaced by the Rev. Max Shennan and attendances grew to around sixty a week. An effective stewardship programme was run and by 1970 St Peter's had enough offerings income to support a vicar. The Parochial District of Pakuranga was constituted on 26 February 1971[5] and in March I was instituted as its first vicar. Eleanor and I arrived with three young boys aged five years to ten months – ideal for a 'nappy valley' area as Pakuranga was in those days.

St Peter's Pakuranga was a dynamic, young and hope-filled community of younger Anglicans many of whom had been envi-

---

3. ADA, P75 Box 1 File GTB710/DLB 79, Pakuranga 1966-1973. The loans were £6000 for the vicarage and £10,000 for the hall.
4. *New Zealand Herald,* 4 September 1967.
5. Diocesan Secretary to Secretary, Panmure Vestry, 10 March 1971, ADA P75 Box 1 File GTB710.

sioned by the Anglican youth movement of the 1950s. A number of resourceful people also arrived from the Church of England. A Church Army children's mission had been led by Sister Elsie Close that summer, boosting the children's and family interest. The early growth was amazing. New people seemed to turn up every Sunday[6] and the Sunday School, which was held in the nearby Pakuranga Heights School, grew until we had to have a waiting list. To staff the Sunday School we taught that it was a 'parent co-operative' and we required each family to provide one teacher (either parent) at least one term every two years. This made life challenging for the superintendents but it seemed to work.

The monthly family services were hectic but exciting experiences as we experimented with family styles of worship and when one parent gathered young people with guitars we began to sing simple contemporary songs beginning with 'Kum ba ya' and 'We shall overcome'.

Another strength was the women's groups. A lively Young Wives Group was already active with younger women joining it. Coffee mornings for young mums were held in the vicarage, complete with pre-schoolers everywhere. How Eleanor coped with the chaos I can't imagine, but she was always calm about it all. An Evening Women's Group was started by Eleanor as this group wanted to go deeper into their faith and it grew rapidly.

We sought a Church Army evangelist to staff our families' work and obtained Capt. Peter Allfrey from 1973. Unknown to us, the Lord had promised Peter that he 'would see spiritual renewal come powerfully in the Pakuranga Parish'. But I hadn't heard that – yet.

For the first few years I felt like I was coachman on a coach where

---

6. An unusual aid to this was a keen parishioner, Brian Freeman, who laid lawns for newly-built houses. He would invite the new residents to St Peter's and it often worked.

the horses had bolted, as I hung on for dear life coping with all the activity, hoping the wheels would not fall off. It was exhilarating but much was being done in our own strength and optimism. Sooner or later reality was going to catch up with us. We needed to find a deeper spirituality behind what we were doing in our own strength.

Into the River

Suddenly it was all just too much. I hadn't had enough holiday – or so it felt – my desk was a sea of work, and I felt I couldn't face another long year of struggle and conflict. I had been the first vicar of Pakuranga for three hectic years. It had been exhilarating and full of promise. Then in the third year every problem imaginable seemed to ambush us. Now I faced a fourth year and I didn't see how I could cope. I can't recall quite how it happened, but that day I found myself on my knees in my small study – a very rare occurrence in those days. With my head in my hands, I prayed out loud, 'O Lord, renew *this* church, and start with me.'

Nothing outstanding happened. No lights. No voice. No apparent change. A little sheepishly I got back on my chair and the day went on unchanged. Or was it? I knew I had at last done something my bishop had challenged us all to do some years before when he had called us all to pray, 'O Lord, renew your church beginning with me.' It had seemed such a trite prayer that in my immaturity I had declined to even try it. Until now. Now it was an urgent, unrehearsed cry for help. I think I wondered what might follow. Nothing much seemed to change for a little while.

About ten days later there was a firm rap on the door beside my study. 'Not another one!' I muttered as I went to answer it. 'Hi, I'm Derek Batts' the stranger said. 'Can I come in and discuss something with you?' Having no option, I agreed. Apparently he and some friends had been running something called a 'Life in the

Spirit Seminar' in another part of the city and he felt 'led by the Lord' to start one in our suburb. Two of my parishioners[7] had been attending it and thought I might be sympathetic. Could he book our hall for a series of nights and offer the seminars to our church and any others from the community? All we would have to do was provide the place and they would do the rest. And he hoped I would be able to come along.

I don't recall quite how Derek explained what a Life in the Spirit Seminar was but I gathered that he had been helping with one being held in the Anglican hall at Kohimarama where the vicar was, in my opinion, a pretty sensible sort of fellow.[8] And it did sound interesting. And, anyway, in those days we let our building to anyone who would pay us some rent, so, why not? Thus are big decisions sometimes made for trivial reasons.

I explained that we would not be able to start immediately as our pastoral assistant and I were about to start a ten-week Clinical Pastoral Education (CPE) course in counselling. He agreed to wait until mid-year. Derek asked if he could pray with me about the seminars; I agreed, and he prayed with considerable vigour and a somewhat fake American accent that the Lord would bless me and the church as we took this step. My modest 'Amen' didn't exactly match his confident praying.

When I put it to the vestry for approval someone suggested that we visit Kohimarama parish to see what actually happened. Another member expressed concern about 'letting that sort of thing into our parish'. So one Monday night most of the vestry went to visit a night of the Kohimarama Life in the Spirit Seminar.

---

7. Joan Rutherford and Joan Dallaway.
8. The vicar was the Rev. John Brokenshire. The Kohimarama vestry agreed to host a LiSS on 18 June 1973. Kohimarama Vestry Minute Book, 1970-76, AADA S10 P44 Box 5/2.

Eleanor and I met before with the vicar John Brokenshire and his wife Sheila who shared how much their lives and ministry had been enriched by being 'baptised in the Spirit' and by experiencing spiritual gifts both personally and amongst some of their parishioners. They seemed impressively sane and positive. Apparently the seminars were being jointly sponsored by the local Anglican and Methodist ministers with support from Wyn Fountain's home prayer group although the seminars were actually Roman Catholic in origin. That sounded reassuring. Then we were given dinner by a leading couple in the parish, Rob Smellie and his wife, who spoke highly of the effect of the seminars on themselves and on John and Sheila. I was impressed that someone as competent as this city barrister – and a synodsman as well – could be taking this so seriously.

When we joined the seminar we found a hall full of people enthusiastically singing contemporary songs of praise some of which we already knew. What impressed us was the confidence with which they sang. A spirit of praise seemed to fill the place which was alive with expectation and a pulsating sense of love. Someone gave a testimony and then Wyn Fountain followed with teaching on 'Salvation' which I found somewhat simplistic but also quite convincing. I recalled how a year or so before, faced with preparing a sermon on salvation from our lectionary readings, I had despairingly said to the Lord, 'I don't even know what "salvation" *means*, Lord.' Now someone was spelling it out for me!

During the small group time John and a few others met with our group to answer our questions. We felt received and loved. Nothing was pressed on us but something very compelling was clearly on offer. We agreed to host one series of the seminars in the parish.

When we got home Eleanor startled me by saying as we prepared for bed, 'Well, are we going to pray together?' We had been married for over nine years but praying together had been a rare and rather private thing, each of us praying our own brief prayers in silence. Rather haltingly we gave it a try. My rather brief contribution was 'Lord, if this is for real, we want it.' Not a bad start really. From that day on our spiritual lives took off. We read all the popular literature of the renewal movement often till 1.00am. Our bibles came alive and we prayed often together. We were onto an enthralling and very fast learning curve.

'Give yourself a party!'

At the same time two other things were happening. The CPE course required ten hours a week training and frequent case studies of our pastoral work. It enriched my understanding of counselling and put me in touch with things in my own life that needed healing and change. I came out of the CPE reunited with my inner self and ready for an adventure. Towards the end of the CPE the group had done a study on the parable of the prodigal son and we were challenged to identify ourselves in the story. I could only find myself in the older brother – not so much in his antagonism to his prodigal brother but in his duteous approach to life. He never kicked the system; he had done all that the authorities in his life had required. He knew neither rebellion, forgiveness nor grace. And he secretly resented his daily obedience and conscientious labour. What had his father challenged him to do? 'Go, kill you own fatted calf. Give yourself a party!'

I came out of CPE resolved to give myself a party on the gospel – and the party would be the Life in the Spirit Seminar. At the same time the parishioners were meeting in sensitivity groups discovering each other and beginning to trust themselves and their needs to each other. Both the CPE and the sensitivity groups were remarkably suitable preparation for what was to come.

The Pakuranga Life in the Spirit Seminar began on a Saturday night in June 1974.[9] About a hundred people gathered, half of them from the parish. Derek Batts had brought in a leadership team of mainly Baptist and Pentecostal friends who rather alarmed the parishioners when they began worshipping with much vigour. The sheer energy of the praise was quite startling but even more was the evidence that these people clearly believed what they were proclaiming. Some of the Catholic writers of the seminars were professionally trained educators. Their training showed in the design of the seminars which included worship in a contemporary free-form style, personal testimony by a team member, straightforward biblical teaching followed by small group discussion led by the group leaders. The evening could end with more worship and a supper.

Significantly the course began with 'God Loves You' rather than the conventional evangelical emphasis on human sinfulness.[10] This starting point related well to the needs of the 1970s when many people felt a lack of love and loss of personal significance. 'God loves you and wants to bless you' was a fresh view of Christianity and one that stood in sharp contrast to the negative messages of the 1960s, either that 'you are a bad person' or 'God is dead so why bother?'

By the third night the teaching was on 'The New Life' which explained how the Holy Spirit is given to the believer and how the charismata, the spiritual gifts, can be received by believers today. On the fifth night people were prayed for to be baptised

---

9. Joan Rutherford maintains that there was an earthquake shock in the area that night and that it was reported in the local newspaper. Interview, Joan Rutherford, 23 May 2010, 2.

10. Some years before, the Anglican Enquiry Centre, based in Nelson diocese, had produced a series of leaflets on faith for unbelievers of which the first leaflet was headed SIN. By contrast the charismatic movement started from the statement 'God loves you'. This was a radical and biblical re-presentation of the faith and very relevant to people's needs at the time.

in the Holy Spirit and to speak in tongues. The concluding evenings introduced the basic principles of living the life of faith in the power of the Spirit.

That first seminar was a wild ride for most of us. Eleanor used to come home each evening thinking, 'I don't think I'm ever going to make it,' but somehow we went back each week. The people teaching it, who included John Brokenshire, were fervent in their conviction that God would fill believers today in the same way he did in the Acts of the Apostles – which they called Baptism in the Spirit – and with the same signs following, especially the gift of tongues. They had enough scriptural evidence to support what they were teaching and witnessing to. It was in fact basic Pentecostal doctrine, slightly modified by the Catholic charismatic connection.

And it made a lot of sense. Rather amazingly the Bible, which we had both known reasonably well, suddenly become electrifyingly alive. We would devour whole sections of it in private reading and were finding witness to the workings of the Holy Spirit wherever we read. How come all this was there and we had never noticed it before? Why had the various sections on the gifts of the Spirit never been evident before? And why had our church never taught us about all this?

It was as if a veil had somehow been stripped from our eyes. Clearly the type of Christianity known in the New Testament period was decidedly different from what we had met so far in the Anglican Way. And these enthusiastic people were saying it could all be ours for the asking! When they began singing in tongues we felt both alarmed and fascinated. When someone spoke up, apparently speaking in the first person for God, we were intrigued and either awed or worried, especially if the message was shouted rather loudly. Anglicans simply do not *do* such things!

Yet God seemed to be there and the parishioners present were starting to experience some of the spiritual gifts. Even before the fifth night, some of them were reporting that they had started speaking in tongues in their private prayers. Others were less sure of themselves but kept coming.

One night in the early stages of the seminar I was alone in the house and I began to pray so easily and delightfully with great love in my heart for God. My spirit soared; my heart was bursting with love and joy and suddenly my whole being was alive with energy like pulsing waves. My body felt electrified and words failed to express the exhilaration that swept my soul. In retrospect I know that was the time of the transformation. That was the occasion of the infilling. At last I had broken through – or was it God who broken through? From that time on *I knew that I knew that I knew,* as the American evangelist Oral Roberts would say. Shortly after, Eleanor and I were visiting with the Rev. Terry Barton[11] who had been in renewal for some time and described what was happening. He smiled and said, 'Oh, it's already happened. I can see that!'

Between the fourth and the fifth nights the seminar process provided for a one-on-one meeting of the group leader with each participant to answer questions and help them prepare to be prayed for. I had many questions of Derek although I had already learned much from the seminars and our reading. I was quite satisfied that God willed to fill believers with his Spirit and that it was biblical to speak of this as being baptised with the Spirit and that charismata would also be received including tongues. But would tongues work for *me*? In my case I had already tried at least *three* times! That was the anxiety for many of us.

---

11. The Rev. Canon Terry Barton was a former chartered accountant and had been Auditor-General for Nigeria before he trained for the ministry. He was a much loved vicar of St Thomas' Tamaki before Bishop Gowing asked him to serve as his personal chaplain (secretary). Terry and his wife Win had a prayer meeting in their home for many years which prayed for renewal in the diocese.

We approached the fifth night with a mixture of expectation and trepidation. I had already tried to bargain with God saying that if it had to be a choice of gifts I would prefer the gift of healing as it would benefit more people but with parishioners coming into this new language I deduced, rightly I think, that God *had* to do it for me, for the good of the church. So I told him plainly that it was past the question of whether I wanted it: I told him it had to happen 'if I am to continue to lead this lot!' The theology was muddled but the aspiration was right.

The fifth night came and the leaders had brought others along to bolster the numbers available to pray with all the participants. A Pentecostal pastor had been brought into my group to make sure I got it. By this time I was satisfied that I had already asked the Lord on at least three occasions to baptise me in the Spirit and it was evident that he had been doing so in preceding months. So I modified the set prayer the seminars provided and I thanked God that he had baptised me in the Spirit and asked him to complete it and to give me spiritual gifts including the gift of tongues.

When the group prayed over me with laying on of hands I felt no great change or event and they encouraged me to speak out in tongues. Now it all got a bit embarrassing. Nothing seemed to be happening – no rush of words – no great flow of anything.

'Just say something – anything,' they said. 'You have to speak – you prime the pump and God gives the flow.'

So I haltingly said, 'Ka – la – ma' and stopped.

'That's good,' they said. 'Add something more.'

'This is ridiculous!' I thought. 'I'm just creating this myself.'

'Ka la ma, ka la ma,' I tried again.

'Keep going,' they said, 'God will give more.'

So I added 'dumba' and felt a complete idiot.

'That's it!' they said. 'You've got it. Just keep using it and more will come.'

'I'm a university graduate with a good mind,' I thought. 'Why am I doing all this? How dumb can I get?' I kept on trying but that was about as far it got that night.

As the small groups came together for concluding worship I was struck by the radiant faces of so many people. They seemed to shine like lights and their smiles were wider than I had ever seen. The concluding worship soared from over a hundred hearts and mouths and when it moved into singing in the Spirit I heard amazing multiple harmonies fill the building. The beauty was beyond description. 'This is what heaven must sound like' I thought as song followed song and prophecies of encouragement issued from some of the team. Whatever had happened to me, a lot had happened to many others. That night the core of the parish was reborn.

Early in the seminars we had been encouraged to start a prayer meeting in the vicarage lounge to keep the group together. We had no idea what to do in such a meeting. Apparently there was more to it than just singing a few songs and having a bible study. We were told we needed to learn how to use the gifts in public and how to 'minister' to each other. One team member offered to come and show us how. Roger Grundy and his wife June came across Auckland each Wednesday to lead our prayer meeting. Roger told us we needed an 'eldership' to pray before the meeting for 'covering' and to 'discern' what the Spirit was doing in the group.

We designated as prayer meeting elders the three pastoral staff members (parish evangelist Peter Allfrey, pastoral assistant Joan Dallaway and myself) and Joan Rutherford who, it transpired, was more than a little responsible for having prayed this holy fire onto the parish, as well as Roger Grundy. We were later joined by Mick Nelson, a long-time Pentecostal, who somewhat to his chagrin found himself in an Anglican church when the Lord finally answered his prayers for his wife to be filled with the Spirit by doing it in an Anglican church. Mick brought helpful awareness of the faults that can occur in a group that is experiencing spiritual power. The decision to introduce the concept of elders was to have further implications for the parish.

The prayer meeting was only a few weeks old by the fifth night of the seminars but the spacious lounge was already quite full of people keen to know more of the ways of the Spirit and the workings of the gifts. The Wednesday after the fifth night promised to be something very special. But before that we had to cope with what was happening in the vicarage. Eleanor and I had both come home from the fifth night with a few words each of an unknown language. (Eleanor promptly wrote hers down to make sure she still remembered them in the morning!)

Derek made his holiday home available to us so we could have a few days to reflect and consolidate what was happening. But something was wrong for Eleanor. Quite uncharacteristically she was sliding into a dark depression. I had never seen her like this before. We were alone in a strange house; I was wanting time apart to keep exploring my new language, and feeling a bit dislocated by it all, and Eleanor was feeling terrible. I did not know what had happened though she believed she was experiencing an absence of God such as she, who had always had faith, had never known.[12] She had been increasing in the presence of the Spirit throughout the seminars, indeed from the very night we had prayed, 'Lord, if this is for real, we want it.' Now it seemed all to have been taken from her and she was in spiritual despair.

After a couple of days I heard her say what many a minister's wife may have wanted to say: 'You will pray for everyone else; why

---

12. Eleanor Battley, personal note. 'For me the two learning experiences were – what it felt like to be separated from God (which I had never previously experienced) – and that I needed to overcome my self-sufficiency and reveal my vulnerability by asking others publicly to pray for me.' Mss notes, Book file, Battley papers.

won't you pray for *me* when I need it?' It was a salutary and serious cry.

With much timidity I laid hands on her and prayed something like, 'Lord, I don't know what's going on here but I ask you to heal Eleanor's spirit and to restore her joy.' Slowly the depression started to lift.

The next day Eleanor asked that we return to Pakuranga so we could attend the prayer meeting. The lounge filled with people bubbling with joy and the singing began but soon Eleanor spoke up, telling them how difficult things had been for her and would they please pray for her? She received prayer and the darkness lifted. Eleanor had been a self-sufficient and reticent person. This experience led her to be open and receptive and to acknowledge her need of others.

From that night on the spiritual gifts flourished in her life and she commonly brought utterances in tongues, interpretations and prophecies in the meetings and ultimately in public worship. She made a deal with the Lord that anything he wanted said, she would be willing to bring. Obedience has always been one of her qualities. It helped, she claimed, that she wasn't in awe of the vicar! I don't think I ever heard Eleanor bring a word that I felt was not authentic and she had countless pictures from the Lord with none of them repeating another. God's creativity is truly awesome.

Photos

St Aidan's Church, Remuera, and baptismal font.

*Battley family at Whakarewarewa c.1947.
Left to right: Jack, Don, guide, Alison, Joyce.*

As M. Jourdain (right) in The Prodigious Snob, *Auckland Grammar Drama Club, 1955.*

As Benvolio (second from right) in Romeo and Juliet, *University Drama Club.*

Beach picnic near Wellington, January 1961.
Left to right: Bruce Gilberd, Andrea and Kevin Barnett, Margaret Nelson, ?, Pat Tanton (later Gilberd), Eleanor Nelson.

Ordination as priest, November 1964.
Left to right: Eleanor, Don, Joyce, Jack Battley.

No Way Back

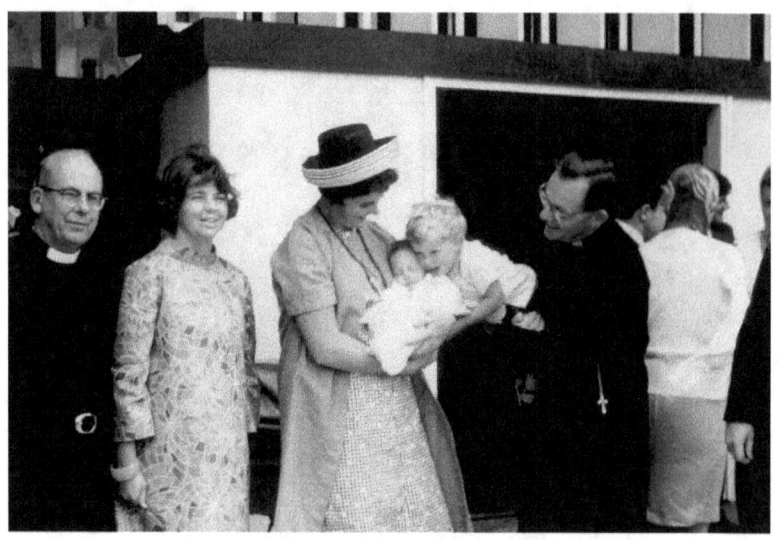

*Baptism of Christopher Battley, All Saints Ponsonby, 1967.
Left to right: Rev. Harry Boyd-Bell, Patsy Burton,
Eleanor, Chris, Mark, Don.*

*Eleanor with guitar.
She led worship this way for 27 years.*

Photos

St Peter's Pakuranga and community.

Action worship, faith-sharing at St Luke's, Melville.

Music ministry at St Peter's.

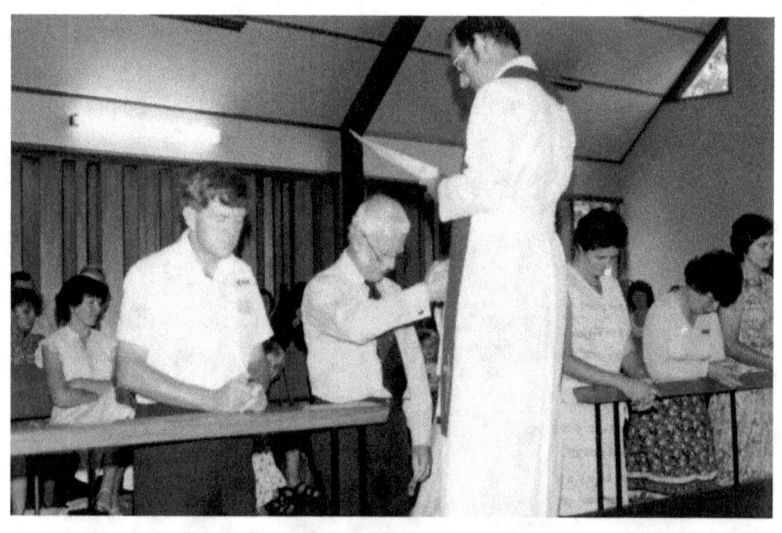

*Commissioning of St Peter's pastoral elders.
Left to right: Michael Guild, Doug Canning, Eleanor,
Joan Rutherford, Geneth Davies.*

*Charismatic High Mass at St Paul's Symonds Street,
Fr David Balfour presiding.*
Source: AADA P106, Auckland Anglican Diocesan Archives.
Published with permission.

*CAM Summer School at All Saints, Palmerston North.
David Harper, and Peter Minson on guitar.*
Photo: Julia Stuart.

*Enthusiastic worship at Summer School 1983.
Kath and Doug Pullar seated at right.* Photo: Julia Stuart.

– 8 –

No Way Back
Living in the Consequences

In preparing for the following Sunday I was faced with a decision: how much of all this was I to tell the parish? Were we going to keep this revival a sideshow in the parish – something that happened on Saturday and Wednesday nights – or was I to go public with it?

The Lord left me in no doubt which way to go. Somehow Acts 20:20 leapt off the page at me. St Paul, on leaving the Christians at Ephesus, declared to them, 'You know that I have not hesitated to preach anything that would be helpful to you but have taught you publicly and from house to house.'

Would I be able to look my people in the eye when I moved on and say, 'I have taught you all I know?' That settled it. If I was satisfied that this was true biblical Christianity I had no option. There was no way back. I had to tell the full truth and teach and minister until all had heard. So it has been from then till now.

From then on I was preaching about the person and work of the Holy Spirit each Sunday[1] and interest and some anxiety was rising amongst parishioners. No sooner had the first seminar concluded than people started asking for a second one. So the staff scheduled another series and placed an advertisement in the local paper. Suddenly I was in deep trouble.

---

1. So much so that after about a year of it one parishioner was heard to say, 'If Don preaches one more sermon on the Holy Spirit, I'll *scream!*'

No Way Back

At the next vestry meeting one member who disapproved of the new developments brought the advertisement and passed it around all the members. Then the attack began: I was accused of going beyond the permission to try just one seminar series (which was true) and of committing the parish to a charismatic style without consultation.

I made my explanation of why the next seminar was needed and probably claimed that we had been ambushed by God and now had to go with the consequences, and sat back. Others spoke of the significance of the seminar for them or their family members. Finally one somewhat conservative man who had attended the seminars spoke up saying, 'Well, I didn't speak in tongues but I am aware that God seems much closer. If it does that for our people, it can't be wrong.' And one member, a professor with a theological degree, added the classic Gamaliel statement, 'If this is of God, nothing will stop it.'[2]

I started to relax – the crisis was ebbing; the next seminar followed and then a third one. By the end of the year about a hundred parishioners had experienced a filling with the Holy Spirit and many had received a variety of spiritual gifts. The next annual meeting elected a vestry with a majority who had been renewed. While tensions continued about the changes that were happening, a clear majority of the leaders were convinced that this was a work of God which had to be pursued. I think the parish's rapid and gentle acceptance of the renewal was helped by it being a very young

---

2. The Rev. Professor Dr Douglas Lancashire was a most interesting person. The son of Lutheran missionaries in China he had been one of the first non-stipendiary Anglican deacons ordained in Hong Kong. He was Professor of Chinese at Auckland University and, when Paul Reeves became bishop of Auckland, was ordained priest and later became vicar of a parish in England. He also observed to me that what was happening looked like another holiness movement.

parish[3] and my being the first vicar. I was not having to compete with traditions laid down by previous vicars.

From the middle of 1974 onwards the parish was in effect experiencing a type of revival, although that expression was not in use at the time. I now consider that what was happening was a quite strong revival – more so than subsequent events which some have wanted to call revival. People were drawn to St Peter's Church without knowing why they were coming. One woman was actually told by a spiritualist to 'go to the nearest church to your home and you will find God there' – and she did.

Original music and praise burst out and people moved rapidly into a wide range of ministries. For once we were actually having some conversion growth and not growing just by transfer growth. The pace became exhausting with lengthy evening services, long prayer meetings and new leadership meetings that went late at night.

As the Holy Spirit worked in people they recognised areas of wounding or distress they needed to resolve. Our counseling ministries expanded and required more of our time as we explored the relationships between client-centred counselling and the revelatory and healing ministries of the Holy Spirit. We found ourselves on a multi-faceted learning curve where every aspect of ministry and church life had to be rethought and reshaped. The reassuring thing was that we were not alone and that others had already faced many of the issues.

By not coming into charismatic renewal until 1974, St Peter's Pakuranga benefitted from the preceding eight years of charismatic trial and error and from the wider forms of church renewal that had been promoted at diocesan and General Synod levels such as liturgical modernisation, increased lay participation in worship and

---

3. Unusually for an Anglican parish, the average age of the vestry would have been under forty.

pastoral ministry, and ecumenical openness. I was much helped and advised by David Balfour from St Paul's and Brian Jenkins at Mt Roskill and at times by Boni at Hillsborough.

Changes in Worship

Moving from traditional to new music styles was not easy and there was considerable pain in some parishes about the changes, some of which had come through synods and some from the renewal movement. At St Peter's the musical changes were not too difficult. As a young mission parish we were worshipping in what had been built as a badminton hall and were already worshipping with a piano and a few guitars singing songs like 'Kum ba ya' ('Come by here') and 'We shall overcome'.

Renewal experience introduced new songs and attracted new musicians. A small choir which sang on some Sundays struggled with the changes and finally split into those who liked the new music and those who didn't. The result was the formation of a music group (it never adopted a more prestigious title) which combined a mix of musicians and singers. Some of the musicians were teenagers who brought guitars, clarinets or trumpets; others were adults, some with professional musical skills, who supplied flute, keyboard, tambourine and recorders.

A challenge with this multi-instrument approach was where to find the person with the skills to make it all work. The leader needed a wide combination of skills – good musicianship; knowledge of the principles of worship and of the repertoire both old and new; some appreciation of the choral tradition; and also enthusiasm for the new possibilities of charismatic praise and of the charismatic gifts. Above all they needed good leadership skills with the ability to cope with the tensions of a group of enthusiastic amateurs mixed with some professionals – never an easy task.

I was perplexed as to how to select the leader. There seemed to be four or five possibilities, each with significant limitations. I adopted an analytical approach – I listed all the abilities needed and scored each person one to ten for each ability. The answer leapt off the page – by scoring a consistent good average plus ten for 'access to the vicar' my wife Eleanor was the clear leader by a high margin.

So was born Eleanor's ministry of leadership in music and worship which lasted for thirty years through four parishes and our time with Anglican Renewal Ministries. Although not a trained musician, she became a capable guitarist with considerable liturgical sensitivity and was gifted in prophetically-led non-liturgical worship.[4] No matter what unexpected thing occurred during a service, Eleanor could calmly bring the group through and keep the worship flowing – such a wonderful gift.

As the St Peter's Music Group developed, members began receiving original songs. Most were not very notable but they were real and from the heart. Each singer had their own style which reflected their musical backgrounds and life experience. An older man sang love songs to God in a Bing Crosby style; the youth sang ballads with a social-conscience edge; Eleanor received mainly songs of prophetic praise; while the professional flautist brought songs with a hauntingly central European flavour reflecting her Czechoslovakian origins. Similar things were experienced in many churches experiencing renewal. The group produced a record and cassette tape of their songs in 1978 entitled 'My Lord Is Jesus'.

Of all the new songs received at St Peter's this song by Alex Palmer best expresses the spirit of those times:

---

4. It was notable in the renewal that many of the leaders were married to gifted musicians. Michael and Jeanne Harper and Graham and Betty Pulkingham both modelled that God-given partnership. We were similarly blessed.

My Lord is Jesus

My Lord is Jesus, he who for me has died,
My Lord is Jesus, he whom they crucified.
Risen from death, his life he gives,
Risen from death, in me he lives.

My eyes are blind, they do not see what they should,
My hands lie idle, ears blocked and tongue of wood,
Till the Lord Jesus lives in me,
Till with his eyes I start to see.

Fill me with love, Lord, fill me with love I pray,
That I may see and hear and do what you say,
That Lord your life in me may grow,
That Christ your love through me may show.

Take me and make me, Father, like your dear Son,
That in the Spirit, Jesus and I be one,
Living in him and he in me,
Saved by his love, in truth set free.[5]

Whenever there has been a spiritual awakening or revival in the Church – and there have been scores of them, at least one each century – a sign that it is a genuine revival has been the upwelling of songs amongst God's people. Examples from the last few centuries include the hymns of the Wesleyan revival, the Moody and Sankey evangelical revival of the nineteenth century, hymns of the anglo-catholic movement and those from the twentieth-century Pentecostal movement.

---

5. From *'My Lord Is Jesus'; Twenty two new songs of faith from St Peters Pakuranga*. © 1978 St Peters Ministry Trust.

People who preferred the older hymnody of the church tended to speak disparagingly of the new songs as 'choruses', saying they would soon be forgotten, unlike the grand old hymns of the past. It is true that a great many songs of the renewal are no longer in use and have been superseded by the constant flow of new ones. Many have been 'songs for a season'.

It is all too easily forgotten that this is how it has always been. It is claimed that the Wesleyan revival produced around 5000 hymns of which fewer than a hundred are in use today. That, I suspect, is the usual survival rate of songs of Christian praise, and the songs of the charismatic renewal are surviving at least as well as that. Some were songs for just one congregation; others swept the world for a time and then faded away. One reason for this is the rapidly changing music styles of Western culture. New music based on the electronic keyboard has been replacing the gentle songs of the guitar-based folk-song era. Some of us lament their passing but technology moves on. Sometimes the styles can be combined – in two parishes that had pipe organs we managed to combine the organ with keyboards and other instruments and get the best of both worlds.

Those who bemoaned the introduction of other instruments in worship seemed to be unaware that the pipe organ was a relatively recent addition in parish churches and that, prior to it becoming affordable, music in parish churches was provided by local musicians as some of the art of the time shows. On an occasion when the St Peter's music group was singing for a diocesan service in King's College Chapel, a fellow priest (Hone Kaa, as it happened) on asking who they were, observed, 'Ah, the people's music.' Just so. A feature of the renewal was that it gave the people opportunity to make and write their own music.

It did irritate us when critics described our songs as choruses – although some of them undoubtedly were just that. Ephesians

5:19 describes singing 'psalms and hymns and spiritual songs' and many of the contemporary songs were just that – spiritual songs of people in love with God; some of them were contemporary psalms and some had the verse progression characteristic of hymns. Good praise comes in many forms and sometimes the repetition of even a single line can be very edifying, as the Taizé tradition has shown. In the early years of renewal we were much inspired by the music of Scripture in Song (an immensely influential New Zealand ministry), Betty Pulkingham's Fisherfolk music and the original music from the St Paul's Singers.

There were other impacts on the worship. First, the preaching style and content changed. While I had always tended to build sermons around the readings for the day (it irritates me no end to hear three scriptures read and then have the preacher preach on something else!) there was now a heightened desire in the congregation to learn from the scriptures and to be fed by them. With so much to teach and explain, the sermons became longer, not to everyone's satisfaction. The well-ordered ten-minute homily went out and people accepted twenty minutes or more of often extempore preaching. For me this was a joy and a temptation. At renewal conferences people would easily listen to biblical expositions of over an hour's length.

Secondly, we had to work out how to operate the charisms in public worship. This proved to be something of a minefield at first. Those who operated in the spoken charisms were new to it and inevitably immature. I felt that if I set tight rules at the start few would attempt anything, yet some guidance was needed. And, curiously, the Lord hadn't been too wise in who he gave the charisms to. I was rather puzzled as to why some who were not leaders in the parish were getting most of the utterances.

After a while I realised that we had been building the leadership out of those who were talented in the world – most of whom were sincere Christians – but the Lord now seemed to be balancing the body out with the charisms going to those who were more prayerful but sometimes less talented in worldly terms. It made for some tension as people with academic or managerial backgrounds struggled with utterances from the carpenters and sales people. Odd that. Seems to ring a bell somewhere.

A further question was how to bring prayer ministry into the Sunday morning worship. We had been learning it in the vicarage prayer meeting and the seminars, but how could it be included in the public worship? And how could words of knowledge be brought? At St Peter's this tended to be left to the evening praise services. And when someone called out a prophetic word – sometimes of a challenging nature – in the morning service it caused concern and anxiety. It took some years to train both congregations and bringers of prophecies into some acceptance, but prophecy never became a significant part of Anglican morning worship.

As the Holy Spirit moved deeper into the life of the congregation a startling thing began to happen. I started to see the New Testament, especially each of the parables, being enacted before my very eyes amongst the people. I saw the rich young man draw close, ask his questions, weigh it up and move away; I saw the widow's mite honoured; I heard the voice of Gamaliel through a university professor; I saw the 'spiritual poor' fed and the fat cast aside (Ezekiel 34:20). I saw the unrepentant adulterers lose their place in the body and those who came repentant for concealed sins restored and raised to leadership. It was an awesome time – long before the word 'awesome' became debased. My perception was that the dynamics of the Kingdom of God were upon us and that all the sayings that 'the Kingdom of God is like …' were being enacted in our midst.

Sharing the Leadership

A significant development was the exploration of forms of shared leadership. In theological college I had been convinced by Ephesians 4:11 that the clear demarcation between ordained ministry and the people was not biblical and that in future mission would require a new shape for ministry.

As a newly created parish we found that the vestry meetings became very lengthy as there was so much to plan for. I noticed there were far more talented and motivated leaders available than could be contained in the vestry. I also observed they seemed to be of two clear types: loyal members who were capable 'money and property' people, and more mission-focused members who were bored by that and wanted to focus on mission and ministry. Clearly we needed both.

In 1972, before the renewal began, I proposed to vestry that we adopt a new structure in which the elected vestry would constitute two bodies: a Finance and Works Committee and a Pastoral Council.[6] Each vestry member would choose which they would serve on and other parishioners would be added to each one. The committees would meet every second month and the vestry would meet on the intervening month. The vicar would chair vestry but a churchwarden would chair each committee. This was adopted in 1973 and increased the core of leaders from fourteen to twenty-four. It was key to enabling us to handle a spiritual revival at the same time as we tackled a building project.

Then questions began to be asked about these 'elders' we had at the prayer meeting and what were they doing in an Anglican parish? Clearly this had to be talked through. By then one or two

---

6. D. H. Battley, *Sharing the Priestly Task*, D Min Thesis, 1986, San Francisco Theological Seminary, 176.

other parishes in renewal were exploring the idea of actually having spiritual elders in addition to the elected vestry. Difficult territory!

I came to realise that elders always existed in any human community – they were the people who held the community knowledge, gave guidance or leadership, and managed conflict or new ventures. Anglicanism had always had elders – we just called them churchwardens, vestry, lay readers, etc.

From that basic sociological insight we realised we did not need to create 'elders' – we needed to recognise those who already existed, and we had indeed already done so to some extent in the development of the two task groups of vestry. What next? As an interim measure we designated a Renewal Leadership Team. Their task was:

1. To foster spiritual growth in the parish, as requested by the bishops of the province in their Call to Renewal, Lent 1977.
2. To develop and oversee renewal programs such as prayer meetings, group bible studies, healing ministries and Life in the Spirit Seminars.
3. To seek the maturation of charismatic renewal and of the spiritual gifts within the parish in harmony with the basic characteristics of Anglicanism.
4. To handle such events and meetings that may occur from time to time in co-operation, as appropriate, with other leadership groups in the parish.[7]

It was led by the vicar with a lay deputy-leader and women were equally eligible. It consisted of the vicar, two churchwardens, five vestry members and two others. It was a transitional step but had not enlarged the team of leaders very much. What was the best solution?

7. Battley, *Sharing*, 181.

By mid-1977 the vicar and vestry were considering the idea of a designated eldership. St Paul's Symonds Street, following the guidance of the Rev. Graham Pulkingham of Church of the Redeemer, Houston, had already formed an eldership within the Anglican governance system. We learned from them. The case for a parish pastoral eldership was put before the parishioners in a paper by me entitled 'Prospect of Eldership'. This was discussed and on 16 October 1977 was approved by twenty-five votes to four. The names of eleven parishioners were proposed to vestry who indicated their support or not in a confidential survey and the top eight (who scored ten or more out of thirteen) were selected, including Eleanor who had one of the highest votes.

It was made clear that the vestry remained the official governance of the parish and the pastoral elders held office by the decision of vestry. This was essential to avoid setting a 'senior-sounding' group above the elected vestry. The vicar and churchwardens were also ex-officio members of the elders' meeting. At the next AGM those elders who had been on vestry did not stand for re-election so that by the time a new vestry had been elected the parish had a dual leadership of nineteen; fourteen on vestry and eight being pastoral elders, four women and four men.[8]

The elders continued to meet throughout the rest of our time at Pakuranga and never seemed to lack matters to work on in relation to spiritual renewal. A number of the women who served as prayer meeting or pastoral elders moved on to ordination. Joan Dallaway, the parish's first lay pastoral assistant, was ordained in 1978; she role-modeled and was followed by Mavis Smith and Geneth Davies in the 1980s, and much later Eleanor Battley was ordained in 2001. Quite a few other people renewed in the Spirit were ordained over the years.

The elders continued to function some years after my departure in

---

8. Ibid, 185,

1983.⁹ They met fortnightly to manage the parish for the five months until the next vicar arrived and the elders continued to function thereafter. People's Warden Doug Canning commented, 'Everyone one was on good behaviour with high levels of cooperation.'[10] But the new vicar had some difficulty discerning what the real function of the elders was and saw it more as the previous vicar's support group.

By 1985 the role of the elders had been re-defined as 'they will provide support to the Pastoral Team in the areas of ministry, education and leadership'.[11] By that time the clergy pastoral team had increased to five: one stipendiary vicar and four non-stipendiary deacons. The vicar deemed this 'an ideal arrangement' but one of the deacons was concerned that the pastoral team might grow too strong over the pastoral elders and commented on the different levels of theological ability in the two groups. When asked, 'Would you say that the existence of the elders partly frees the staff to reach out into the community?' the vicar replied, 'Yes, I would. Most definitely' and the theological student deacon commented, 'If you took that eldership out and tried to function with only the pastoral team and vestry a lot of the activities wouldn't get off the ground.'

It seemed significant that those who held an episcopal licence were out in the community representing the church's pastoral ministry while the unlicensed pastoral elders were active in guiding and supporting members of the gathered congregation. This seemed like an appropriate outworking of licensed and un-licensed pastoral ministries.[12]

---

9. See Transition section, Battley thesis, op. cit. 189-193.

10. Interview with D. L. Canning, former People's Warden, 6 June 1985. Cited in Battley, *Sharing*, 189.

11. Parish of Pakuranga, Agenda of Pastoral Elders Meeting, 2 May 1983, *Sharing*, 190.

12. Battley, *Sharing*, 191-192.

Doubling the Building

In the midst of all this renewal activity we set about enlarging the church building by adding a meeting lounge, classrooms and a chapel. The original building had been designed as a community hall to generate community contacts and included only a kitchen, toilets, entrance and a small room which served as a chapel and robing room. During the week the hall doubled as a kindergarten and every Saturday it had to be converted into a worship area with a moveable altar, benches for communion rails and hard stacker chairs. It allowed us a flexible worship style, and the family services in such a setting were often memorable, but, as one ex-mariner observed, it felt like 'ward-room worship'.

We had a lot of fun in that hall but every Sunday had to send the children across a busy road to the local primary school for their classes and we worshipped surrounded by pre-schoolers. The original idea had been that the parish would ultimately build a 'proper' church alongside the hall but changes in zoning prevented that. Apart from relocating, we had no option but to enlarge what we had and to convert the hall into a worship area.

By 1975, only four years after getting their first vicar, the parish was ready to build a major extension for about $48,000 – the equivalent of about $500,000 today.[13] Most of the work was done by parishioners: a parishioner architect designed it; an airline pilot served as unpaid clerk of works; two parish carpenters were employed to construct it, and some materials were obtained by church members at wholesale rates. It was a happy achievement which gave parishioners a task to unite around while tensions about spiritual renewal were worked through. We used to pray where the

---

13. Howick parish had generously given us the proceeds of the sale of a church section on our common boundary, which met about half the costs.

new chapel was being built and had the distinct impression we were building it around a special presence of the Holy Spirit that is still there.

When the job was done the people's warden surprised me by saying the job wasn't finished – we still needed to build offices and he showed me where they could be. I was bit gob-smacked at the financial implications and took it to the Lord to ask for special financial provision. A few weeks later a recently joined parishioner, whose life had been deeply blessed by the Spirit, called in to say the Lord had told him to sell his boat and to tithe the proceeds to the church. He gave me a cheque for $5,000 dollars – about half the cost of the offices. So does God provide for what God orders.

But it wasn't always plain sailing. Something that got to me was that people kept moving away or going to other churches after they had been blessed at St Peter's. I protested to the Lord one day, 'Lord, how are we ever going to build a big church if you keep moving people away?'

His reply was, 'Who said anything about building a big church?'

I said, 'Well, it's obvious, isn't it?'

And he replied, 'No, it's not. What is obvious is that I have set you on a corner so people can find you easily. When they arrive, you have two years to bring them to me and get them Spirit-filled. After that it's my business whether they stay or go. I just promise you that you will always have enough people to do what has to be done.'

So it was. St Peter's remained a mid-sized church, with a constant flow-through of people. What was a bit less acceptable was the attitude of a near-by Baptist minister when I protested about his attracting our people. 'Well, the sheep will go where the grass is greener,' he said. A bit hard to take. Competition from Pentecostal and Baptist churches got a bit fierce at times although the support from the local Assembly of God pastor, Cecil Mulvey, was loving and strong. We enjoyed very supportive relationships in the Pakuranga Ministers Fraternal (as they were called then). All in all, the 1970s at Pakuranga were exciting days which changed many lives and produced many servant-hearted ministers for the church's mission. And we were not alone on the renewal journey.

– 9 –

Spreading Waters
Renewal Floods Auckland Diocese

The adoption of the Life in the Spirit Seminars had major impacts for charismatic renewal through the diocese of Auckland and the country. A 'strawberry runner' effect took place with seminars generating new seminars in nearby parishes. People empowered by the seminars in one place travelled to other parishes to conduct further seminars and new bonds in the Spirit were generated and remained special to participants for many years.[1] In south-east Auckland, for instance, while St Peter's continued to offer the seminars for many years using their own people, Derek Batts and his colleagues moved on to conduct seminars at St Andrew's Presbyterian Church, Howick and at St John's Co-operating Parish, Bucklands Beach.[2] Members of Howick Anglican Parish attended the Pakuranga seminars including the vicar Michael and Evelyn Houghton, and some assistant clergy.

The Rev. Lloyd Cullen, vicar of Papatoetoe, attended a seminar at Pakuranga and then invited St Peter's people to conduct seminars at Papatoetoe which people from Otahuhu also attended. The

---

1. The Rev. Paul Gravelle, a non-stipendiary priest with a teaching ministry, says that he conducted around eighty Life in the Spirit Seminars between 1974 and 2010, ministering to between one and eighty-seven participants each time. Interview, Paul Gravelle, 2.
2. Interview, Derek Batts, 21 July 2009, 3.

Rev. Neil Fuge initiated seminars at Papakura in 1975.[3] The Rev. Richard Colegrove introduced the seminars at Pukekohe in 1974 where they quickly became ecumenical and attracted so many people they had to be based in the town hall.[4] People and clergy attended from Tuakau and Bombay parishes.[5] A seminar was also held at St Paul's East Tamaki and Murray Spackman offered the seminars at Clevedon in 1974-75.[6] The Rev. Chris Pryor, on becoming a non-stipendiary priest at Manurewa, brought the seminars from Devonport and a vigorous renewal got underway in the Manurewa parish in 1977.[7] Almost all the parishes of south Auckland were impacted by Life in the Spirit Seminars in the years 1974 to 1978.

At the same time the seminars spread in other directions. In addition to the seminars which started at St Paul's and Kohimarama in 1973, seminars took place at St Martin's Mt Roskill[8] and Devonport from 1973,[9] St Margaret's Hillsborough from 1973 or 1974, All Saints Ponsonby from 1974,[10] St Jude's Avondale and St Thomas'

---

3. Interview, Neil Fuge, 24 August 2010, 2.

4. Interview, Richard Colegrove, 30 September 2010, 1.

5. Interview, Jim Withers, 9 November 2010, 1. 'We did them together with people from both parishes attending.'

6. Interview, Murray Spackman, 13 October 2010, 5.

7. Interview, Max Scott, 5 November 2010, 3.

8. Interview, Brian Jenkins, 5 November 2010, 5. Bishop Bruce Moore recalls attending a seminar in Mt Roskill attended by Bill Subritzky and Professor John Morton.

9. Paul Gravelle recalls using the seminars with Chris Pryor at Devonport in 1973 and introducing them to New Lynn in 1974. Interview Paul Gravelle, 24 July 2009, 2. David Guthrie says they were 'used consistently as the instrument to renew the congregation'. Telephone interview, David Guthrie, 18 February 2011.

10. Interview, Bishop Bruce Moore, 2

New Lynn in 1974[11] and subsequently at Te Atatu and Henderson from 1975.[12] Martin and Valerie Bridge experienced a seminar at Henderson in 1977 and commenced them at Mangere Bridge from 1978.[13]

Use of the seminars extended to Dargaville and Ruawai[14] and at Maungaturoto and Paparoa[15] from 1975 to 1981. Bill Subritzky, who owned a farm at the Bay of Islands, paid to have speakers flown to Kerikeri in 1976 to conduct the seminars while Arthur Mead was vicar there.[16] Speakers included John Brokenshire, Wyn Fountain, Owen Woodfield, Don Battley, Brian Jenkins, Richard Colegrove and Peter Lloyd. Extensive use was made of the seminars around the Coromandel parish in Bill Smith's time (1973-81). Jim Withers introduced the seminars at Birkdale-Beachhaven between 1977 and 1980.[17] One seminar was presented at Blockhouse Bay in 1977 by people from St Paul's but their use of partisan terminology had a divisive effect and, following that, Bob Barrett developed his own course 'Foundations for Faith'.[18] One seminar was presented at Glenfield in 1977 or 1978 by the Methodist minister John Salmon but these did not continue.[19] Seminars were held from 1979 at Massey and

---

11. Max Scott recalls attending a seminar at St Jude's in 1974 while he was still a student. Interview, Max Scott, 5 November 2010, 1.

12. Interview, Derek Lightbourne, 31 May 2010, 2.

13. Interview, Martin and Valerie Bridge, 12 October 2010, 1-2.

14. Interview, Ann Dodd, 15 October 2008.

15. Interview, Murray Spackman, op. cit., 9.

16. Interview, Arthur Mead, 9 June 2008.

17. Interview, Jim Withers, 9 November 2010, 2.

18. Telephone interview, Bob Barrett, 22 February 2011.

19. Interview, John Salmon, 24 August 2010, 1.

the Whenuapai Air Base;[20] Torbay[21] and Titirangi from 1980;[22] Waiuku;[23] and Green Bay Community Church.[24]

Use of the seminars continued during the 1980s including Whangarei between 1980-83;[25] Te Atatu 1982 and 1984; Manurewa 1988-1991;[26] Kaitaia from 1985;[27] Point Chevalier and subsequently One Tree Hill[28] and Meadowbank.[29] Further presentations were made at Tuakau, Clevedon[30] and Birkdale-Beachhaven.[31] By the mid-1980s fully half the parishes of Auckland diocese had used the seminars, some just once but most on a recurring basis. This was an unprecedented uptake of a teaching programme which had no official endorsement and was promoted by word of mouth and by the publications and conferences of the charismatic movement. In 2010 Peter and Lorraine Lloyd presented the LiSS again in Birkdale-Beachhaven parish and found them 'as effective as ever'.[32]

20. Conversation with parishioners, Massey Parish, 13 February 2011.
21. Interview, Peter and Lorraine Lloyd, 21 May 2010, 4.
22. Peter Philip confirms that LiSS were not used at Titirangi in his time as vicar. Telephone conversation, Peter Philip, 22 February 2011.
23. Interview, Bruce Richardson, 12.
24. Interview, Paul Gravelle, 3.
25. Interview, Neil Fuge, 4.
26. Telephone interview, Mark Beale, 22 February 2011.
27. Interview, Harold Clark, 3 March 2010, 1.
28. Telephone interview, Ian Nairn, 23 February 2011.
29. Telephone interview, Colin Ruge, 24 February 2011.
30. Interview, Eleanor Keys, 8 November 2010, 1.
31. Interview Peter and Lorraine Lloyd, op. cit., 7.
32. Ibid.

Prayer-Breakfast at Bill and Pat's

Soon after the end of the Pakuranga Life in the Spirit Seminar in 1974, John Brokenshire invited me to join a group of renewal Anglican clergy who met monthly at Bill and Pat Subritzky's home in Mt Roskill. They met early on Saturday mornings and key members included Brian Jenkins, John Brokenshire, 'Boni' Boniface, Peter Philip, David Balfour, Bill and a few others. I recall Boni introducing me as 'our newest recruit'.

It was a very different kind of group from the formal archdeaconry clergy meetings where people guarded what they said. In this group members spoke of what was happening to them in their experiences of the Holy Spirit and how renewal in their parishes was developing. Members prayed for each other with laying on of hands for blessing, wisdom, strength or healing. This helped us gain spiritual resources for the challenges before us and for healing situations in our lives and parishes.

Bill set the lead in praying with words of knowledge and prophecy. He would not allow an expressed need to go past without intentional prayer being brought into the situation. His boldness challenged us to grow further in the spiritual gifts. We shared a vigorous sense that God was creating a dynamic renewal in the churches and that we were a team working together to further that work in the Anglican Church and bonds quickly developed between us that in most cases lasted the rest of our lives.

We were all involved in bringing changes into churches habituated by long histories of Anglican conformity and most of us ran into difficult challenges or outright opposition. Occasionally a priest might also have been questioned by the bishop about a complaint from a parishioner and the weight of these things could be heavy. Bill was not slow to give advice, frequently in the form of a 'word from the Lord', but he was frequently right. This ministry to each other was followed by a breakfast prepared by Pat Subritzky. Bill and Pat were generous hosts who shared their attractive home with many people. Those morning prayer-breakfasts became the precursor of a sequence of Anglican connections, and their successors were still meeting forty years later. They set me on a journey that defined much of the rest of my ministry.

From the bonds formed on those mornings we gave support to each other's Life in the Spirit Seminars and organised inter-parish and diocesan renewal events. This may sound ordinary but it was innovative at the time. Clergy mostly kept to their own parishes and had little participation in any other. The dynamic of the early renewal changed this hugely. I was especially supported and coached by John Brokenshire, Boni and David Balfour. David in particular helped me marry the charismatic dimension to the sacramental and liturgical principles of Anglicanism.

Bill and Pat also hosted a weekly open prayer meeting in their home which was soon attended by scores of people, so much so that not only was the large lounge and dining area full to capacity but the meeting was relayed to a downstairs area. On my first evening there I was seated on steps down into the lounge when a word in tongues was spoken by someone and my heart immediately began to pound as I began to receive a stream of words in English in my head. Aware that this was probably the interpretation of the tongue I protested silently, 'No, Lord, this is just my *first time* here!'

No-one else brought an interpretation and Bill insisted, 'Someone here is receiving the interpretation of that tongue.'

Finally I yielded and uttered an interpretation rather loudly. I was promptly summoned forward to be delivered of a 'spirit of terror' which really surprised me.

Although nothing much was manifested during the prayer ministry I knew that I had been assaulted in a school shelter shed as a five-year-old and had been terrified by the experience and began stammering about two years later. A feature of Bill's prayer meetings and his subsequent ministry has been a focus on discerning what is believed to be demonic presences in people or places and delivering people from them.

I was not offended to be so treated and was fascinated by the varied ministries I witnessed in Bill's home over many evenings. And that's how we learned – being surprised by the Spirit and led on by bold leaders. I went for many evenings, sometimes taking parishioners or Eleanor with me. There was sung praise with a talented pianist on the piano, a teaching word from Bill or another teacher, words of knowledge followed by prayer ministry over the people identified, often with convincing words of prophecy frequently delivered by Trevor or Laurel Hare. No wonder so many people came. Bill and his assistants would continue to minister to people individually long into the night after the meeting had ended.[33]

How Bill ever sustained a demanding professional life as well I cannot imagine. But he did, including faithfully attending a weekly 7.00am Communion service in his parish church of St Martin in Mt Roskill.[34] I became progressively more exhausted as the year went on with all the extra late night meetings but I have no regrets about it. I changed from being a dutiful son of the church to being a remade son of God who was fully confident in the Christian faith.

---

33. Brian Jenkins recalled that Bill's main supporters were Trevor and Laurel Hare and himself. 'Trevor had been raised a Catholic ... (and) had a great sense of the supernatural ... the prayer-meeting would close down about half-past nine and everyone would get a cup of tea which was quite a logistics event and then Trevor and Bill and I would see people who wanted to see us personally ... so we would do a lot of ministry afterwards in Bill's study which would go on into eleven, twelve, sometimes one, two, sometimes three o'clock.' Interview Brian Jenkins, 5 November 2010, 2-3.

34. Although Bill tended to put down his pre-charismatic days as an Anglican, he was a faithful believer and worshipper, as his vicars of the time have testified to me. See Interview Brian Jenkins, 1.

The Auckland Anglican Charismatic Core Group

An inter-denominational renewal group had existed since the late 1960s and may have been called the Auckland Charismatic Renewal Group (ACRG). This earlier group grew, I believe, out of the group that had organised the Auckland visit of Dennis Bennett in 1966 and had included Wyn Fountain, Derek Batts, Ken Prebble and Boni. They had worked to introduce charismatic beliefs and experience into any denomination and showed impressive lack of denominational bias.

It was as the renewal grew within denominations that needs arose for leaders in particular traditions to meet to discuss issues specific to that church. Thus dispensationalism was not an issue for Anglicans whose tradition did believe in the active ministry of the Holy Spirit, nor was prayer for healing foreign, as the ministries of the Guild of St Raphael and the Order of St Luke were established and fairly widely accepted. Anglican tensions were around baptismal theology, the introduction of spontaneity in worship which had been firmly controlled by the Anglican Prayer Book, and the effect of adding enthusiastic prayer meetings into the almost prayer-less life of Anglican parishes. Many parishes experienced the 'worship wars' of bringing guitar-based music into services dominated by pipe organs and four-part harmony hymns. But permanent changes were wrought and became widely accepted.

In February 1976 Brian Jenkins wrote as chairman to all members of the breakfast group advising that we had become the Auckland Anglican Charismatic Renewal Committee; that the goal had changed from spreading renewal to encouraging the growth of local parishes in renewal, to build up the local body of Christ. We were taking 'what authority we had, or hadn't got' and going to act. The immediate suggestions were: residential weekends for clergy; meetings with charismatic clergy and a some lay leaders on

Friday nights; a Pentecost weekend at the cathedral; a seminar on deliverance; and a get-together during synod. We invited CAM to provide a Summer School in Auckland for 1977 in cooperation with ourselves. CAM agreed and invited Michael Harper, Bob Frost and Leonard Evans as key-note speakers. Brian commented that he observed 'an increasing amount of spontaneous and, I believe, Spirit-inspired activity developing at the local regional level'.[35]

It soon became apparent that the group was more wish than action so after a couple of inconclusive meetings I volunteered to be secretary – such has been my life-time avocation.[36] Brian was delighted to accept and so began a long-standing friendship and partnership in ministry. The group spent more time in planning and probably less in prayer ministry than before but by then the needs for mutual support were decreasing and planning of Life in the Spirit Seminars and diocesan renewal events increasing.

In May 1976 the renewal in Auckland diocese received a major boost from a renewal mission led by Archbishop Bill Burnett of Southern Africa.[37] After having been a leading anti-apartheid church leader and a central executive member of the World Council of Churches, Bill Burnett was baptised in the Spirit in 1972.[38] He became an ardent advocate of renewal. He spoke many times in the diocese and had wide-ranging impact. Bishop Gowing was clearly impressed and spoke favourably at length in his synod address later that year saying,

---

35. ANG 076/6/17

36. Letter DHB to B. Jenkins 14 September 1976.

37. The Mission was probably promoted by the Diocesan Committee for Evangelism where Boni was convenor. Brian Jenkins was by then Archdeacon of Hauraki. Burnett was in the Archdeaconry of Auckland May 20-21 and Hauraki May 22. Keven Hall was also involved and Terry Barton as priest assistant to the bishop. Circular from the Ven. E. G. Buckle, AADA S10 P44 Box 11, file 2.

38. Michael Harper, ed. *Bishops' Move*, Hodder, 1978, 10.

> In many striking and wonderful ways there has been granted to us – men and women and young people, renewal: the Holy Spirit of the Lord has been at work and many have become more fully conformed to the likeness of Jesus. I am talking of things I know and which I have seen... I am able to say, 'I know these things have happened; I know that what the Archbishop called 'release of the spirit' has happened.[39]

The Burnett Mission was probably the highpoint of the charismatic movement in Auckland diocese.

Encouraged by these developments, the renewal group renamed itself the Anglican Charismatic Core Group (ACCG).[40] It listed eighteen members, including six laymen. A residential weekend at Manly was held over 6-9 March 1977 with around fifteen participants.[41] A Pentecost renewal weekend was run on 27-29 May at the cathedral using our own speakers, and worship leaders from St Paul's and St Peter's.[42]

A residential consultation of thirty-two clergy from the upper North Island dioceses was held at St John's College 22-25 May 1978 with addresses given by Peter Philip, 'What is the Good News?' (invite Christ into the current crisis in your life), Richard Colegrove, 'Urgency in the Gospel' (there is bound to be conflict); Brian Jenkins 'Encouragement in the Gospel Through the Church' (killing the sacred cow of professionalism); Herbert Boniface 'Beyond the Honeymoon' (including the value of elderships); John Brokenshire 'Wholeness in Spirit, Soul and Body' (submis-

---

39. Address by the Rt Rev. E. A. Gowing to the Third Session of the Forty-first Synod of the Diocese, 4 July 1976, 9, AADA 9A. Gowing E. A.
40. Notice of Meeting, 18 October 1976, ANG 076/6/17
41. Letter D Guthrie, 3 February 1977, ibid.
42. Notes on Meeting 27/4/77, ibid.

sion allows the Holy Spirit to work); Cecil Marshall 'To Reach and Teach Others', including his experiences of the Spirit drawing people together across the denominations so 'that charismatic clergy and pentecostal pastors are getting together and that there is a tremendous amount of brotherliness'. Observing the amount of prayer ministry being sought by the priests, the writer of a report on the consultation, Geoff Ginever, observed,

> It seemed amazing ... that a group of clergy had so many needs, ranging from deep inner hurts and feelings of loneliness and insecurity and despair to articulated repentance, ministry of healing, and even ministry for deliverance. If such are the needs of a group of shepherds, expressed in an environment of real trust and love and sharing, how great must be the needs of the sheep in the pews ... and the needs of the sheep who have strayed from the fold.[43]

This report evidences that by 1978 barriers between clergy were falling, that the priests were coming to trust each other and forming new bonds and that spiritual healing was happening through these events – steps beneficial to the development of a movement of renewal. And we were doing it for ourselves, under God.

While these developments were growing in Auckland, similar things were developing throughout the country. Clergy and parishes were being impacted in Dunedin (St Matthew's in particular); Christchurch and Rangiora; Nelson, especially at All Saints; Wellington diocese especially at Palmerston North, Whanganui, Belmont and Tawa. Renewal was also experienced in Waiapu, espe-

---

43. Report 'Towards Wholeness: Learning to Live in a New Dimension. A Consultation of Anglican Clergy from the Dioceses of Auckland, Waikato and Waiapu', May 1978, ANG 076/6/17

cially at Gisborne and Kawerau. Harvey Smith reports that between 1974 and 1981, under the episcopate of Paul Reeves, renewal was widely accepted in Waiapu diocese:

> Apart from (one priest) there was never any antagonism to the charismatic renewal in the Diocese. It was accepted as one of a number of renewals taking place in the Church… The gifts of the Spirit became widely accepted and understood. The more spectacular gifts were not widespread apart from healing prayer which in some form or other took place in every parish.[44]

Little renewal was seen in Waikato diocese possibly because the bishop, Archbishop Allen Johnston, was not sympathetic. But the pulsing heart of it all was at Palmerston North.

My first introduction to the CAM Summer Schools was in January 1975, the third such event at Massey University and All Saints Church in Palmerston North. By then attendances had burgeoned to over a thousand.[45] To attend, we towed our caravan down and stayed in the nearby civic campground. The teachings were riveting, especially in the power of their scriptural expositions – never had I heard scripture being opened up with such confidence and insight. The massed singing in All Saints Church was extraordinary in its power and grace.

---

44. Email Harvey Smith to DHB, 21 June 2019, 3. Harvey reports that at least nineteen clergy from the diocese attended the Francis MacNutt priests' retreat in response to Harvey's encouragement, including Bishop Paul Reeves and future bishops Brian Davis and Godfrey Wilson.

45. See Williamson, 168 where she analyses the records for 1974 to 1979. By 1977 attendances totalled 1,333 including 550 Anglicans and 460 Catholics.

But we encountered one problem that was to have future impact – they made no provision for children, and with three children aged five to eleven cramped in a caravan, how were we to manage them? Eleanor and I had to choose who attended which session while the other entertained the boys – a less than ideal conference experience. It seemed to me that being focussed on serving 'leaders' in a non-inclusive time meant focussing on ministers and emerging students, but not on the needs and resourcing of families.[46] This would soon become a pressing issue. It was also a current view at the time that baptism in the Spirit was not for the young, and that it could even be harmful for people under sixteen (and there had been issues about overzealousness and some emotional instability). It would be twenty years before we worked out how to include children in what was happening. But the 1975 Summer School further enlarged our vision and hope for renewal of the church by the Holy Spirit.

By Lent 1977 the bishops had caught some of the new energy when they issued 'A Call To Renewal' to the whole Church, citing 'a deep sense of the need for Christian evangelisation today (as) there is now an urgency to proclaim Jesus Christ as Lord of all life'. They hoped that 'In every diocese, efforts will be made to help the Church respond to God's Holy Spirit in His renewing work'.[47] They would have been thinking of renewal in a broader spiritual sense than just the charismatic movement, which some of them actively disliked. But such calls gave energy to the charismatics.

---

46. Dale Williamson reported that the CAM Summer Schools 'alienated some young families by not providing childcare'. Williamson, *Uncomfortable Engagement*, 168.

47. 'A Call To Renewal', Letter from the eight bishops, AADA S10 P44 Box 14/1. J. Brokenshire Sundry Correspondence, February 1977.

The 1978 Anglican Pre-Lambeth International Conference on Renewal

Through Cecil Marshall, by then Director of CAM, we were advised of an Anglican International Conference on Spiritual Renewal that the Rev. Michael Harper and others were planning to hold at Canterbury in the UK just prior to the 1978 Lambeth Conference. We were all encouraged to get there if we could. This set in train planning for my first sabbatical leave[48] to include attendance at the conference.

Eleanor and I set off in late May 1978, leaving our three boys in the care of parishioners. We visited renewal contacts in Singapore including Bishop Chui Ban It, then toured Israel with friends from Pakuranga, went to Greece, cruised the Aegean and visited Istanbul and then to Rome to attend an Anglican-Catholic course known as ROMESS, and on to London. Our three boys, Mark, Chris and Phil, were brought from New Zealand by Archdeacon Ted and Mona Buckle who were on their way to the Lambeth Conference. Where I rather expected tearful reunions, three bright-eyed lads strode confidently through Heathrow with rucksacks on their backs ready to take on Europe.

The conference was held at the University of Kent on a hill overlooking the historic cathedral and town of Canterbury, the centre of Anglicanism. We settled into two student rooms having with Kiwi ingenuity smuggled three boys in to sleep on the floor and fed them privately before we joined the conference food queues for our meals.

The Canterbury Conference had been organised by the Rev.

---

48. By then the diocese had a policy that stipendiary clergy should take three months' paid study leave every seven years. I had had one unofficial leave in 1969 when I was selected as a Rotary Group Study Exchange team member for a visit to Indiana.

Michael Harper, the leader of the UK renewal agency the Fountain Trust and by Episcopal Renewal Ministries (ERM) of the USA. ERM had an interesting history. Early in charismatic renewal in the American Episcopal Church, key people had teamed up to form the Episcopal Charismatic Fellowship (ECF). A subsequent review of that ministry led to it being renamed Episcopal Renewal Ministries. The name change signified a maturing vision of the task – the emphasis needed to be on the renewal of the church, not just on the charismatic label, and the function needed to be on ministry to others, not just fellowship of a group. The witness of ERM at the conference had wide-ranging consequences.

People had been invited to the conference from most parts of the Anglican Communion and around 350 people including twenty-seven bishops from Britain, Africa, the Americas, Oceania and a few from Asia attended. Priests and laity came from all around the Communion. The sheer range of those attending showed that the renewal had spread rapidly around the Communion and was becoming a force to be reckoned with.

For many of us it was our first experience of the widely international character of the Anglican Church, an experience that was usually only given to the 'top brass'. But here we were, grass-roots missioners of Christ's church, all drawn there by the excitement and challenge of new experiences of life given by the Spirit of God. Hope and expectation for the spiritual renewal of the church were tangible; excitement rippled through every event and personal conversation. The worship sessions were thrilling experiences of contemporary praise with outstanding expositions of scripture, and workshops[49]

---

49. The workshop subjects were: Evangelism, Revival and Renewal, Parish Renewal, Ministry and Leadership, Liturgy and Worship, Ecumenism, Community and Fellowship, Spiritual Gifts and Healing, Social Action. Conference papers, Battley papers.

which addressed the key topics of the new spiritual life and of parish renewal.

Leading speakers of the renewal included Terry Fulham, Bishop Frey of Colorado, John Howe, subsequently bishop of Florida, from the USA, and Colin Urquhart and David Watson from the UK.[50] Towards the end Michael Harper introduced his vision to create Sharing of Ministries Abroad (SOMA), a ministry which he would lead for sending faith-sharing teams throughout the Anglican Communion. The conference ended with a renewal eucharist in Canterbury Cathedral where bishops including the archbishop of Southern Africa, Bill Burnett, and many others famously danced in the aisles with the joy of renewal in the Spirit.

At one point during the conference people met in their national groups and were encouraged to consider what the renewal in their situation needed from them as leaders. My notes of the meeting record that a national gathering in New Zealand was already scheduled by Ray Muller for 17-19 October. We discussed how to provide coordinated leadership; relations with the episcopate – we were concerned that there was little dialogue with bishops and we needed to correct that; concerns about theological training which was unhelpful to people we sent for training and did not equip them for leading parishes experiencing renewal; how to develop ministries between parishes; how to cope with adventism in the movement; and particularly what kind of agency could be formed. Could New Zealand sustain an Anglican charismatic ministry when we already had CAM? Might the term Charismatic Renewal Services as used by the Catholic charismatics in the USA be helpful?

In this meeting was birthed the idea, following the example of ERM, that an Anglican renewal ministry could be beneficial across the country but with Anglican leaders of CAM present it was not

---

50. 1978 Europe Tour Notes and Diary, Battley papers.

sensitive to pursue it. The idea had been voiced and I for one was convinced it was needed. There were many issues involved theologically, liturgically and politically in the Anglican Church that an interdenominational ministry like CAM could not adequately address.

In the background to this issue was a tension about the interdenominational character and strengths of the charismatic movement and its impact on the denominations. Many denominational boundaries had been crossed in the early renewal. Baptists led Anglicans into baptism in the Spirit; open-minded Pentecostal teachers taught many of our early leaders. The anglo-catholic David Balfour was deeply influenced by Pentecostal pastor Peter Morrow in Christchurch; Ken Prebble had been led into renewal by Baptist layman Wyn Fountain; Ray Muller had been impacted by the Roman Catholic renewal at Ann Arbor in Michigan[51] and consequently the CAM Summer Schools were planned and conducted by inter-church teams which included Roman Catholic priests and lay leaders. This brought richness to the events but did lead to difficulties about sharing of Communion. With many Catholic charismatics sharing the same spiritual renewal as their protestant friends, all wanted to share in one Communion, which the Catholic bishops forbad giving rise to unhappy experiments such as having parallel celebrations in adjacent buildings, or even two tables at one event with separate administrations.

From 1966 to 1978 there had been constant cross-fertilisation between denominations and multi-denominational worship at conferences. I can still hear Peter Philip boldly proclaiming at one such event, 'This is *real* ecumenism!' and that's how we experienced it, but was it real and could the renewal transcend the chasms of denominational history and culture? A consequence of the specifically

---

51. Interview, Ray Muller, 1 June 2010, 1.

Anglican Canterbury renewal conference was to focus us on the needs and potential of charismatic renewal in the Anglican context. Subsequent events were to confirm that we needed to do our own work within the Anglican Church but that there would be losses as a consequence. The 1978 Conference energised us not just for parish renewal but also for church-wide renewal.

After the conference our family toured parts of England visiting key renewal centres, crossed to France for a camping tour and returned to the UK for some more visits before Eleanor and the boys flew home while I set off for a quick visit to some American parishes. I visited the Church of the Resurrection in Dallas, Oral Roberts University (we had met a staff member on the Aegean cruise) and St Luke's, Akron, Ohio where the Rev. Chuck Irish, leader of ERM was rector. With his quiet manner and wide vision, Chuck became a role model for me and I learned a great deal from him. The 1978 sabbatical journey had been very enriching for all the family and opened new ideas that defined the rest of my life.

– 10 –

Joining the Streams
Developing Anglican Renewal Ministries

I arrived back in New Zealand at the end of September 1978 with my horizons greatly widened and a vision derived from ERM and Chuck Irish for a New Zealand-wide Anglican renewal ministry. But how to get there when CAM was doing excellent work and was led mainly by Anglicans?

The Tawa Anglican Conference

In October, renewal leaders gathered at a national conference of Anglican renewal leaders which Ray Muller organised in Wellington. Most of those who had attended at Canterbury were there and a few others. It was held at St Christopher's Tawa where Ray had become vicar after four years with CAM in order to create a model renewal parish. Ray's vision was strongly for parish renewal – that it was not enough to lead some people into personal renewal. If this rediscovery of the energies of the Holy Spirit was authentic it had to develop into full parish renewal, not only encompassing most parish members but also reshaping everything the parish did and how it found direction and exercised its mission to the community. This had already been modelled by several Episcopal parishes, some English churches[1] and a few in New Zealand.

1. The high-profile ones in the USA were at that time St Paul's Darien,

Ray brought to the Tawa conference Baptist minister Murray Robertson from Spreydon Baptist Church in Christchurch. Murray had already led that church into many of the things we aspired to and was an excellent interpreter of both the theology and the praxis of parish renewal. If I recall aright, no decision was made about a new renewal ministry but we agreed that we should keep meeting at least annually.

January 1979 saw many of us refreshed with the ecumenical aspect of renewal when we attended a CAM-sponsored priests' and spouses' renewal retreat led by Dominican priest Francis MacNutt from the USA.[2] Four hundred attended at Massey University, Palmerston North. Based around the theme of 'inner healing', the retreat went deep with many hurt or hopeful leaders. Priest's wife Sheila Brokenshire, reporting how people from many denominations shared their needs and prayed for each other, described the experience as

> a time when the Holy Spirit was truly present in the hearts of men [sic], as old hidden hurts, bitterness and anger fell away and left us freer to serve Jesus and each other.[3]

At least nineteen clergy attended from Waiapu diocese including Church of the Redeemer Houston, St Luke's Seattle and St Luke's Akron but there were many others. In the UK key churches included David Watson's parish of St Michael-le-Belfrey in York and Colin Urquhart's parish in Luton. Some of these parishes were well known because books had been published about them.

2. Francis MacNutt's book was a definitive resource for many of us in the 1970s. Francis MacNutt, *Healing*, Ave Maria, Notre Dame, 1975.

3. 'Retreat at Massey' article by Sheila Brokenshire, Kohimarama parish magazine, Lent 1979, AADA S10 P44 Box 17/3.

Bishop Paul Reeves and Dean Brian Davis.[4] CAM's interdenominational influence was spreading, but the needs of Anglicans were also increasing.

The Aucklanders kept the idea of an Anglican agency alive and in May 1980 I wrote on behalf of the Auckland Charismatic Core Group to David Harper and others that:

> Where until now we have felt that the formation of a distinctive Anglican charismatic organisation was not called for, it seems now that something is required ... We are also concerned that the bench [of bishops] still appears to be on the defensive and unaware of the extent and significance of the phenomenon. The Anglican leaders [of renewal] therefore need to be more related to each other to achieve a variety of goals.[5]

We proposed that a few of us get together to discuss these issues and come up with some action. In response, the Rev. Peter Stuart of Eastbourne parish expressed some of our concerns:

> I sense a mood of people in the Renewal (lay and clergy) to discover where they are in relation to the Anglican Church. I believe there is a lot of confusion, woolly thinking and occasional bitterness creeping into the freshness of the new life in the Spirit, and it is directly related to the lack of leadership being provided by the Bishops and by the clergy about where the renewal is going *in the Church*... The time has come to lead our lay people firmly away from those aspects of Pentecostal teaching which cannot be reconciled with

---

4. Email Harvey Smith, op. cit.
5. Letter DHB to David Harper, 7 May 1980, ANG 076/1/1.

the Anglican way. Otherwise all we are doing is acting as a recruiting agency within the Anglican Church for Pentecostal churches, and introducing division into our own church.[6]

Archbishop Paul Reeves

Then a new urgency entered the situation. Not all Anglican clergy had been handling their new experiences of the Holy Spirit wisely. The whole thing had been highly impactful and non-Anglican theological ideas were widespread. These included issues surrounding the age for baptism and styles of worship, and how to interpret and expound the scriptures and even qualifications for church membership and church leadership. The pressure of simplistic interpretations of scripture was considerable and most of us were feeling the pressure and some uncertainties about how to combine our new insights and convictions with our duties as Anglican priests. Even lay leaders felt this pressure and sometimes were less well equipped to manage the challenges.

Inevitably a few clergy took steps too far and parish conflicts broke out and landed on a bishop's desk. Unfortunately in Auckland three of them happened in the same area to the new bishop of the southern region of the diocese of Auckland, Bishop Godfrey Wilson. One was a baptismal crisis where a priest of decidedly low-church convictions decided that he no longer believed in infant baptism so when requested to do them, he was alleged to have poured water over the child declaring, 'I dedicate you...' Consequently the parents were unsure whether their child was properly baptised. Such things are bishops' nightmares and the matter was only resolved by the priest resigning and the bishop being left with serious concerns about where charismatic ideas were taking the clergy.

6. Letter from Peter Stuart, 14 May 1980, ibid.

Another crisis swung more around a priest challenging people's involvement in freemasonry (a concern many of us held). When this interconnected with a battle about the times and nature of Sunday services it became a damaging conflict which left wounds for many years. The priest concerned not only resigned his parish but also left the Anglican ministry. In a third case a fine priest with catholic convictions lost confidence in infant baptism and solved his crisis by resigning and taking on assistant priest roles. Such a succession of crises, all in one area, raised concerns for the two bishops[7] and for renewal leaders.

In early 1980 I wrote a letter of concern to Archbishop Paul Reeves, who I had known and liked for many years and was then bishop of Auckland, expressing my concern about both the theological difficulties some of my colleagues were showing but also my concern about apparent episcopal reactions. How could we calm this down? The result was a phone call from Paul suggesting I come in so we could talk it all through. I hadn't foreseen this but it was obviously the appropriate response. I followed this invitation up with a more comprehensive letter on 13 June in which I said,

> All [the unfortunate parish situations] can be traced back to attempts to impose forms of pentecostal teaching and practice upon Anglican parishes. Less visible are the clergy who have caught the fire but got burned themselves and have turned from it. Even less visible is the movement of 'spirit-filled' Anglicans to pentecostal churches as the fire cools in their church or as the priest draws a line beyond which he will not go.[8]

---

7. Bishop Paul Reeves became bishop of Auckland in 1979 and Godfrey Wilson assistant bishop in the southern region soon after.
8. Battley to P. Reeves, 13 June 1980, ANG 076/1/1.

I listed six matters that could cause division[9] and another five that could cause confusion but not division[10] and expressed a concern about 'the heartbreak of the clergy' who have sustained 'rape' by Pentecostals[11] or were living with a vision they didn't have the leadership to effect. I offered three ideas – selection, preferably by bishops, of perceptive visiting resource people to address issues of theology and charismatic practice; the need to gather New Zealand leaders to work together on these issues; and the possibility of bishops creating a 'Council of advice or care for charismatic renewal'.

Paul was superb when we met: genuinely interested, sympathetic to the charismatics, not wanting anything polarised. He commented that he had been a lecturer at the theological college in 1966 when the students had been going into the city to hear Dennis Bennett and had gone himself to see what it was all about. He had also attended the priests' retreat with nineteen of his Waiapu clergy with Fr Francis MacNutt a few years before.[12]

Whatever Paul's personal reservations about some aspects of the renewal might have been, his key principle was 'as long as we all keep listening to and learning from each other' which I said was fine by me, because we felt we were decidedly not being listened to

---

9. The six were the authority of scripture; the nature of spiritual rebirth; issues of re-baptism; the exorcism of persons; issues of ethics, especially homosexuality; and episcopal discipline of charismatics.

10. Adventism; healing vs. suffering; baptism in the Spirit and confirmation; the nature of the congregation; priorities in mission in a context of increasing diversity.

11. Meaning the theft of members.

12. At that retreat MacNutt's colleague, Fr John Bertolucci, had given offence with some injudicious remarks about lack of spirituality amongst bishops. Fr John, to his credit, made amends publicly for his error next day but it was an unfortunate example of the tendency at that time for charismatics to speak disparagingly about church leaders who did not share their enthusiasms.

in much of the diocesan life. Then he surprised me by asking 'So what do you think we should do?' By now we were looking at it as a New Zealand-wide set of issues as he was now archbishop – in those days we had only one.

I replied off the top of my head that I thought he and I should convene a New Zealand-wide consultation of the recognised leaders of the renewal plus some of the bishops. He agreed and asked me to set it up. We agreed on a selection of possible participants and in July, under the letterhead of the Auckland Anglican Charismatic Core Group, Brian Jenkins and I on the archbishop's behalf invited twenty leaders from the seven dioceses to a consultation in Wellington in October.

First National Consultation on Renewal

Nineteen of us met with Bishops Paul Reeves and Ralph Matthews from Waiapu Diocese at Eastbourne parish on 28-29 October 1980.[13] In order to ensure some disciplined thinking before the meeting I asked each renewal leader to bring a written statement addressing three questions: *What I believe the charismatic renewal offers the Anglican Church in New Zealand; Key areas where I think the renewal needs help or discipline – and where such help might come from; My hopes for Church renewal for, say, five years.*

Dale Williamson on summarising these written statements many years later observed:

---

13. The nineteen were: from Auckland, David Balfour, Dr Keven Hall, Peter Philip (from CAM), Capt Peter Lloyd (C A) and myself; from Waikato, John Greer; from Waiapu, Harvey Smith; from Wellington, John Anderson, Ray Muller, George Spargo, Peter Stuart and Charles Waldegrave; from Nelson, Archdeacon Malcolm Welch; from Christchurch, David Harper, Wallace Marriott (Latimer Fellowship), Allen Neil, Martin Warren; and from Dunedin, Harold Clark whose airfare had been paid by his bishop, Peter Mann.

The written responses were broad ranging and showed reasonably deep understanding of the charismatic movement in the NZA, calling into question the judgement that there was poor theological reflection within the movement … These papers also indicated a clear willingness of these leaders of the movement to critique it.[14]

Recurring themes included the need for deeper theological reflection and careful handling of scripture in a more scholarly way to counter Pentecostal literalism; acknowledgement of judgemental or overconfident attitudes by some charismatics; a lack of emphasis on social justice issues; and particularly the need for better understanding by the bishops and the institutional church of the potential, gifts and needs of the movement.

As an example, I wrote,

> Charismatics have sought to maintain a low profile partly because of fear of rejection and partly out of fear of dividing the church … Charismatics tend to be unsure of how they are perceived by their superiors. Much energy is consumed in coping with such uncertainties. Leading charismatics tend to move with an uncertain step endeavouring to be responsible to diocesan leadership and to maintain a creative role in the diocese, yet seeking also to service and to keep alive a spiritual awakening which seems precious in their eyes but is all too seldom given official affirmation.[15]

---

14. Williamson, 271. Content of the conference is summarised by Dale, 271-276.

15. Battley, 'Observations on Charismatic Renewal', a paper prepared for the 1980 Eastbourne Conference, 2, ANG 076/1/1. Reading this 35 years later, it is an accurate description of my own feelings at the time.

There was recognition that the bishops varied considerably in their view of the renewal, from openly supportive (Bishops Peter Mann and Peter Sutton) to tolerant, to critical to plainly hostile. But our underlying desire was that the bishops should recognise the inherent truth in charismatic renewal, back it, and share the financial resources of the church with it. Most of us were by then aware that we were paying twice for everything – our parishes were often paying substantial levies to the diocese which then funded resources that did not fit the renewal, and then we were paying ourselves for every conference or resource we needed. There was a growing sense of injustice about this – a matter which we never really resolved. We were tempted to feel cynical about a church which said so much about social justice but was not above discrimination within its own life.

The conference worked on issues of inclusion and mutual appreciation. Dale Williamson concludes that:

> Regarding the relationships between Charismatics and non-Charismatics, on one hand it was decided that Charismatics were asked to value good relationships above doctrinal agreement, showing tolerance and respect for differences in the Church. On the other hand, it was recognised that the wider Church needed to acknowledge the contribution charismatic spirituality was making to the ministry and direction of the Church.[16]

Discussion ensued on the need for bishops to receive good information; recognition of their concerns about some of the speakers being invited into the country; and the limits of what bishops as authority figures could deliver in pastoral care. 'This meant

---

16. Williamson, 274.

there needed to be peer care, charismatics caring for each other.'[17] Theological issues discussed included authority and interpretation of the bible, infant baptism, how God speaks to the church, ethics and social issues.

The final evening, discussion centred around how Anglicans involved in the renewal could best be involved in all levels of the church. Recommendations for managing leadership in the renewal had come from each diocesan representative: some advocated the appointment by bishops of mutually acceptable liaison persons; others the formation of an Anglican renewal service group. It was generally agreed that 'encouragement and directive is desperately needed'. Both options were discussed[18] and Paul asked us what we felt was the best way forward. We recommended that each diocesan bishop appoint a diocesan liaison priest for the charismatic movement and those priests be authorised to meet as a national oversight group under the leadership of an approved leader. This was the way the Catholic Church was meeting the same need by creating charismatic service groups which were recognised by their bishops.

I doubt if we had thought at all deeply about this idea – it was just what was current with the Catholics – and probably many of us hoped to be the recognised key person. The attraction of it probably was that it would give us the benefit of both options – official recognition and standing, yet a network that was ours to lead. But would this really have been a good way to go? Certainly it would have provided a structure for accountability and for a certain amount of intervention if needed. But what if a bishop had chosen someone other charismatics had reservations about?[19]

---

17. Ibid, quoting Keven Hall's report on the 1980 Eastbourne Conference, 2, ANG 076/1/1
18. Williamson, 275.
19. As sometimes happened in the Catholic Church.

Archbishop Paul was requested to ask the bishops, at the next bishops' meeting, to 'look at ways of setting up appropriate liaison within their dioceses relating both to the bishop and the renewal'.[20] It was agreed that we would meet in a year's time, with additional participants and some theological teachers and some people from Tikanga Maori.

'Anglicans in Aotearoa' and Other Events

Before the second conference two significant and very different events occurred. The Board of Missions convened a New Zealand-wide Anglican motivational conference on mission which they called Anglicans in Aotearoa. Every parish was invited to send three representatives, two of them lay persons. The event was held in Lower Hutt in August 1981. Not surprisingly, probably a majority of the lay people as well as many of the clergy were charismatics or some type of evangelical. The worship was placed under the leadership of a renewal priest, Derek Lightbourne, and a multi-instrument group.[21]

On the opening night the worship burst into open singing in the Spirit which swept through the gathering.[22] The line-up of the bishops on stage looked surprised and even bewildered by it, though a couple of them knew what it was. The evening continued in similar style but afterwards Derek was requested to not allow anything similar to happen again. Those of us in renewal leadership were astonished by the outbreak of singing and pleased to witness it

---

20. Williamson, quoting from Keven Hall's report, 5-6.
21. Interview Dale Williamson with Stephen Brooker, 1 January 2007, 2.
22. It has been claimed that a group of Pentecostals had gathered in the gallery and set it off. I find this improbable – it was probably a group of fired-up Anglicans who just responded to the moment.

but even then I thought, 'Oops! What will happen now?' The conference proceeded sedately through its addresses and workshops. I recall feeling that a barrier had been broken through that night and if the church could follow through on what was evidenced an era of spirit-empowered mission was possible.

Dale Williamson assesses that the event was 'a high point in the life of the New Zealand Anglican Church' and also a high point in the relationship between the charismatic movement and the wider church. Yet, she observes, there is little evidence that the energy for mission and acceptance of the charismatic movement generated filtered out into the wider church.[23] The enthusiasm engendered amongst those who attended was not necessarily accepted by the people in the parishes. Organiser Stephen Brooker described the lack of positive response as 'the institution at its most soul destroying'.[24] This was not necessarily the bishops' fault. But that evening's worship showed the renewal leaders that we were close to a tipping point in the renewal's favour, but it alarmed some of the institutional managers.

A background to all these events was that the 1981 Springbok Rugby Tour had taken place in New Zealand that winter and had bitterly divided the country, including many of the churches. Many courageous anti-apartheid Christians and ministers had taken part in street protests and playing-field invasions but, in the main, charismatics had distanced themselves from the protest movements (though probably not approving of apartheid either) and thus became distanced from the more protest-oriented Anglicans. They were tense days in nation and church. It was in this setting that we reconvened for the second consultation.

23. Williamson, 277.
24. Brooker interview, 2.

The Second Consultation on Charismatic Renewal

In October 1981 twenty-six renewal leaders met for three days at Wallis House, a retreat and conference centre in the Hutt Valley. Four bishops and the Warden of St John's College, Canon Dr Raymond Pelly and lecturer in Maori studies Canon John Tamahori attended. The Maori stream was represented by Canon John Tamahori and Rev. Wally Davis of Porirua. The four bishops were Archbishop Paul Reeves, Bishop Ralph Matthews from Waiapu and Assistant Bishops Godfrey Wilson from South Auckland and Max Wiggins from Wellington, who had been a bishop in Tanzania. Participants included three Anglican members of CAM, Cecil Marshall, David Harper and Peter Philip.

The conference objectives were: Communication, leading to understanding; Clarification of theology, leading to correction; Co-ordination, leading to future action. Particular attention was given to renewal and the place of scripture in the church and baptismal issues and these were discussed widely. Issues of theological training at St John's College were discussed with Raymond Pelly, our view being that as St John's was the only theological college for the province it had to accommodate all points of view but that, despite that being the policy, charismatic renewal was in fact the Cinderella amongst the renewal emphases at the college. The warden responded that there did not appear to be persons who had charismatic experience and advanced theological teaching to qualify for appointment to college staff although some could be involved on a visiting lecturer basis (a response which stimulated some of us to undertake advanced study to acquire the necessary qualifications). A working group was appointed to meet with the warden and faculty of St John's College to discuss how the charismatic witness and learnings could be adequately represented there 'as all future Anglican clergy would need to be able to minister amongst charismatic Anglicans'.[25]

Reports on the renewal were received from each diocese and the Pihopatanga with each raising a range of issues. It was agreed we needed to study the Church Growth movement and to continue meeting and to offer an open conference within two years.[26]

On the leadership question[27] the archbishop reported that the bishops had discussed our proposal for the appointment of liaison persons and a national leader and he advised us that the bishops had decided 'that they did not want to appoint chaplains to a theological party within the church'. This is the expression he used at the meeting. Paul's letter to me does not actually use this expression. He wrote:

> On the questions of a relationship with the episcopate, the Bishops preferred that there be liaison within a diocese rather than the appointment of some Provincial representative. I would have to say that not all Bishops are likely to want a Diocesan liaison person.[28]

25. D. Battley, 'Report on the Archbishop's Consultation on Theology and Leadership in Charismatic Renewal, Wallis House, Lower Hutt, New Zealand, 19-22 October 1981', 19. ANG 076/1/2.
26. Ibid.
27. It is noticeable that there is nothing on this part in the report on the conference.
28. Letter, P. Reeves, 26 February 1981, ANG 076/1/2. The minutes of the Bishops' meeting also confirm this. Under the confusing heading of 'Report on Pentecostal Consultations' (!) they thought that while 'the suggestion of a regular liaison between a Bishop of the Province and the Provincial Committee of the Pentecostals was not thought to be desirable …
It was felt, however, that at the Diocesan level, a representative by the Charismatic Renewal Group, with whom the Bishop could liaise, might

This was a disappointing response for us and it became part of the folk memory of that generation of Anglican renewal leaders that this was the moment that the bishops 'dropped the ball' on the renewal. We believed we had proposed something that would put the renewal more under the oversight of the bishops and would provide a good measure of accountability and coordination. We felt the bishops had responded in a partisan way, viewing the charismatics as a 'party' in the church rather than a renewal with potential for all. It was they who pigeon-holed us. We were not a single 'party' at that time – some of us were from the catholic stream (Peter Stuart, David Balfour, Brian Jenkins); some were evangelicals (Cecil Marshall, David Harper); some were theological centrists by nature – we just had a common experience of the grace of God to share with the church.

The response from the bishops also left me with the realisation that this church had an additional level of governance that is unaccountable, restricted to one order, and is basically inconsistent with Bishop Selwyn's principle that governance should be by a partnership of bishops, clergy and laity. Power accretes where humans meet and the justifiable meeting of the bishops to harmonise management issues they have to handle carries the temptations to govern by privy council.

On later reflection I now believe we should have been our own advocates and have met with the bishops collectively to present our proposals (not that I doubt Paul's genuineness). However, the bishops had now opened the way for us to do what most of us actually preferred – to create our own renewal agency.

---

well be helpful'. Provincial Bishops' Meetings 1980-89, 17-20 Feb 1981, Item 6, ANG 103/1/6. Used with permission. These kinds of appointments did in fact eventuate in some dioceses over the next fifteen years.

The conference concluded with positive views – Paul Reeves said, 'I feel supported and enriched.'[29] A number of working groups had been created and a date set for a third conference in 1982. As a result of the two consultations, bonds of fellowship and shared vision had been formed between key leaders across the country – and that was a potent set of connections.

The Birth of Anglican Renewal Ministries NZ

Following the second conference I became convinced that we would have to set up something ourselves and at some time during the next year I drafted a possible constitution for an Anglican renewal ministry probably to be called Anglican Renewal Ministries New Zealand with the convenient mnemonic ARMNZ. This was not a new idea – we had discussed the idea in England in 1978 and had held it in abeyance while the archbishop's consultations took place.

Most of the renewal members of the consultation met again over 18-21 October 1982. Paul Reeves had told me he saw no need for him to come for a third time and I failed to invite any other bishops or theologians in time. I forget whether it was due to overwork or a subconscious desire to have the meeting to ourselves.

We met again at Wallis House and first discussed developments in SOMA which Michael Harper had initiated in 1978. SOMA had recently held an ecumenical international conference in Singapore with further conferences planned in Fiji (within the area of the Anglican Church in New Zealand and Polynesia) and later at Nairobi in 1983. Members expressed a sense of loss and disappointment at SOMA becoming another interdenominational ministry and were concerned at the change of direction following

29. Consultation Report, 1981, op. cit., 17.

the Anglican focus of the 1978 Canterbury Conference. We asked, 'If SOMA does not carry out an international ministry among the Anglican Communion, then who is going to do this?'[30]

We were informed of a coming teaching tour by Herman Riffel organised by CAM, discussed questions of the devotional life, mid-life ministry crises, overwork and rest, loneliness and stress amongst renewal clergy, and the need to support lay leaders. Baptism and re-baptism were discussed again noting the 'power issues ... which caused Pentecostal and Baptist churches to insist on baptism by immersion and re-baptism of those baptised in infancy, which was regarded as a type of "spiritual one-up-manship"'. Hurt was expressed about the harm this caused to the Anglican renewal movement.

Malcolm Welch reported that a proposal for a 'Service of Thanksgiving for the Birth and Blessing of a Child' he had presented to the Bishops' Meeting had received a negative response.[31] These discussions highlighted the need for closeness and support among leaders and we agreed to sponsor a priests' renewal retreat programme which David Harper was asked to promote.

The next day we addressed the core issue of national leadership and asked, 'So what do we do now?'

Peter Stuart promptly said, 'We have no option, we have to form Anglican Renewal Ministries and do the job ourselves.'

I said, 'Funny you should say that, I have a draft constitution in my satchel!'

We worked all the next day in utmost harmony revising every

---

30. Report on the Consultation on Charismatic Renewal held at Wallis House, Lower Hutt, October 18-21, 1982, 1, ANG 076/1/3.

31. In time, such a service was included in *A New Zealand Anglican Prayer Book: He Karakia Mihinare Aotearoa* in 1989, but without any explicit blessing.

clause until we were satisfied with it. Peter Stuart saw to it that we had a good theological statement about renewal being within the historical order of the church, and that it had to be renewal of the church, society and creation. Wallace Marriott introduced the principle of unanimous decision-making which Terry Fullam[32] had been teaching with much conviction.

We agreed to name the ministry Anglican Renewal Ministries NZ (ARMNZ).[33] After further prayer, confirming scriptures were received.[34] As there were few organised constituencies from which delegates could be elected[35] we designated ourselves as the initial Council which would have power to call members to itself.[36] The next day we all signed the constitution. We were challenged by what we had been led to do and it certainly re-directed my life and

---

32. The Rev. Terry Fullam was an Episcopalian rector of St Paul's Darien and an inspiring scriptural teacher.

33. This name incurred a little criticism. At a subsequent meeting with the bishops, one of them, well known for his anti-war convictions, challenged me about our choice of such a militaristic title. I explained the evolution from EFC to ERM to ARM (in England) to ARMNZ, ARMA, (Australia) and so on, but the comment said something about how some experienced the renewal.

34. The scriptures were Luke 10:1-9, Psalm 78:1-4, Psalm 98:1-3, Isaiah 43:1-13 and Ezekiel 3:27.

35. Just two regional groups existed at the time, the ACCG in Auckland and 'Group 70' in Christchurch. It was called Group 70 just because it had been formed in 1970.

36. The minutes note that three papers on 'Reflections on Renewal' (D. Battley), 'Reaffirmation of Baptism', (M. Warren) and 'Acceptance and Reconciliation' (A. Neil) and subjects brought forward from the previous meetings – ministries of prayer, approach to St John's College, church growth, relations with Latimer Fellowship, Post-ordination training, submissions to the Prayer Book Commission and General Synod, social action and Christian responsibility – were not discussed due to shortage of time. These all became part of the tasks of ARMNZ.

empowered many others. Yet there was a lingering sense that we had been pushed to the side and left to find our own way within a church which had substantial structural and financial resources. We would have to pay our own way.

When I subsequently reported to Paul Reeves what we had done he said to me, 'Thank you for doing this.'

Later, a couple of bishops affirmed that this was the right way to go about the task. 'Keep it right out of the power-games of General Synod or it will die!' Bishop Penny Jamieson later said to me.

And yet, the question remains: had we and the bishops failed to adopt the better option – official recognition and leadership of such a dynamic phenomenon within a church which usually works through official staff? It was noticeable that other fields of change that came from General Synod were granted budgets and staff, the Bi-Cultural Commission and the office of the Social Justice Commissioner being two obvious examples. Had the charismatics just been elbow-jolted to the side, to be denied recognition, access to funds, and left to sink or swim? We had certainly submitted the situation and our needs to the bishops, but met, in the main, rejection.

An unfortunate event illustrates the ambiguous situation the charismatics existed in. Just as we achieved ARMNZ with some episcopal support, the Auckland diocesan newspaper *DioScene* published a very critical paper written by Bishop Godfrey Wilson from his difficult experiences in South Auckland. The paper had been written for confidential use by the Bishops' Meeting, but had subsequently been given to the Auckland archdeacons and was published by *DioScene* without Bishop Godfrey's knowledge. It was a slamming condemnation of most things the charismatics held dear. Entitled 'More Ways than One? Exploring Sectarianism', Godfrey expressed concern about:

A growing sectarian spirit within our Church ... about clergy basing their ministry on a fundamentalist understanding of Scripture; embracing a narrow judgemental approach to moral issues; seeing their chief allies in Pentecostal groups, and individuals, and subtly denigrating the Anglican Church and causing division in the parishes they served.[37]

The paper expanded on all these concerns. It was a not unreasonable expression of concern to fellow bishops in a private meeting, although distinctly one-sided, but as a major article in a diocesan paper it was a brutal attack on the renewal. The shock of it lasted for a long time and probably made it impossible for Godfrey to ever be elected a diocesan bishop – the charismatics simply had too many numbers in synods by then. Brian Jenkins responded with a firm letter to the paper expressing 'considerable concern' about the article. In addition to defending the renewal against all Godfrey's critiques, Brian stated:

My real concern is the trend to narrow down the Anglican Church, to exclude one particular form of Anglicanism which happens to be uncomfortable. The effect, I believe, of the Bishop's paper will be to polarise people rather than reconcile them, to so correct them through the 'teaching role' of the bishops, that they will never hear him.[38]

Godfrey responded with a letter in which he explained the paper was never intended for publication and that for a public paper he

---

37. *DioScene*, Vol. 2, No. 4, December 1982, 3, Kinder Library BX 5752 DIO
38. *DioScene*, Vol. 3, No. 1, September 1983, 2.

would have expressed things differently, and expressed his appreciation of the good aspects of the renewal.[39] But damage had been done and the charismatics knew they had much work to do to be fully accepted in their own church. And I was left wondering what actually went on inside the Bishops' Meeting, which never reported back to the church. Did we have government by privy council?

The question of institutional acceptance of the renewal became the research subject of Dale Williamson's Ph D thesis, 'An Uncomfortable Engagement: The Charismatic Movement in the New Zealand Anglican Church 1965-1985'. Writing twenty-five years later, Dale's assessment of this situation was:

> The NZA missed an opportunity by not embracing the Charismatic Movement wholeheartedly. The Charismatic Movement brought a fervour of spirituality, evangelism and energy that, no doubt, was somewhat dampened by the lacklustre response from the wider church. Furthermore, charismatic parishes grew at a time when many Anglican parishes were in steady decline. The NZA's acceptance of the Charismatic Movement as a subgroup reduced the movement's impact on the NZA.

On the creation of ARMNZ, Dale observed,

> The creation of ARMNZ did not mean that the dream of charismatic leaders to renew the wider Anglican Church through charismatic spirituality and practice was dead. It did mean, however, that this goal would be continued to be worked towards from outside the institutional NZA structures

---

39. *DioScene*, Vol. 3, No. 2, November 1983, 3.

rather than from within them. ARMNZ, as an agency independent of the institutional church, did have one advantage. It had the freedom to set its own direction.[40]

In that hopeful spirit ARMNZ headed into the future.

40. Williamson, 285.

– 11 –

Shooting the Rapids
Travelling the Country

I returned to Pakuranga parish from the third consultation facing mountains of work. Not only had the formation of ARMNZ set up a range of tasks – not all of which had to be done by me – but I was also undertaking a part-time doctoral programme and was facing the fact that my time at St Peter's was done and it was time to move on to another parish.

Involvement in the Doctor of Ministry (D Min) arose in part from an awareness that the brightest of the more liberal clergy seemed to get scholarships for advanced study and then got onto the church's internal career escalator (oh yes, it has one!) while the charismatics seemed to get by-passed. I first applied for funding to do a D Min in Church Growth at Fuller Theological Seminary (an American evangelical college) and was turned down for funding as it 'was not Anglican enough'.

I was pointed in the direction of San Francisco Theological Seminary (SFTS) and a St John's Trust post-ordination scholarship was granted for their D Min programme. So for two northern summers I attended summer schools in San Francisco on the course work of ministry review and academic courses on Johannine biblical studies, and evangelism and church growth. The Johannine study was exciting but the latter was distinctly disappointing.

The core of the Doctor of Ministry was the research study and a consequential thesis and for this I had chosen to examine the use of elderships by charismatic Anglican parishes in New Zealand and overseas. Theologically this required an examination of the relationship of the Anglican understanding of ministerial priesthood and its relationship to the priesthood of all believers, which Anglicans also profess.

Experiments with elderships had developed at St Paul's Symonds Street, St Margaret's Hillsborough and St Thomas' New Lynn, and we had heard or read of others overseas at places like St Michael-le-Belfrey, York and the Church of the Redeemer, Houston. I had also trialed my own version at Pakuranga. I thought eldership was an important development for the expansion of ministry resources in Anglican parishes and as a counter to the clericalism that is inherent in Anglican culture. When I travelled overseas I interviewed Anglican clergy who had developed elderships and gathered nine American and South African examples and, from published reports, twenty-three English cases, to which I added ten New Zealand ones. But the D Min project was interrupted by a change of parish.

I never fully reconnected with St Peter's after the 1978 study leave. I had seen too much and my vision had been internationalised. Much as I loved the Pakuranga parish my heart now held a wider vision. By 1982 I had been at Pakuranga for eleven fulfilling years which gave me great satisfaction but a wise older colleague said to me, 'To serve in a position for more than ten years, a priest needs to know they have the vision and the energy for the next ten years.'[1] I realised I had neither and was losing effectiveness. My GP (a parishioner) even said to me, 'What you need is new challenge.' So when the Papatoetoe parish came vacant on the resignation of its vicar I applied and was duly selected as its next vicar.

---

1. The wise colleague was the Rev. Francis Foulkes, biblical scholar and warden of St John's College.

The Next Renewal Parish

St George's Papatoetoe was a parish in arrested renewal, evidenced in particular by a gaping space between the congregation and the high altar – some twenty feet of space each way. The vicar and vestry had managed to remove all the choir pews and the choir but had no way to fill the yawning space. Musically the mid-morning service sang guitar-based choruses before the service started and then reverted to four hymns sung with the organ. The worship was stuck between the classical and renewal traditions just as the parish's identity was stuck between its catholic background and its previous vicar's new-found charismatic evangelicalism.

The building was, and still is by New Zealand standards, a quite substantial basilica capable of seating 250 people but its main service had shrunk to about 80 worshippers. I found in it a beautiful spirit of prayer, especially in its side chapel where previous vicars had prayed faithfully. Our family of five arrived in January 1983 to take up residence in a large modern vicarage which suited a family with three teenage boys. I grieved deeply for Pakuranga for over a year but found loving and faithful leaders at St George's who wanted all that the family and I could bring them.

Eleanor had left Pakuranga very reluctantly saying, 'I could stay here all my life,' but she could see I needed a new task. She thought she might be able to stand away from music ministry but within a month she had been asked to lead a combined music ministry and move the parish forward in worship. And so it happened all over again – the multi-instruments, this time with a full pipe organ and supportive organists with Eleanor skilfully blending the best of the new music with the richest hymns. The worship burst into life and my preaching took off again, usually expounding the three scriptures of the day. The mid-morning service soon stretched out to ninety minutes or more. Some former parishioners returned and new ones turned up; the mid-morning service was soon numbering around 120 with significant impact on offerings.

A presenting issue was the lack of a centre in the worship; musicians stood to one side; the old pulpit (an un-removable idol) to the other side and nothing in between. We purchased a lightweight moveable lectern and placed it in the centre, from which all the liturgy, readings, sermon and prayers were read. ('Goodness,' the loyal lay reader said, 'he's standing between the people and the altar!' – but he soon got used to it). At the offertory the lectern was moved aside and communion was celebrated from the two-ton stone altar at the far end.

As I had been presiding at communion facing the people for the past twelve years I was no longer comfortable having my back to them, so I soon wanted a freestanding communion table in the vacant space with communion rails around it. I wasted little time in raising the idea and the leaders were open to working it all through. A few worshippers may have been concerned but we won them around. Fortuitously the church's 25th anniversary was coming up the next year and with the mortgage cleared, the church could be consecrated. The building needed extensive interior maintenance and funds were in hand for this as well as a steady income from an opportunity shop staffed by loyal volunteers. We set about a renewal and renovation of a fine building. First we experimented with a temporary communion table and improvised kneelers to see how a semi-circular sanctuary would work. This type of sanctuary redesign was not a new thing – liturgical renewal from the 1950s had been advocating that the communion table be brought closer to the people, preferably in a circular or gathering layout.

An issue, however, was what to do with the large stone altar and the original fixed altar rails. As the altar had been lifted in by a crane before the roof went on, it had to stay and it is there to this day – and the rails remain also. The new half-circle sanctuary platform in front of them has removable rails, and the area can be cleared for dance, drama, or choirs. After trialling all this in 1983 we let the refurbishment contracts and by mid-1984 the scaffolding was in for the repainting of the high ceiling.

In doing all this in my first eighteen months I had defied an old saying in Anglicanism: 'When you arrive in a new parish, change nothing for two years, as you will gradually learn there are good reasons why things are as they are.' Such are the arguments for stasis. There is an alternative wisdom: 'When you arrive in a new parish, walk around with a notepad and write down everything you need to fix. If you don't, you will get used to the faults and fail to fix them!' I favour the latter course and did it with a vengeance at Papatoetoe.

A further issue was leadership structures. Again the vestry had much work to do, but some of the leaders had a passion for ministry development. I could see a need for an eldership but it was far too soon to venture such a reform. I proposed a Leaders Meeting which was simply a gathering of those who led a ministry. Some of them were on vestry also and coped with two meetings a month.

The Leaders Meeting soon had its hands full with spiritual development, pastoral strategy and worship issues. I felt greatly affirmed when the 70-year-old leader of the Mothers Union said one night, 'This meeting is the single most valuable innovation Don has brought us.' Beneath that I heard her saying, 'For all these years I have led women's ministries in this church and have never been allowed to sit with my peers and discuss how we could work together. Now I am able to do so.' I think that her inclusion enabled her to bring her generation along with the changes we were introducing. I have long suspected that many vicars continue with keeping their lay leaders apart so they can't gang up on the vicar about something – the old 'divide and rule' British syndrome. Hopefully that has been changing.

On arriving at Papatoetoe I found myself the sole pastor where at Pakuranga we had four – two ordained and two lay volunteers. I had to get to know all the new households by personal visits and manage an overhaul of the parish life at the same time. I was so caught up in administration that in order to get out to the people I had to resolve, 'I will make *one* significant pastoral contact a day, even if I have to start the visit at 5.00 p.m,' and so I gradually got amongst the people but it was a tough challenge. The bishops saw the need and sent me a newly ordained assistant, Mark Harper, in the second year.

When I needed to replace the parish administrator, a very able Pakuranga parishioner, Jean Martyn, resigned her career in the civil service to join me as parish administrator, much to my relief. In the midst of all this we ran Life in the Spirit Seminars, healing services, home groups and received visiting ministries including Chuck Irish again. The unfinished D Min thesis lay in the background haunting me.

A significant development was that I teamed up with the vicar of Mangere Bridge, the Rev. Martin Bridge, who would come over to talk and pray with me. I had first met Martin and his wife Valerie at the ministry night of a Life in the Spirit Seminar at Henderson in 1977, and subsequently Pakuranga and Papatoetoe people had assisted them with the seminars at Mangere Bridge. Martin looked to me as a bit of a role model just as I had looked to David Balfour and Brian Jenkins. I liked Martin's steadfast dedication to the priesthood and his fine mind. Neither of us foresaw what the Lord was planning for each of us.

The Development of ARMNZ

In parallel with all this parish development, ARMNZ was beginning to roll. The inaugural ARMNZ Council meeting was held on

21 October 1982 and I was elected chairman and Ray Muller secretary. Additional members were selected for geographical coverage;[2] organisational decisions were made and an inaugural National Conference was planned to be held at Tawa in May 1983. A supportive comment from Michael Harper was recorded:

> Something important is emerging – God is directing His people away from the slippery slopes of non-denominational renewal which is a cul-de-sac leading nowhere – into a new commitment to denominational renewal, and that is where the anointing is now resting.[3]

At its next meeting in March 1983 we agreed to import and on-sell the ARM UK course *Saints Alive!* which was an English adaptation of the Life in the Spirit Seminars; invited the Revs Chuck Irish and John Howe from ERM as our next conference speakers; and set goals for the year including to publish 5000 copies of a paper on Charismatic Renewal and the Renewal of the Church.[4]

The May clergy and spouses National Conference commenced with a short salvo from the bishop of Wellington, Sir Edward Norman. When Ray Muller as the host welcomed those attending he said he had something he had to present and read a short letter from Bishop Norman declaring that the conference was 'unauthorised' and ordering all Wellington clergy to return to their parishes

---

2. A representative from Tikanga Maori had been appointed – the Rev. W. (Wally) Davis from Porirua.
3. Minutes of the Inaugural Meeting of ARMNZ, 21 October 1982, 4, ANG 076/2/1
4. Minutes of a Meeting of the Council of ARMNZ, 30 May to 2 June 1983, ibid.

where they were paid to be. A nervous laugh went around the conference and, as far as I know, no-one left.

A day later one of the older priests, Doug Pullar, vicar of Hawera, met with the bishop to explain why he was attending. Reportedly the bishop said, 'But you're not one of them are you?' to which he stoutly replied that he was. We had no more salvos. Visiting speakers at the conference were Chuck Irish, Ron Jackson and John and Karen Howe, all from Episcopal Renewal Ministries, who taught on parish renewal. At the following Council meeting information was shared from ERM; goals were set for 1984 including conferences in different parts of the country, parish renewal weekends, and gathering clergy together locally. It was noted that we needed to be able to pay a conference organiser where possible. The work was expanding rapidly. Council meetings continued twice yearly for many years and from 1985 an Executive met between Council meetings to keep work moving.[5]

In October 1983 Eleanor and I attended an ERM conference in Dallas where we saw the twenty Canadians present resolve to form Anglican Renewal Canada. In our next meeting the ARMNZ Council worked on relations with CAM to avoid duplication; discussed relations with the Province; and appointed the Rev. Colin Brown as our theological consultant.[6] Conferences were planned for Hamilton and Christchurch in June 1984 and we resolved to issue a newsletter to supporters four times a year.[7] The first ARMNZ newsletter was published in mid-1984 to promote the June conferences. Six more were published and circulated to a

---

5. ARMNZ Executive Minutes 1985-1989, ANG 076/2/3.
6. Colin Brown was a theological lecturer in Christchurch.
7. Minutes of a Meeting of the Council of ARMNZ 5-6 October 1983, ANG 076/2/1.

Shooting the Rapids

growing mailing list over the next four years.[8] In the first issue my editorial said:

> Few of us have found it easy to straddle the distance between full-blooded pentecostalism and our inherited Anglicanism ... Most of us have lived with an identity struggle – a struggle that has borne much positive fruit. We have sifted the pentecostal witness and found much of it to have good correlations with the Anglican heritage. We have sifted the heritage, and perhaps come to varied conclusions.
>
> At the very least we have cause to be thankful for the openness of Anglicanism; the witness of the Prayer Book to the place of the Holy Spirit in the life of the believer; the heritage of scripture enshrined in the Prayer Book, the evangelical movement and modern scholarship; and the commitment to healing, exorcism and the sacramental acts of the Anglo-Catholic movement. It is no wonder that spiritual renewal has found a ready response throughout the Anglican Communion.
>
> Today the renewal movement is becoming conscious of its Anglicanism – of a desire to be visibly present within the Church, relating to the heritage yet pointing to a new future. We cannot revert to what we were before the Spirit revitalised our lives but we no longer feel aliens to our own home.[9]

The newsletter was renamed *NETWORK* in 1988 and was published thirty-eight times over the next decade.

---

8. NETWORK Master file, Battley papers.
9. Newsletter of the Anglican Renewal Ministries of New Zealand, (undated), 'Of Identity and the Kingdom', Battley papers.

ARM Auckland and Others

In the early 1980s the Auckland Core Group seemed to lose its way and its focus: it convened meetings to pray about its future – a sign of uncertainty. One document written in 1983 said:

> Over the past few years the Renewal has lost its way to a large extent. People are relating to the 1980s on the basis of a 1970s experience. Our concern is to help people explore what God is saying to us in the 1980s with a relevant spirituality to undergird that exploration. We are aware that similar explorations are taking place within other facets of the life of our church and community.[10]

In 1983 the ACCG renamed itself Anglican Renewal Ministries Auckland (ARMA). A press release for diocesan use stated, 'With diocesan agencies showing increased awareness of the needs of the renewal movement the ARM Auckland committee aim to fill any gaps in the resourcing of renewal.' It announced a Day of Renewal to be held in South Auckland and a planned ministry tour over Pentecost 1984. It stated an aim to have 50 percent lay members.[11] Similar groups subsequently developed in the Waikato (WARM) and Dunedin (SOAR – Southland-Otago Anglican Renewal). In Christchurch, Group 70 became CHARM. Each group then had the right to nominate members to the ARMNZ Council. The ARMA clergy met monthly on Friday mornings for a prayer

---

10. Paper written by Rev. Harry Poole, Harvey Smith and Keven Hall, probably early 1983, ANG 076/6/17. All three writers were from the anglo-catholic stream of the renewal which seemed to be more uncertain than the evangelical-led sector.
11. ANG 076/6/17 1980-82.

breakfast and conducted renewal events around the diocese, supplied speakers to Life in the Spirit Seminars and sponsored days of renewal and occasional evenings of praise in the cathedral.

My diary from 1983 shows a steady flow of ARM-related events – parish renewal weekends, Council meetings, LiSS ministry evenings, ARM prayer breakfasts, ARM Auckland meetings, a lecture on renewal at St John's College, a marae weekend, a meeting with CAM, and visiting speakers coming and going. Regional and national ARM conferences occurred. It is not surprising that by 1984 the Council was discussing making a staff appointment 'the nature of the appointment to cover teacher, encourager, publicist and administrator capable of arranging conferences'.[12]

At that meeting we were surprised to receive a request from SOMA to contribute a fixed sum to their budget. We side-stepped any financial commitment but requested closer consultation. The relationship between ARMNZ and SOMA continued to be a source of tension as we wanted the SOMA work to be contained within ARMNZ but Michael Harper saw it differently. In time they created SOMA-NZ which sent ministry teams overseas for some years.

In June 1984 ARMNZ held renewal conferences in both islands, in Hamilton and Christchurch, and Canon Colin Buchanan from the UK was guest speaker at both. The bishop of Waikato, Brian Davis, attended the Hamilton conference and was interested and supportive. Brian represented a new generation of bishops – those who had become bishops after the charismatic renewal began and had had some experience of it. The newer bishops were aware they had been elected to dioceses with significant numbers of renewal people in them and, whether the charismatics had supported or

12. Minutes of a Meeting of the Council of ARMNZ 1-2 March 1984, ANG 076/2/1.

opposed their election, the bishop would have to work with them. Brian Davis in particular had an open, well-educated evangelical background. He had attended the priests' retreat with Fr Francis McNutt in 1979 when he was Dean of Waiapu. After the retreat I was reflecting on the presence of the Waiapu group and the Lord said very clearly to me, 'Keep your eye on that young man – he's going to be bishop of Waikato, bishop of Wellington and archbishop of New Zealand.' He became a much-loved friend.

From 1984 ARM area representatives brought reports to Council on renewal development in each area. The Rev. Edward Subramani, who had led renewal boldly in Fiji for some time, initiated an ARM group in Polynesia. We were advised of a proposed SOMA conference on renewal for September 1985 and a subsequent ARM Conference in Derbyshire. The ARM network was becoming a focal point for consultation both locally and internationally.

Valuable ministry tours by visiting speakers were run every year – including Chuck Irish and John Howe (1983), Canon Colin Buchanan (1984), Bishop David and Mary Pytches (1985 and 1987), Chuck Irish and Ron Jackson (1986), Dr George and Eileen Carey (1987). Although responsibilities were shared between Council members, it became difficult to fulfill all the projects the Council aspired to.

On the Move Again

During the 1984 Hamilton conference, the Rev. Paul Davidson, senior assistant priest from Christ Church parish, Whanganui, asked whether I knew anyone suitable to be the next vicar of that parish, which had been a leading renewal parish in the 1970s. I made a few tentative suggestions and then unguardedly blurted out, 'I might even come myself.' The emotional background to what was a disloyal act against Papatoetoe I can't clearly recall, I just know I wasn't coping very well with the new triple episcopate in Auckland diocese.[13] Despite Paul Reeves' kindness, I was never really sure where I stood with them.

When I got back to Papatoetoe parish we were into the renovation of the church interior with scaffolding to the high ceiling while we worshipped in the parish hall. The consecration service was scheduled for October and a mission was to be conducted by David Harper and others from CAM in September. In about August, an invitation arrived for me to be the next vicar of Christ Church Whanganui.

I was gobsmacked by this – unable to decline but not free to accept; both Paul Reeves and Godfrey Wilson, my local bishops, were overseas so I could not talk it through with them. I began to experience extreme ambivalence: after a Sunday I would say 'There is NO WAY I could leave these people – or this work'; then from about the middle of the week the interest in the work to be done in Whanganui would build up again.[14]

When we went down to Whanganui for interview and to learn more about the situation, we were warmed by the maturity and spiritual passion of the leaders. When we expressed a concern about Eleanor losing her teaching job in Auckland the people's warden asked what she taught. 'French and Latin,' she replied. 'Well, I'm deputy principal of the high school and can tell you we are desperate for teachers of the romance languages. I'm sure we can get you a part-time position,' he replied. As we drove away I asked Eleanor what she thought and she replied, 'I feel ready for a new adventure.' A few days later I noted in my diary from Acts 7:3, 'Leave

---

13. The three bishops were Archbishop Paul Reeves, and assistant bishops Godfrey Wilson and Ted Buckle.
14. We later learned that the parish had held fasting and prayer on Wednesday mornings for the next appointment.

your family and country and go ... so he left (and) God made him more.'[15]

We finally made contact with Paul Reeves by phone and Eleanor took the call.

Paul asked her, 'Do you think he wants to go?'

And Eleanor said, 'Yes.'

Paul agreed that I should accept.

I also went to see Bishop Ted Buckle to put the quandary before him. He clearly thought I should go and said, 'There is a bigger purpose being worked out here' and that I did not need to worry about Papatoetoe – it would be safe. What he was not free to tell me was that Martin Bridge, who was on study leave in the UK, had written to tell the bishops he did not feel called to continue at Mangere Bridge and would be available for another appointment. So it was that my prayer partner succeeded me at Papatoetoe and that Martin and Valerie had nine very fruitful years there. Martin was gracious enough to say some time later that I had achieved changes in two years that would have taken him five.

Later I learned about what we now call 'transitional pastorates' – where a priest is appointed to a parish with special needs for a short period to bring healing or transition. Unwittingly I had done a two-year transition pastorate at Papatoetoe but new horizons beckoned.

Following a parish mission in September led by David Harper and Ian McCleary from CAM, the parish celebrated a triumphal Consecration Service on 27 October where Paul Reeves preached on Hope. He and I knew that I would be announcing my departure the following Sunday. Three months later, Eleanor and I and Chris and Phil moved to Whanganui, leaving our eldest son Mark behind to study at Auckland University. For the four of us who moved to Whanganui a new adventure was beginning which would expand all our lives.

15. DB 1984 Diary, 4 September.

– 12 –

Running the River
Whanganui to the Vineyard

Christ Church Whanganui

The parish of Christ Church Whanganui[1] is what the Americans call 'a cardinal parish'.[2] The first church for the European settlers was built in 1843 and opened in January 1844.[3] From then on the CMS missionary to the Whanganui area, the Rev. Richard Taylor, conducted services on both sides of the Whanganui river, the Maori mission services at Putikiwharenui and elsewhere in the region and English services in the settler township. Over succeeding decades Christ Church birthed new churches throughout the growing city and district. By 1985 the city had five Anglican parishes and Christ Church parish had four churches and a school chapel to service. To cover the nine services a week required four priests and a team of lay preachers.

The parish had a long-standing evangelical heritage and in the 1970s had been swept by charismatic renewal led mainly by some

---

1. At the time I was there, Whanganui was known by its old spelling, Wanganui, but it has since been corrected with the addition of the 'h'. I have chosen to use the correct spelling.
2. Cardinal meaning both founding and the centre of a network of churches born from it.
3. J. B. Bennett, 'Christ Church The Continuing Story', Wanganui Newspapers Ltd., 1978, 35.

gifted assistant clergy. The Rev. David McGregor in particular was a fine musician and liturgist and Christ Church had become a leading centre for renewal-style Anglican worship attracting worshippers from many denominations. Unfortunately the very popular vicar at the time had an all-too public ministry breakdown and had to be removed by the bishop which left the parish badly hurt. A vicar with pastoral gifts was then appointed and the cost of pastoring a wounded and slowly declining parish broke his health within five years. In fact, the preceding four vicars had all had health or ministry collapses. I approached the role of vicar there with some trepidation but also hope.

We were warmly welcomed especially by Paul Davidson and his wife Helen, who was a great-granddaughter of the missionary Richard Taylor, and by the newly ordained deacon Tony Gerritsen who had worshipped as a theological student with us at Pakuranga. My friendships with Paul and Tony became life-long.

Paul was a contrast to me – he was from a farming background, had been converted as a young man in a milking shed, served as a CMS missionary in Pakistan and Afghanistan, was ordained by Paul Reeves in Waiapu Diocese and was a steadfast evangelical and charismatic with strong organising skills. Once we had decided a project he would say, 'Right, leave it to me!' and it would be organised. Tony was different: a talented intellectual but open to the working of the Holy Spirit. Tony went on to be chaplain at Whanganui Collegiate, headmaster at a church school in Tonga, archdeacon for ministry and then mission in the Wellington diocese and then manukura/principal at St John's Theological College. In addition the parish had a non-stipendiary priest in artist Ted Lewis, an active retired priest in Colin Venimore and a number of lay readers. It was a richly talented church.

Our five years at Christ Church were an exciting, demanding and fulfilling time that I remember with gratitude. We had been advised that they had a parish mission all planned for six weeks after we arrived and, a little ominously, the theme was 'Coping with Stress'! Again David Harper and CAM led the mission. This certainly fired the charismatics up and a number returned from other churches. The parish had 1,700 households on its roll so we needed to offer ministry right across the Anglican spectrum yet were free to reclaim dynamic charismatic worship at the main Sunday service and in the evening. Evensong was also offered at one of the other churches. Eleanor's worship experience was again called on despite the parish having some experienced musicians. The parish flourished and more was to come.

The Vineyard Movement

The 'more' walked into Christ Church in February 1986 through the Rev. Barry Kissell, a Kiwi who had been converted nearby years before and wound up being ordained in the Church of England where he served with Bishop David Pytches, the vicar of St Andrew's Church, Chorleywood in London. David Pytches, Barry Kissell and many others in the Church of England had been strongly influenced by a new version of the charismatic movement emanating from the Vineyard movement led by Pastor John Wimber in California. Although there was little that was really new in the Vineyard movement, other than its emphasis on the loving 'father heart' of God, their faith and manner of praying for whole congregations brought great spiritual blessing wherever they went.

In one weekend, Barry and his team from Chorleywood brought inspiration and an increased anointing of the Holy Spirit to the expectant people who came to Christ Church for teaching and worship sessions. Their style was relaxed, humorous and very confident before God. A distinct feature of the Vineyard style was not to lay hands on people but to pray blessing on people with hands held just above them. For some reason this seemed to increase the spiritual blessing experienced.

While I tended to be a bit critical of what I called the 'hovering hands' style of prayer ministry, it spread widely as a slight change in the exercise of prayer ministry. I heard John Wimber explain once that their style of prayer ministry came about because the first building they worshipped in lacked air-conditioning and got very hot so they learned to not place hands directly on people and found that more seemed to happen as a result. I missed the direct nature of touch in the previous 'laying on of hands' style of praying with people and still prefer it.

Wimber claimed that this was a 'third wave' of renewal – the first being the earlier Pentecostal movement and the second the charismatic movement. Michael Harper said to me a little exasperatedly, 'There's no such thing as the "third wave" – it's still the charismatic movement!' I agree with him and the Vineyard's wish to revise many proven practices of the charismatic movement was a bit annoying and confusing. CAM adopted this enthusiastically and many of CAM's subsequent conferences were led by Vineyard teams. Vineyard led five teaching conferences in New Zealand and the first three reached over 10,000 people: August 1986 (Signs and Wonders); November 1987 (Power Evangelism); December 1988 (Power Healing) (Melbourne); February 1989 (Establishing the Kingdom of God); October 1991 (Holiness Unto the Lord).[4] The Wimber teams also introduced many new songs which emphasised a sentimental 'I love you Jesus' style. I found it wore thin rather quickly. But the Vineyard style was meeting spiritual and emotional needs for people to find love from God where their families had failed them.

Something from Chorleywood and the Vineyard that did influ-

---

4. Vineyard file, Battley papers.

ence ARMNZ was their modelling of faith-sharing teams. They would send out teams of six to eight people with perhaps only one ordained person but with worship-leaders and people who could teach, testify and pray for others. The faith, grace and joy exhibited blessed congregations strongly, and they made good use of words of knowledge to encourage people to come forward for prayer ministry. Christ Church soon took this up and began to send teams to other parishes and ARMNZ soon followed doing weekend ministries around the country.

Around this time the parish leaders sent me away for a month to complete the Doctor of Ministry thesis to get it out of the way.[5] For some time I had been interviewing clergy who had experimented with elderships, meeting both Kiwis and people overseas or from reading their writings. By 1986 my prime conclusion was that there was no one eldership model to apply across parishes, but that each parish had to shape the idea as suited their size and resources.

For Christ Church parish I proposed yet another model which I called Functional Departmentation.[6] Rather than going for a spiritual eldership to oversee spiritual activities as at Pakuranga, or a Leaders Meeting to coordinate ministry design and management as at Papatoetoe, we chose a model of action teams for areas of ministry, each headed by a member of the vestry or staff team. These

---

5. The pursuit of this qualification was related to the charismatics' perception that we would not be admitted into senior leadership roles in the church unless we could match the academic abilities of the leading liberals. Some of us put a lot of time and energy into acquiring extra qualifications for this reason, including Ray Muller and Martin Bridge (D Min), Dale Williamson (Ph D), John Marquet (M Min) and others.

6. D. H. Battley, *Sharing the Priestly Task – A Search for Models for New Zealand Anglican Parishes*. A Doctor of Ministry thesis on the theology and organisation of sharing ministry between laity and clergy in the Anglican Church in New Zealand. San Francisco Theological Seminary. June 1986, 261ff.

leaders reported into a team meeting. The parish was blessed with a wide range of talented leaders so competent leaders were not difficult to find. For a while it worked well, but the problem became replacing leaders when they moved away, frequently on to St John's College for ordination training.

The arrangement did not last beyond my time as vicar, as was quite often the case with unofficial elderships. But the renewal interest in elderships was a creative search for better ways to share ministry leadership and was explored in many renewal parishes.

Spreading Influence

Over the next three years the renewal movement was resourced and fired up by ministry tours by Bishop David and Mary Pytches, Barry and Mary Kissell, Bishop-elect of Bath and Wells Dr George and Eileen Carey, John Wimber and a Vineyard team, Tony Higton, John and Joyce Huggett, and John and Paula Sandford.

George Carey's visit was very significant. I first experienced George in 1985 as the bible expositor at an ARM Conference in the UK. I was impressed by his clear grasp of scripture (he was expounding the high Christology of Colossians); he had been a successful parish priest and had published a book about the renewal of his parish called *The Church in the Market Place*.[7] He had a Ph D in New Testament and was at the time principal of Trinity Theological College in Bristol. I invited him to come to New Zealand for ARMNZ and he accepted willingly. By the time he arrived in New Zealand he was bishop-elect of Bath and Wells. This was top credibility!

George and Eileen ministered very impressively at Kaitaia,

---

7. George Carey, *The Church in the Marketplace: How renewal and a spirit of sacrificial love came to a city church*, Kingsway, Sussex, 1984.

Ngaruawahia Christian Camp, St Luke's Rotorua, St John's College Auckland, All Saints Palmerston North, All Saints Hataitai, a Nelson clergy school, an ARMNZ and Latimer conference in Christchurch, and a one-day conference in Dunedin. We had no idea we were hosting and being encouraged by a future Archbishop of Canterbury. He was warm, humble and real. The then vicar of Kaitaia, board member Harold Clark, told me that Kaitaia parish was launched into renewal in one weekend by George and Eileen's ministry.[8]

A consequence of the expanding activity in both parish and ARMNZ was that my life became even fuller, with some diocesan committee work as well.[9] In October 1986 I reported to the Council, 'The task of Chairman plus National Coordinator is a time-consuming one with a large parish to lead as well. My staff are very supportive. There are times I can see that ARM could be a full-time job.'[10] By 1987 the Council was managing visits by George Carey, Michael Harper, Bishop Owen Dowling of Canberra, the importation of resources such as 'Basic Christianity' from ERM and 'The Changing Church' programme from the UK, and was planning a national conference in May. Bank accounts totalled less than $1,000. In May 1987 the Executive resolved 'that we cannot hope to increase our effectiveness on our present spare-time basis and recommended to the Council that we employ a full-time staff member from January 1988'.[11]

---

8. Harold Clark, *To God Be The Glory*, Polygraphia 2011, 74.

9. An example of the kind of clash that could occur was that on the very morning Barry Kissell and his team were delivering a new anointing of the Holy Spirit to Christ Church parish I was in Wellington at the Standing Committee meeting that ended the candidacy of recently nominated bishop for the diocese.

10. Chairman's Report for year ended 30 Sept 1986, ANG 076/2/1.

11. Executive Minute 8, 13-14 March 1987, ANG 076/2/3.

Over the next year the Council explored how to support a National Coordinator when they had neither a house nor the necessary income stream. For a time the Executive was thinking about a part-time National Coordinator who would work also in a parish. Plans were made for members to attend the next international renewal conference at Canterbury UK just prior to the next Lambeth Conference, and a New Zealand-based national conference was planned for later in 1988.[12]

In 1987 Eleanor and I were able to buy our own home in Whanganui. This fulfilled a long-term dream and we were able to buy a house with sub-divisible land adjacent to a couple who had a vision to develop a Christian community within the parish. On subdividing the land we sold three sections on the open market but retained four others for parishioners wishing to form a community. Couples who shared the vision soon bought in and built their own homes, each with a room available for guests to stay.

Our goal was to create a healing community, Te Puna Wai Ora,[13] where weary renewal people could come to heal and recover. Eleanor and I extended our home to provide three offices. As this all developed I could see a clash of calling developing. Was my future to be with the parish and the community and the diocese, or with ARMNZ? I had no wish to leave such a dynamic parish and its opportunities for outreach in renewal but I also had the vision for ARMNZ as a national agency strong in my heart.

By early 1988 the ARMNZ leaders were feeling upbeat about what they were achieving. I had attended a Provincial 'Disciples in Mission' Conference in February on behalf of ARMNZ and reported to Council that:

---

12. Executive Minutes 11 September 1987, ibid.
13. Meaning 'Spring of Life'. It was in an area of Whanganui known as Springvale.

Renewal is much more widely affecting the Church of the Province than it was at the time of the 'Anglicans in Aotearoa' conference of a few years ago ... that probably more than 50% of the delegates were 'spirit-filled' (and) the climate for consultation with the bishops is now very encouraging ... The whole church is now much more open and sees the need for evangelism if the church is to survive. We are now beginning to see the fruit of the work (of) ARMNZ influencing the whole Church of the province.[14]

As our opportunities expanded, the question of staffing became insistent. Ideas for funding an appointment included seeking individual supporters, contributions from parishes and subscription membership. A national consultation was planned for 17 to 20 October at Waikanae to consolidate our support base to be followed by a visit to the Bishops' Meeting on 26 October.[15]

Canterbury '88

In June-July 1988 many of us had the opportunity to travel again to the UK for the second Canterbury Renewal Conference convened by Michael Harper and SOMA. On the way, Eleanor and I were able to visit Edward Subramani in Fiji, ARM Canada in Ottawa and Toronto, and ARM (UK) in Yorkshire. As we Kiwis had been receiving so many faith-sharing teams from the UK and the USA we decided to offer a team to the UK and twenty-four of us conducted renewal ministries to a number of parishes in Somerset where George Carey was by then bishop.

The Canterbury conferences were a more complicated process

---

14. Executive Minutes 1 March 1988, ANG 076/2/3.
15. Executive Minutes 3 May 1988, ibid.

than the one in 1978. There was firstly a SOMA Leaders' meeting, then an ARM Leaders' meeting which were followed by an open conference. I subsequently reported to the ARMNZ Council that:

> The Conferences were challenging, diverse, enriching and at times exhausting experiences. The theme 'The Church in the Valley of Decision' did not really come alive but the vision of the leaders for Holiness, Unity and World Evangelisation were testified to powerfully in the leaders' conference and taught with insight in the open conference... The one-day ARM conference was inhibited by the attendance of many people from nations without ARM groups but they may have caught a vision that will bear fruit.

Of the overall experience I observed:

> The prevailing vision from the conferences is the call of World Evangelisation over the next decade. The SOMA vision continues to be for sending faith-sharing or renewal teams for short visits to indigenous churches ... It is stimulating to engage in such endeavour (but) I do wonder whether successful evangelisation will not require much more than that. I would have appreciated hearing more about overall mission strategy for the next decade.[16]

I also attended a renewal-style UK clergy training programme 'The Changing Church' led by John Finney and Roger Vaughan where I felt very much at home. I was keen to bring the course to New Zealand and subsequently reported this to the NZ Theological Education by Extension Director, David Moxon, who was very supportive.

16. Chairman's Report for Year to October 1988, ANG 076/2/2.

This idea became our 'Church Alive!' ministry training experience.

I noted to the Council that our penetration of the Anglican institution had improved with Ray Muller being appointed Parish Ministry Consultant and Peter Stuart as Canon Theologian for Wellington diocese, Malcolm Welch as Vicar-General for Nelson Diocese and myself as alumni member of the St John's College Board of Governors. Archbishop Brian Davis, who was always supportive of us and was our episcopal advisor, met with the council for two hours in April 1988 and told us that the image of the renewal was now 'quite good ... especially as the cases of damage to parishes and clergy have diminished in the 1980s'. There was fruitful discussion about issues of the healing ministry and deliverance, which the archbishop accepted as real 'having seen some powerful things happen under my own ministry'.[17]

National Conference and Bishops' Meeting 1988

Our post-Canterbury national conference was held in October and was attended by eighty leadership people. In addition to hearing key Kiwi speakers, including Archbishop Davis, extensive discussion covered areas such as resourcing all parishes seeking to move in renewal – and the need to do this on a zone basis; equipping clergy better and identifying resources; the Changing Church Course; ministry in Fiji and South America; being heard better within the church; renewal and evangelism; and renewal of baptism vows.[18] The proposal to employ a National Coordinator was supported enthusiastically and many participants pledged financial support before the conference ended.

17. ARMNZ Newsletter, No. 6, May 1988, 3, ARMNZ Network file.
18. Report of the Consultation of Anglican Renewal Ministries NZ held at El Rancho, Waikanae 18-20 October 1988, ANG 076/2/2.

No Way Back

Later that month we reported in writing and by a delegation to the six-monthly bishops' meeting stating that:

> There has been significant change in the climate between the renewal and the rest of the church in New Zealand. In the early 1980s aberrations in the renewal were causing suspicion and repressive reaction in some places, and militancy in some other areas of the church were pushing charismatics into defensive attitudes. In a number of dioceses these tensions have eased considerably and we thank those bishops who have helped this process. Parishes experiencing charismatic renewal usually act more responsibly when their abilities are recognised and utilised creatively.[19]

First National Coordinator

By November the Executive was in a position to advertise for a National Coordinator with the job description, 'To coordinate the resources and activities of ARMNZ working closely with Executive and accountable to Council.'[20] The position was open to clergy or lay people. The selection committee consisted of chairman Ron Legge, archdeacon Malcolm Welch, Cecil Marshall and Brian Jenkins with the selection to be discussed with archbishop Brian Davis.[21] Only one enquiry was received and was subsequently withdrawn.

The committee then asked me to apply which I did with both high motivation but also hesitation and some regret as it meant

---

19. A Report to the Bishops of the Church of the Province of NZ from Anglican Renewal Ministries NZ, October 1988.
20. Executive Minutes 2 November 1988.
21. Executive Minutes 3 February 1989.

stepping out of the 'career path' of ministry within a diocese where I was well regarded by the bishop. My appointment was received by the next Council meeting 'with great pleasure and enthusiasm'.[22] With around half a monthly stipend being pledged by our first forty supporters, funds were building up to launch the appointment. I announced my resignation to the parish at the end of April and was to start the appointment in August. Ray Muller said to me, 'The people will love you for this.' The whole country now lay open before me.

22. Council Minutes 21-23 April 1989, ANG 076/2/1.

– 13 –

Riding the Wave
The Growth of ARMNZ

I commenced as full-time National Coordinator[1] with ARMNZ in September 1989 and Eleanor ceased secondary teaching to be available to travel with me. We remained in our own home in Whanganui developing the new community that was gathering around us. I found at first that my time was taken up with the basic administration of developing a charity which was dependent on donations and offerings but we soon received invitations to conduct ministry visits to parishes.

For a long time my heart had been for the smaller parishes who were moving in renewal but did not receive visits from overseas speakers.[2] In the first twelve months we ministered to forty-eight parishes or other ministries either ourselves or with small faith-sharing teams or utilising overseas speakers like David and Mary Pytches, Barry and Mary Kissell and Rosemary Green.

We visited parishes from Auckland to Poverty Bay to Invercargill and the West Coast. It was exhausting but exhilarating and we found that what we had suspected was true – the smaller parishes

---

1. The title National Coordinator was derived from Episcopal Renewal Ministries in the US. They had chosen the term rather than Director which the British seemed to prefer.
2. Many such parishes had been lovingly visited by the Rev. Cecil Marshall when he was Director for CAM. Cecil was very supportive in introducing me to many of those parishes, especially in a tour we shared of the South Island.

were hungry for input and ministry. They loved Eleanor's music ministry which they found accessible and sensitive to New Zealanders' music preferences and their leaders appreciated teaching and counsel from a couple who had been in the renewal in small and medium-sized churches. So often overseas speakers had spoken (sometimes a bit pridefully) of how they had grown renewal churches into large congregations – but for most New Zealand churches that was seldom achievable.

By this time ARMNZ had a two-level structure of a national council and coordinator and regional renewal groups that networked their areas. Such groups were often developed by the council members. Nelson Diocese considered they were a diocese in renewal with an early Pentecostal-Anglican, Derek Eaton, as their new bishop. Each regional group met as they wished, planned local renewal events and conferences which they often ran themselves and worked with the National Coordinator in utilising overseas speakers. Thus connection and local empowerment were developed.

The council continued to be a valuable meeting-point for the regional leaders and provided opportunities to consider the wider picture and to maintain relationships with similar agencies overseas. A number of key initiatives were initiated by the council and developed by the executive. ARMNZ imported and on-sold resources in renewal, especially the 'Saints' series published by ARM UK: 'Saints Alive!', 'Saints for Healing', 'Saints in Worship', 'Saints in Evangelism' and 'Crash Christianity'. These were widely used for some years.[3] John Minns served for many years as our secretary-treasurer and the on-seller of the imported resources.

During the first year with a staff person we paid our way, being sustained by significant surpluses from our visiting speaker tours.

---

3. In six months in 1991 these resources were sold to 47 parishes. ARM(UK) Publications, ANG 076/2/2.

We applied to the St John's College funding system for a grant but were told, 'Your entity is not recognised as a Provincial entity and therefore is not responsible/accountable to any provincial body.' I observed to Council that

> the renewal movement is now in a trap partly of its own making. The fact that the movement has never found (or been given?) an official place within the church's structures means that we can be starved of resources and kept in a marginalised position. Independence has both its advantages and handicaps... As things stand, the likelihood of our getting funds from the province seem poor.[4]

This issue was never resolved to our satisfaction and for a long time we felt we were being made to pay twice for what we needed. In 1989 I was elected to the Board of St John's Theological College as the alumni representative. While it was useful to be there to see the complexities of the set-up – which by then was being deeply affected by the bi-cultural partnership issues, and how to fit Polynesia into that concept – I was not able to achieve very much for the renewal. One person on a board has limited impact – but we were there.

The Decade of Evangelism

By 1990 leaders of the major churches had announced a Decade of Evangelism. The call to make the 90s a decade of evangelism was heard and put forward by leaders of the charismatic movement – initially Father Tom Forrest, International Director of the Catholic Charismatic Renewal, who proposed it to Larry Christensen of the

---

4. National Coordinator's Annual Report year ending 30 September 1990, 3, ANG 076/2/5.

Lutherans and Michael Harper of the Anglican Church. They commended it to others and presented it to the top leaderships of their three churches, each of which adopted it.

I commented to our top half consultation in September 1991, 'It is as if we have given birth to a baby and the whole tribe has agreed to bring it up,' and added, 'there may be moments when we may wish they would give it back to us and let us direct its growth!'[5] Despite the charismatics' enthusiasm for it, nothing remarkable came of the Decade of Evangelism in New Zealand.

Mission to Polynesia

In preparation for the Decade of Evangelism, ARMNZ was invited by the Chair of Polynesia's Evangelism Council, ARMNZ Board member Archdeacon Edward Subramani, to launch the decade in the diocese of Polynesia. It fell to me to recruit a large enough team to do the task. Some Australians joined us from SOMA Australia and we aimed to send twenty-eight Kiwis all of whom had to pay their own travel costs. In total we achieved a team of forty people. About the context, I said in a recruiting letter:

> Last November seven of us ministered in Fiji and found it a heartwarming experience. Many are very keen for the things of God and faith is high. Much of the diocese is, however, quite traditionalist and except for the few 'renewal' parishes the usual sensitivity is needed in presenting change to traditionally-minded people.[6]

---

5. An Address by the ARMNZ National Coordinator to the 'Top Half' Consultation at Keswick Conference Centre, Rotorua 30 September 1991, ANG 076/2/2.
6. Letter DHB, 16 February 1989, SOMA file. Battley papers.

We arrived to conduct a Diocesan Renewal Conference in the Suva Cathedral from 19-23 May, then went out in small teams to minister in every parish in Fiji, returning for a Thanksgiving Service in the cathedral on 1 June. The services in the cathedral were outstanding – the building was frequently full and their singing powerful. The then Dean, Winston Halapua (subsequently Archbishop of Polynesia) said to me wonderingly, 'How do you *do* it? I have spent years trying to get these people to sing – you just get up there and off they go?' (It was, of course, about the fresh spirituality, and the freedom from tradition). Extension teams then went to Tonga but a ministry to Samoa had to be cancelled due to a high-profile funeral happening there. The visit had been extremely testing but quite inspirational.

More energising experiences followed. In September 1990 Eleanor and I and forty-eight other Kiwis attended an Anglican Congress on World Evangelisation in Singapore. Despite its grand title it was an offering by the dioceses of Singapore and Sabah and showed the dynamic approach to evangelism of those dioceses. Most of the 850 participants were from South East Asia and the Pacific. The Singapore diocese, having been led by a charismatic bishop and clergy team, had grown exponentially. I was impressed and a bit envious of what had been achieved but was aware of the cultural differences between them and us. I subsequently reported to the Council:

> The Singaporean Anglicans are a particular breed of Anglican which represents, in my opinion, a synthesis which may not be found in very many other places. They are mainly first-generation Christians, most of them converts from other faith groups in Singapore. They therefore know the difference that Christ has made to them and are able to testify to it. Most of them will be bi- or multi-lingual and their

churches have church services for different language groups. They therefore have the ability to communicate cross-culturally. They live in a society which has with considerable success melded English, Chinese, Malay and Indian roots into a dynamic modern culture (which) is both Western and upper-income Asian... Each of them expect religious life to require moral discipline. None of them have yet been affected by the Western approach to rationalism in religion... This needs to be remembered both by those Westerners who would criticise Singaporean Anglicanism and those admirers of it who would like to replicate it in Western churches.[7]

I instanced also the stark contrast of Singapore having at the time 2.9 million people packed in an area the size of Lake Taupo with churches of over 1,000 members while we had to minister over a much larger country containing many small churches. 'By contrast,' I observed, 'New Zealand is still an intimate society,' and asked, 'If the Decade of Evangelism is to have effect within New Zealand do we need to study small church evangelism rather than large church strategies?'

Away from Whanganui

By 1991 it was clear that our remaining in Whanganui was not working well for the new vicar, the parish or the community, and I was finding that working out of Whanganui was not really convenient. In late May Eleanor and I moved, in quite some pain, to our holiday home at Rotorua to await clarity on where to live next. ARM Auckland made a strong bid to have us return there.

7. A Report to the ARMNZ Council on the Anglican Congress on World Evangelisation held in Singapore, Sept 1 to 6, 1990, ANG 076/2/2.

In the meantime Eleanor and I travelled to the ERM Evergreen Conference Centre in Colorado for their ministry training programme; then to Scotland to visit and minister with SERF (Scottish Episcopal Renewal Fellowship) and then to an ARM conference on 'Partners in Renewal' at Canterbury, followed by an interdenominational Theological Conference on Renewal held at Brighton. Our tour concluded with a course on evangelism and apologetics led by Canon Michael Green at Regent College, Vancouver. The whole trip was an impressive experience of how thoroughly charismatics were facing up to issues of theology and practice of ministry.

Prophetic Leadings

Throughout this time I had moments when God spoke into my mind with leadings and new ideas. An example is this from 6 April 1991:

You see but the beginning.
Now let your imagination flow in me as I reveal to you
things that are to come.
You are not to shorten my arm by limiting what I can do
to what you deem possible.
Am I not the Lord of the whole earth?
Do not all his cattle and wealth belong to me?
I can provide and I will provide on the day that I appoint.
Have I not done so? Why should you doubt?
So write down what I speak into your heart,
Receive it by faith; let the people know and wait for me
to show the way.

So write now:

1. Importation, distribution and sale of resources
   Distribution Secretary. $10,000 capital.
2. Publication of a magazine (not a newsletter)
   - by beginning of 1992
   - DHB as editor
   - professional editorial advisor
   - designated contributors
   - funded by specific donations
3. Full-time administrative secretary – knowing all the inside works.
4. Zone or regional leaders – not salaried but approved by supporting church.

Cluster the key workers.

There is still more.[8]

From moments of inspiration like this, new steps came.

Speakers Tours and 'Church Alive!'

Each year saw new developments which increased the impact of ARMNZ on its constituency and on the church. Visiting speakers of international standing came through the country, but not always as guests of ARMNZ, and added insights and energy: Eddie Gibbs introduced us to the principles of church growth, Fr Rick Thomas with Catholic Charismatic Renewal Services challenged us on radical options for the poor; and Ann White taught on healing of memories. Anglican Tony Higton from TIME Ministries International visited those parishes which were using his course 'Called To Serve'. Tony was not willing to let ARMNZ be agents

---

8. Mss document, ANG 076/2/2.

for his programme; in imperialist style he wanted to retain control. Some of the parishes which took his material on board did quite well as a result.

A more influential visit was a tour by the Rev. Roger and Sally Vaughan from England. Roger and I had a lot in common in churchmanship, intellect and spirit and he was one of the creators of the 'Changing Church' training course in the UK. He and Sally were in New Zealand from mid-September to early December 1991, spending part of the time on holiday, but they taught extensively and were keynote speakers at our first 'Church Alive!' residential training course held at Tea Pot Valley Camp near Nelson in November 1991. ARMNZ designed its own course but drew on the English model.

I included in our design process Ray Muller and Martin Bridge who had recently gained Doctor of Ministry degrees in church growth, Church Army evangelist and trainer Peter Lloyd, and Paul Williamson who had been ministry officer in Dunedin diocese. We also drew on the support of David Moxon, the TEE Director at the time. While 'Church Alive!' never became an official training course of the church it was given some funding from national training funds. Participants had to pay their own fees and accommodation costs. By the end of 1991 the subject of developing some type of alternative training centre or theological school with an evangelical/renewal base entered our discussions.[9]

In 1992 Lee and Audrey Buck and the Rev. Kevin and Sharon Martin from Episcopal Renewal Ministries visited in August to speak at our second 'Church Alive!' course. Both had been key presenters in the ERM residential course at Evergreeen Colorado. They conducted two of Lee's 'Dare to Share' evangelism week-

---

9. This project was subsequently adopted by AFFIRM and contributed to the development of Bishopdale College in Nelson.

ends at Ngaruawahia and Balclutha, taught at the two 'Church Alive!' schools at Rotorua and Living Springs, Christchurch and ministered in Avonhead and Temuka parishes. Lee was a much appreciated, confident lay teacher and evangelist.

The content of the Church Alive! course was indicative of the needs of renewal clergy and lay leaders at that time. The 1992 Church Alive! included:

Introduction to Church Growth 1 & 2 (Ray Muller)
Biblical Perspectives of Leadership (Lee Buck)
Developing your Lay Ministry (Lee Buck)
Styles of Leadership (Kevin Martin)
The Seven Stages of Parish Renewal (Kevin Martin)
Developing an Evangelism-oriented Parish Lifestyle (Don Battley)
Charismatic Issues in Ministry (Don Battley)
Management of Change (Don Battley)
Church Sizes and Church Growth (Peter Lloyd)
Surviving as a Clergy Spouse (Eleanor Battley and Sharon Martin)
Ministering as a Couple (D & E Battley, K & S Marin)
Burning at Both Ends – Ministry Survival (Panel)

Worship-based evening sessions were 'Dare to Share Your Faith' (Lee Buck), 'In the Presence of the Lord' (Eleanor Battley), 'Leading People to Baptism in the Spirit' (Lee Buck), 'A Ministry of Healing' (Team). The evenings always included prayer ministry. Sixty-one people plus the presenters attended in 1992.[10]

By 1992 ARMNZ was in full swing. We conducted ministries in

---

10. Church Alive! Clergy and Lay Ministers In-Service Training Programme, 2-7 August 1992, Battley papers.

over fifty locations, including the two Church Alive! courses. Andy and Audrey Arbuthnott visited from the London Healing Ministry and ministered in twenty-four locations in five weeks. Jean Martyn, who had been my administrator at Papatoetoe, became ARMNZ administrator from April and as a result ARMNZ had two initiators and ministry managers. Jean made significant contributions to the development of ARMNZ.

ARMNZ Tenth Birthday

By October 1992 ARMNZ had existed for ten years and we called a tenth anniversary conference at Keswick Conference Centre, Rotorua, to celebrate and reflect. As keynote speakers we invited leading New Zealanders to make the event our own. These included Bishop Derek Eaton of Nelson; church growth consultant the Rev. Dr Ray Muller; Bill Subritzky, by then a world-renowned evangelist; Professor John Morton, a leading ecologist and Professor of Zoology at Auckland University; and the Rev. Francis Foulkes, biblical scholar and evangelical leader. The theme of the event was 'Where has the Spirit brought us to? Where is the Spirit leading us?'

Two hundred and twenty people attended, indicating how response to the ministry had grown. The financial statement of that year showed that annual income had risen from $59,000 to $108,000 and costs from $66,000 to $114,000 plus sales of resources from $16,000 to $34,000 p.a. There was much to celebrate.

In my opening address, having acknowledged the founders and their vision, I asked 'What have we learned from the Renewal Movement?' I named the increased reality of God and God's gifting for witnessing, and observed,

A Decade of Evangelism is no new thing for those in renewal – we have been doing it for *two* decades already. Now the church thinks it needs to tell us how to do it!! Let us learn what we may, but don't unlearn what God has shown you.

I spoke of the restoration of the charisms to the church; the new music ('an ancient sign of authentic renewal') and less controlled approach to worship; and the vision of a church that grows. Again, I said,

Church growth is not new to the renewal movement – our current interest in that movement is primarily that it gives us clues to the blocks we encountered and couldn't negotiate. Again, I feel a bit cynical or sceptical about the church's current interest in church growth... When we had real spontaneous church growth not too many of our leaders were interested. We were even judged for breaking the mould and not being properly Anglican. Now that the surge has faded, they want to recreate it! It was all happening in the 70s, for heaven's sake!!... Sometimes I wonder if the Anglican Church has an inbuilt death wish, that it can shaft so much good growth.

I moved on in a more positive note to affirm the role of faith-sharing teams as a positive contribution we could make to the Decade of Evangelism and then reflected on the role of suffering in our witness:

We have also learned to suffer for the truth's sake. It is an odd thing that somehow we were led to expect that being anointed with the Spirit of the Lord would mean joy without sorrow. That is certainly not biblical ... the curious thing for us has been that it is not the world that hates us, so much as large parts of the church!... It has been very, very painful for many of us, lay as well as priests, to come into the power of the Spirit in a church which values control above creative liberty, tradition above God's current moving, and intellect above the gift of faith.

More and more I find myself living in two distinct churches: a church of renewed faith, prayer, unity, hope, scriptural joy, and outgoing mission – until I encounter the rest of the church and it feels more and more like an alien world where people are aggressive, angry, competitive, alienated from each other and especially from us, and I wonder how these different visions of what it means to be a Christian can co-exist in one church.[11]

I then acknowledged that we needed to be aware of others seeing similar faults in us – including narrowness and judgementalism. I wondered whether we were caught in a 'Cinderella syndrome'. Other more positive comments followed.

Biblical scholar Francis Foulkes presented a very thorough and balanced address on faith and fundamentalism; Professor John Morton shared his passion for a sound theology of creation and the care of creation; Bill Subritzky gave a comprehensive testimony of his journey into faith and Holy Spirit-empowered ministry and followed it with a 'no punches held back' critique of the Anglican Church (which presaged his later withdrawal from it over the LGBT issue).[12] Bishop Derek was encouraging and inspirational. It was an interesting and diverse panel of speakers which evidenced the wide

---

11. ARMNZ 10th Birthday Conference 1992, ANG 076/5/9.
12. Bill Subritzky's Address at the ARMNZ National Conference October 1992, 14-21, Battley papers.

range of Anglicans who had experienced the baptism of the Spirit and had then followed their spiritual gifts into a variety of ministries. A range of workshops were led by our people. The conference concluded with a joyful celebration dinner and worship time.

Nineteen-ninety-three was a steady-as-she-goes year with about forty-eight in-parish ministries conducted by Eleanor and me, including an extensive tour of the South Island involving twenty-three contacts, and a short but high-impact ministry visit by Michael and Rosemary Green. They ministered at Auckland, Whangarei, Hamilton, Rotorua, Dunedin and New Plymouth. The highlight was Michael conducting a School of Evangelistic Preaching and Christian Apologetics at Waikanae attended by eighty clergy and lay preachers.[1]

The regional groups grew stronger and WARM conducted a Waikato/Bay of Plenty renewal conference in July.

But the major event in 1993 was the birth of AFFIRM.

---

1. *NETWORK* Magazine, No. 20, 7, Battley papers.

Photos

*Four founders at ARMNZ's tenth birthday, 1992.
Left to right: John Greer, Peter Stuart, Don, Ray Muller.*

*ARMNZ staff. Left to right: Peter Taylor (computers), Don,
Alan McLean (accounts), Sue Thomson (administrator).*

Summer Wine camp site at Lake Taupo Christian Camp.

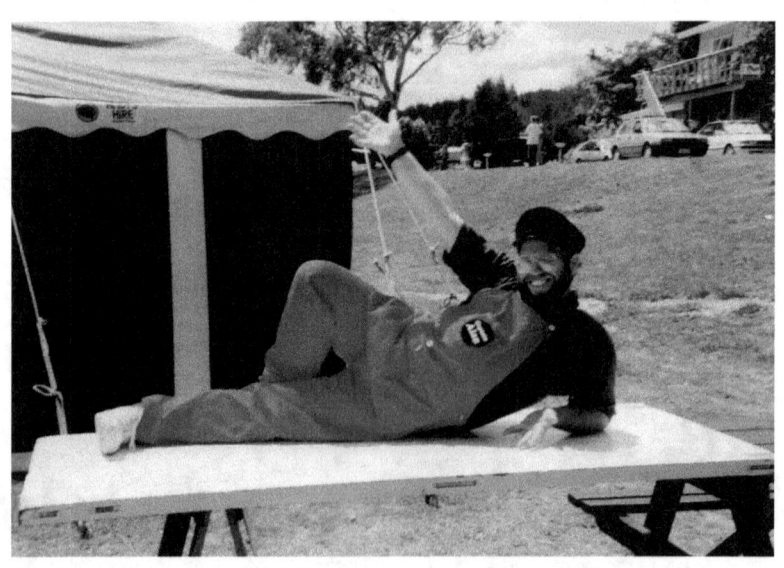

Capt. Alan Price welcoming campers.

Scenes from the Big Top at Summer Wine.

Decade of Evangelism mission to Fiji with Sisters of the Community of the Sacred Name. Left to right: Ralph Richardson, Eleanor, Sisters, Don, ?, ?, Pamela Richardson.

Pamela ministering in clowning. We learned that the children were frightened by the white face, white being a sign of death in Polynesia.

Photos

In Rwanda. Hongi between Canon Bert Karaka and Canon Jerome Munyangaju.

Memorial Service at a mass grave site being led by team leader Don Brewin of SOMA.

AFFIRM Conference at Waikanae, 1993.
Photo: Godfrey Boehnke.

Kristen Williams, youth leader and speaker.
Photo: Godfrey Boehnke.

Photos

AFFIRM leaders. Left to right: Peter Lloyd (CA),
Bob Robinson (CMS), Don (ARMNZ), Les Brighton (Latimer Fp),
Brian Jenkins (CA), Dale Williamson (ARMNZ).

Signing of the AFFIRM Covenant.
Rev. Rosemary Anderson and Don. Photo: Godfrey Boehnke.

Eleanor's ordination, St John's Bucklands Beach.

Thirty-fifth wedding anniversary.

– 14 –

Uniting the Rivers
Affirming Orthodox Faith

Affirming Orthodox Faith

In November 1991 a meeting occurred which had far-reaching consequences. I had received a letter from the evangelical society Latimer Fellowship asking whether, given the similarities of our objectives, ARMNZ and Latimer should somehow combine for greater impact. I replied that I had a number of one-to-one relationships to manage and I didn't really need another but was willing to meet. So on 1 November some from ARMNZ met with leaders of Latimer in Christchurch. I soon realised that part of the situation was that Latimer, who had a valuable but costly publishing ministry, were in financial difficulty partly because the evangelical stream was becoming dissipated by the charismatic movement.

A word of explanation may be needed. The term 'evangelical' has had numerous meanings in Christianity. Based on the word *evangel* (for gospel), every Christian is by definition 'evangelical' because we have all accepted and are called to serve God's gospel. But over the centuries, especially since the Reformation, the term has come to mean those who particularly hold to the core reformation principles, especially the high authority of the scriptures and the need for personal conversion. At times Anglicanism has streamed itself into evangelical, central or broad-church, and anglo-catholic streams defined in part by preferences in worship but often also according to theological emphases.

Two strong movements in contemporary Christianity have muddled this over-tidy classification: the liberal-modernist movement and the charismatic movement. Both have drawn committed support from all three streams. The charismatic movement in particular fell upon catholics and evangelicals equally – leading each towards the convictions of the other, and even central-churchmen like myself found themselves caught up into it, somewhat to their surprise and often their joy. So ARMNZ would not have considered itself an 'evangelical' organisation. (I well recall Brian Jenkins declaring indignantly, 'I'm not an evangelical – I'm a *catholic!*' – yet he wound up being director of the very evangelical Church Army).

But by the 1990s something had happened amongst the charismatics: the anglo-catholic charismatics seemed to have lost their way (St Paul's was by then a shadow of its former self) and the evangelically strong charismatics were dominant by sheer numbers and by their ability to expound the scriptures competently. Some of us had abandoned all the previous labels and focussed simply on what we saw as a new and more biblical model of Christianity – the original charismatic style of the Book of Acts – or at least, what we thought it meant. Whatever our earlier convictions, we were drawn by the experientiality of the charismatic movement into a more dynamic and open style of confident faith. We had become 'new evangelicals', deeply convinced of the inherent truth of foundational Christianity.

I believe it was I who, after listening to the Latimer leaders, many of whom were charismatics, suggested we should look at something wider than a partnership but rather an alliance of all the evangelically-oriented voluntary societies to see how we could work strategically together.

Again, an explanation: while the Anglican Church has strong

formal structures – synods, dioceses, parishes, chaplaincies, it has long accepted the right of its people to form voluntary societies that are created to act in particular areas of mission. The classic example, of course, is that Anglicanism was brought to New Zealand by a voluntary society – the Church Missionary Society. Many others have existed over time. We agreed to sponsor a meeting of the evangelically-oriented voluntary societies early in 1992.

This 'Consortium' meeting was held at Ron and Jean Legge's home at Raumati over 2-3 March 1992. It was attended by twelve representatives of Latimer Fellowship, Church Army, ARMNZ, Church Missionary Society in New Zealand and Church Growth Resources. Concern was shared about the evident decline of the NZA (the Anglican Church in Aotearoa, NZ and Polynesia); we recognised that our societies tend to be reactive rather than proactive but that 'we have in common the desire to see live, growing, enriched churches, reaching out in evangelism'. We agreed that a coalition of these groups was important; that there was value in publishing various materials; and to maintain regular consultation with each other. An open conference was proposed for August 1993.[2]

The representatives met again from 29 April to 1 May 1992 and considered a wide range of subjects: the role of voluntary societies and the modality/sodality tension in the church; how serious was the crisis in Anglicanism; youth and children's work; generating new communities of faith; the need for a common theology for mission; change-agency roles; dangers of deism and clericalism; the relation of scripture, tradition and reason; authority and hermeneutics; gospel and culture and the fundamentalism debate.

Theological education suitable for evangelical and charismatic candidates for ordination was a significant concern because there

---

2. Summary of Discussions at Consortium held at Raumati 2 & 3 March 1992, AFFIRM papers, Battley papers.

was no choice for such people in New Zealand except outside the Anglican system. We saw a crisis coming to replace older clergy in the evangelical and charismatic parishes. We agreed to pursue these goals:

- To start training people while they were laity in parishes
- To encourage people to do pre-St John's study
- To encourage at least a few to get overseas study
- To continue representations to St John's and monitor it
- To train people long-term up to Ph D for theological faculty or ministry officers
- To provide post-St John's in-service courses.

All these objectives have, in time, been achieved.

The idea of forming some kind of organisation to pursue these goals jointly developed, and it was agreed to formulate a statement of faith and a covenant. After a time of prayer the name Anglicans For Faith, Intercession, Renewal and Mission – AFFIRM[3] – was agreed to.[4]

The AFFIRM founders met again on 6-7 September in Christchurch following a national church conference called 'Partners in Mission' (PIM). We were very discouraged by the PIM event. There had been some cheap scoring off evangelicals and charismatics which had not been appreciated; the focus of the event had been on management rather than mission; discussion of a statistical analysis presented by Ray Muller had in general been explained away rather than faced up to. Ray had presented a paper to Wellington Diocese entitled 'What Sort of Future?' in April

---

3. At first AFIRE (E=evangelism) was suggested but members thought this sounded too Pentecostal. Mission was the right word as the church already had a five-fold definition of mission which we could support.

4. Notes of the Second Meeting of the Consortium at Raumati 29 April – 1 May 1992, AFFIRM Battley papers.

1992. A statistical analysis of the 1991 census, it showed severe falls in all Anglican statistics which showed us to be 'in a very weak position'. Ray concluded, 'The challenge for the Anglican Church is how to effectively evangelise, involve, nurture, train and deploy those in the under 40 years age group.'[5] I recall being deeply disappointed by the Partners In Mission experience and being convinced we had to create a new climate of faith and hope.

The societies reported that each of them was in principle supportive of the AFFIRM project. Time was spent revising a draft of a covenant which we hoped, 'though not saying everything that could be said, nonetheless represents the *central thrust* of the issues that have brought us together'.[6]

The meeting discussed a paper requested from Dale Williamson on 'The Work of Women, Men, and God', noting that some women were in 'double jeopardy' – of being put down as conservatives as well as women; and that we needed to develop good hermeneutics to liberate scripture from an earlier evangelical rigidness. Work was put into planning the coming AFFIRM conference and developing the Latimer magazine into a larger AFFIRM magazine.

AFFIRM Council met again on 29-30 January 1993 following a Vision NZ Congress. We noted an old paradigm/new paradigm contrast between the Anglican Partners in Mission Conference and the Vision NZ experience. The Anglican event had been a low-expectation and defensive experience; Vision NZ was energetic and confident in the future. Council's time was spent on planning the coming conference and the proposed magazine.[7]

---

5. Twenty-five years later, the statistics are even more dire.
6. Record of a Meeting of AFFIRM at Sister Eveleen House, Christchurch, 6-7 September 1992, ibid.
7. Minutes of a meeting of AFFIRM, Raumati South, 29-30 January 1993.

A Confessing Movement

AFFIRM was formally launched in August 1993 with a National Conference at Waikanae attended by 240 people from all around the country.

In the chairman's opening address, I stated our concern about widespread anxiety amongst our constituents about trends in ethics in our church, and that we ourselves experienced major concerns about the modelling the church was giving to new converts and the treatment 'reborn' or 'renewed' members experienced from some clergy and from some diocesan selection or training programmes. I then said:

> All these factors, and others, have led the leaders of these voluntary societies and ministries to say it is time to stand together and to raise up a confessing movement in this church. In simple language, I think that is what is happening. What is in this AFFIRM project for the voluntary societies, by way of mutual support, envisioning, etc., is incidental.

I described a confessing movement as not being primarily about confessing our sins, necessary though that might be, but 'to publicly own and acknowledge; to profess faith in God and Christ and to obey his will'.

> Throughout the history of the church there have been a range of 'confessing movements' within the churches: obviously the Apostolic Church which confessed Christ to Jew and Gentile alike, but also the early monastic movements, St Athanasias and the anti-Arians, the Franciscans, the Reformers, the early evangelicals, the German Confessing Church in the Nazi era, to name only a few from Western Christianity.

I cited a recent talk by Professor Keith Ward from the UK who had said that there are two types of theology: Critical Theology and Confessing Theology. They are both needed ... and Confessional Theology is quite valid. Confessing Theology is convinced of the basics of the Apostolic Faith and seeks to present it positively with all the resources of argument, conviction and persuasion it can muster. I continued:

> We need to become again a convinced, confessing church, and to realise that that is always how the Christian faith has spread and survived. It is time for many to challenge this church to be faithful to its task of confessing God and Christ in a rapidly secularising society...
>
> The future of the church does not lie in rewriting the Christian confession so that it accommodates to the blindness and paganism of secularism... The church's future lies in a bold confrontation with the emptiness of secularism – and in offering to New Zealanders, whose lives have been made shallow by secularist education and life assumptions, the depth and height and breadth of a vision of life lived in the experience of a living God and a risen Christ.

AFFIRM, I said, recognises the need for a rediscovery of confessional theology and positive apologetics and we rejoiced that there were already people of advanced theological training at the heart of the AFFIRM project. We saw this as a long-term project for at least a generation, and so welcomed the participation of fifty younger leaders at the conference which 'fills us with hope for the future'.[8]

The conference followed four themes, one each day: 'Faith in

---

8. D. H. Battley, Address for AFFIRM Conference: 'We AFFIRM the Apostolic Faith', Battley AFFIRM papers.

Crisis', 'Church in Transition', 'Mission in Crisis' and 'We AFFIRM the Gospel of God'. Strong presentations came from able speakers including Professor Billie Abraham from the USA; Pastor John Smith (of God's Squad motor cycle ministry in Australia); Archbishop Brian Davis; Dr Bob Robinson, General Secretary of CMSNZ, who voiced 'an enormous cry of anguish from a church in decline'; church growth consultant Rev. Bob Barrett; and Captain Peter Lloyd, Rev. Lorraine Lloyd and Rev. Brian Jenkins of Church Army. A feature was twenty discussion groups which discussed and reported back in writing on 'Concerns I feel about life in the Anglican Church at present' and 'Some things I would like to see given priority by the Church in the next five years'. A youth conference ran concurrently.

The AFFIRM Covenant was signed on behalf of the four founding societies and by the conference participants who included three bishops. The Covenant declared that AFFIRM 'seeks to recall the Church to biblical faith, the life of prayer, spiritual renewal and effective mission' and stated that the members held in common the creedal beliefs of the Anglican Church and affirmed especially:

a. The love of God as the source and motive of our life and mission
b. The Lordship of Jesus Christ over the church and the world
c. The authority of the Bible as God's living word to individuals and communities
d. The Holy Spirit's gifting of all Christian women and men for their varied ministries
e. The centrality of evangelism within the whole mission of the church
f. The need for continuing renewal of local congregations as living communities of faith and love
g. The priority of prayer and worship as undergirding all Christian life and action.

Having announced itself as 'a new confessing movement in the church', AFFIRM invited membership of other mission societies and of members of the Anglican Church who wished to subscribe to the objectives.

The conference issued a concluding Conference Statement:

We, 240 members and leaders of the Anglican Church, representing every diocese in New Zealand, have spent four days together in prayer and consultation. We wish to:

a) *express* our concern about current trends in belief and ethics in this Church. We see these leading to the discouragement and disillusionment of many key members of this Church. We are aware that some of the most dedicated people in our parishes are close to leaving because of their anger, disappointment and sense of betrayal;

b) *declare* our commitment to the Church in its weaknesses and its strengths. We are determined to work, together with all who share our concerns, to recall the Church to
  - an orthodox and biblical faith
  - a renewed dependence on the Holy Spirit and prayer, and
  - effective mission and evangelism;

c) *state* our belief that a radical reshaping of the church is required as the church moves into the next century. We seek to contribute to that search and journey.

Four voluntary societies (Anglican Renewal Ministries, Church Army, Church Missionary Society and Latimer Fellowship) and Conference members have signed a Covenant to create AFFIRM (Anglicans For Faith Intercession Renewal and Mission) to work together to fulfil these aims. We seek to relate openly to the leaders and members of the Anglican Church in Aotearoa New Zealand and Polynesia as we share our common journey.

Waikanae 29 August 1993.[9]

The conference was deemed a great success by many and insightful letters came in from participants such as the Revs Bob Glenn, Bruce Nicholls and James Worsfold. The South America Mission Society (SAMS) indicated their intention to join AFFIRM.

The next meeting of AFFIRM Council identified fields of immediate action. Latimer Fellowship, which had experience in publishing, had already published the first AFFIRM Magazine, *AFFIRM: New hope for the Church today*, a challenging exercise for them, and the magazine became a constant source of effort and concern. The magazine was edited for a time by Les Brighton, the General Secretary of Latimer Fellowship, but the load soon wore him down. The magazine had 1,100 subscribers by the end of 1993 and 1,600 by 1994.[10]

Council also considered ways that parishes and individuals could become members; how to provide in-service training for clergy and lay leaders; and whether they could achieve an alternative theological training college. We were trying to build a coordinated strategy between the societies but without funds or a full-time staff person to drive it.[11]

Presbyterian evangelicals liked the AFFIRM idea so much that

---

9. AFFIRM Conference 1993, ANG 076 /5.00/10.
10. Documents in AFFIRM Executive file, 1993-1996, Battley papers.
11. I recall Ray Muller commenting to me that AFFIRM wouldn't achieve much because no-one was willing to support a staff member to drive it.

they requested permission to use the title (which we agreed to with some reservations given the possibilities for confusion).[12] Soon after, joint AFFIRM meetings began in Auckland between representatives of the Anglican AFFIRM, Presbyterian AFFIRM and the Methodist Aldersgate Fellowship, which soon became Methodist AFFIRM.[13] Methodist AFFIRM published a small magazine until 1997 when they were overtaken by the crisis in the NZ Methodist Church over ordaining homosexuals in relationships and the subsequent formation of the Wesleyan Methodist Movement in 1997-8.[14] We then helped with joint AFFIRM meetings which issued into a sequence of AFFIRM theological pamphlets.

At the same time Anglican AFFIRM published their AFFIRM Magazine; the first issue was in October 1993 and the magazine continued to be published for some years at much cost to the Latimer Fellowship and its staff. Publication ceased after eight years and twenty-three issues.[15]

The Mood of the Times...

From *The Church of England News* (3 Sept 1993):

> Anglo-Catholic society Ecclesia commends the breakaway Anglican Catholic Church (from USA) as an option for people who cannot accept priesting of women.

---

12. *Introducing Presbyterian AFFIRM,* undated, Battley papers.
13. First Methodist AFFIRM Conference, 8-10 November 1995, Aldersgate Fellowship file, Battley papers.
14. Wesleyan Methodist Movement file, Battley papers.
15. Final issue, *AFFIRM: New Hope for Today,* Vol 8 No 2 Winter 2000, Battley papers.

Letter from Michael Harper and others to explain why he and others plan to join the Orthodox Church because the CofE is 'already in a state of apostacy'.

US parish clergy call a conference of the Episcopal Church which was attended by 1,000 people in what 'looked like becoming a serious grass-roots revolt'. Rev. John Shuller of East Tennessee said, 'Those numbers represent real people – parishioners, friends, parents and children of us all. I think we've lived a long time in a kind of denial about decline.' He added that resistance to change in the church was evidence of that denial.

Bishop Terence Kelshaw, of the diocese of Rio Grande laments that the Episcopal Church in the USA seems to be moving from being a fellowship of believers to being a politically-driven advocacy group which excludes from Episcopacy anyone who clearly will not advance the political agenda ... and closes doors at the entrance into ordained ministry against those who will not accept such plans.

Book Review 'Affirming the Bible without Affirming Fundamentalism' – essays in defence of orthodox faith. 'We are now witnessing a thorough-going revision of the faith inconsistent with the evangelical, apostolic and catholic witness... In the name of inclusivity and pluralism, we are presented with a new theological paradigm which rejects ... the doctrinal norms of the historic creeds and ecumenical councils.'

An Auckland AFFIRM committee was formed in February 1994 from leaders of CMS, Church Army and ARMNZ located in

Auckland. Their goals were to be a focus for Anglicans for biblical and orthodox Christianity; to be a loose-knit association of people on the AFFIRM project; to build partnership between the societies; and to get involved in the diocesan structures.[16] The group met and acted for some years. It subsequently became Mainstream Auckland.

By May 1994 AFFIRM Council was monitoring the sexuality issues that were being introduced to General Synod (GS) and the Inter-Diocesan Conference (IDC) and were requesting some involvement in their proposed commission on sexuality. This issue became a long-term focus for AFFIRM, which was in some ways regrettable because it distracted AFFIRM energies from wider issues of mission, ministry and preventing church decline.

A Short Hailstorm – Bishop John Spong

A continuing nuisance to us were the recurring visits to New Zealand of Bishop John Spong from the USA. He had come to prominence around 1987-88 when he wrote controversial articles for the Episcopal Church (TEC) on sexuality followed by a book *Living in Sin? A Bishop Rethinks Human Sexuality*. This was followed by a polemical book *Rescuing the Bible from Fundamentalism* (1989), in which he suggested Paul was a body-loathing yet celibate homosexual; *Born of a Woman* (1992), in which he said that the virgin conception was a ridiculous concept and that Mary was in fact probably a rape victim; and then *Resurrection: Myth or Reality* (1994), in which he claimed that the idea that Jesus was alive occurred in the head of the fisherman Peter about six months after Jesus' death.

---

16. Notes of a meeting of leaders of the AFFIRM Societies to plan AFFIRM Auckland, 23rd February, 1994, AFFIRM – Auckland file, Battley papers.

Spong's previous promotional visits had caught the New Zealand churches rather unprepared but in 1994 we were more ready for him. Already many overseas scholars had written about the shallowness of his arguments and weak scholarship and his book on the resurrection was no better. One example was UK systematic theologian Alister McGrath who critiqued Spong in *The Renewal of Anglicanism*. Spong, McGrath said, treads a path which 'just about everyone else has abandoned as outdated and irrelevant'. The book on fundamentalism is 'as aggressive in its modernity as it is selective and superficial in its argumentation and intolerant and dismissive of the views of others'. McGrath observed:

> One cannot help but feel that the reasoned argumentation we have come to expect of the Anglican tradition has here been replaced by a special pleading and petulant assertion, more characteristic of the fundamentalist groups to which Bishop Spong takes such exception. Spong creates a fantasy world, in which his own vision of a politically correct culture leads him to impose political and social stereotypes upon the New Testament with a fierce and uncritical dogmatism and a lack of scholarly insight and responsibility... Many had dared to hope that this kind of thing was not typical of Anglicanism.[17]

Despite the publication of numerous critiques of Spong's works, many New Zealand clergy and lay leaders flocked to his lectures and on one occasion I experienced a group, stocked with clergy educators, actually cheering him.

What was going on in the intellectual life of so many clergy? How could they be so accepting of such confused thinking? In

---

17. Alister McGrath, *The Renewal of Anglicanism*, SPCK, London, 1993, 44.

1994 AFFIRM published a paper 'How Reliable a Thinker is John Spong?'[18] drafted by Francis Foulkes and myself and edited by a number of AFFIRM leaders which summarised some of the scholarly critiques of Spong's books, including assessments by Alister McGrath and Tom Wright. We sent copies to the Waiapu clergy who were to hear him at their clergy school and I received a stinging rebuke back signed by many of them.

Auckland AFFIRM presented four public seminars in Auckland to rebut his thinking on the resurrection. Archbishop Brian Davis weighed in with a sound article for *The Dominion* newspaper in which he used some of our quotes and stated:

> To my mind Spong's understanding of the Easter event fails to adequately explain the remarkable and lasting birth of resurrection faith. He also asks us to accept a re-arrangement of the Easter events that demands credulity rather than informed faith.[19]

AFFIRM Times had said in June:

> The Council has real misgivings and concern about the visit, and about the fact that several of our bishops seem actively involved in the invitation. Some other of our Anglican leaders disapprove of his coming – but why should AFFIRM have to go to all the time, trouble and expense of expressing that disapproval for them?'[20]

---

18. AFFIRM paper, *How Reliable A Thinker Is John Spong?*, Jack Spong file, Battley papers.
19. B. N. Davis, *Response to Bishop Spong*, Jack Spong file, Battley papers.
20. AFFIRM *Times*, June 1994, AFFIRM Times file, Battley papers.

We were gladdened by the archbishop's support but I never enjoyed these conflicts and they tended to harm the mission of ARMNZ which was to win people's confidence, not alienate them.

Tensions amongst charismatics were building as a result of the increasing pressure to change sexual policy in the church. By 1994 some conservative clergy were pondering the possibilities of leaving what was beginning to look like an apostate church. The Rev. Lloyd Williams of Kawerau-Edgecumbe wrote to me, 'We are living in strange days where the once unthinkable soon becomes normal.'[21] ARMNZ Council even found itself considering options of alternative or parallel jurisdictions (that is, seeking an arrangement where we could have our own diocese and bishop) and I recall the Rev. Mike Hawke protesting such thinking saying, 'Woah, guys! You are talking about tearing apart every parish in the country!' Such have been the tensions we have lived with for over twenty-five years.

AFFIRM Developments

It became necessary to show our conservative members that we were willing to stand for their concerns. We arranged a short lecture tour by Alister McGrath, by then principal of Wycliffe Hall, Oxford, which was sponsored in September 1995 by Auckland AFFIRM. Alister spoke at St John's Theological College and Auckland Synod. His addresses included 'The Renewal of Anglicanism', 'Apologetics in a Modern Context', 'Bishop Spong and the Fundamentalism of the Left', 'Faith, Doubt and Experience', 'Making Sense of the Cross', and 'Christian Confidence in an Age of Pluralism'.[22]

The joint Affirms sponsored an AFFIRM Theological Con-

---

21. Letter Lloyd Williams to D. H. Battley, 20 December 1994.
22. Alister McGrath September 1995 file, Battley papers.

ference held at St John's College on 29-31 August 1995.[23] It was attended by a hundred people[24] and was entitled 'Orthodoxy: Foundations For Faith Today'.

Speakers were scholars of standing: Rev. Dr Stephen May, Lecturer in Systematic Theology at St John's College spoke on 'Being Orthodox Today'; Rev. Dr Harold Turner of the Gospel and Cultures Trust on 'Orthodoxy in NZ – An Analysis'; Rev. Dr Sue Patterson, a post-doctoral researcher at Princeton, USA on 'Orthodoxy and the Person of Christ'; Rev. Graham Redding, Presbyterian minister on 'Orthodoxy and the Doctrine of God'; Rev. Dr Paul Trebilco, Professor of N.T. at Knox College on 'Orthodoxy, Scripture & Tradition'; Rev. David Kettle, Tertiary Chaplain at Massey University on 'Orthodoxy, Church, Worship & Mission' and Dr Andrew Howie, Researcher in Christian Ethics on 'Orthodoxy and Ethics in a Pluralist Society'. We deliberately set the idea of orthodoxy out there to challenge the church. We were asking 'Does the NZA even see 'orthodoxy' (right belief) as a necessary standard for today's church?'

In May 1996 AFFIRM made a substantial submission to the Tikanga Pakeha Commission on Sexuality. Co-authored by the Rev. Francis Foulkes and myself, it was signed by twenty-two leading Anglicans, most of whom were office holders in the AFFIRM societies. In a carefully balanced submission which covered many aspects of the same-sex debate, we advised that:

for this Church to move to accept homosexual priests having

---

23. AFFIRM Council Minutes 20-22 February 1995, Item 9, AFFIRM 1995 file, Battley papers.

24. Methodist AFFIRM magazine Oct 1995, Vol 1 Issue 4, Methodist AFFIRM file, Battley papers.

sexual partners living with them, whether in the vicarage or their own homes, would be unacceptable and damaging to the unity of the church. Conversations we have had with priests and lay people indicate that there are priests who would leave the Anglican ministry and lay people who would move out of the Anglican Church if such a development were to be permitted.

We added,

We do not consider this issue is in any way analogous to the priesting of women. Women are 50% of the human race and there were strong theological and missiological reasons to make that change. The homosexually partnered percentage is less than 2%. The church's presbyterate is a special role for which the church ought to require special standards. We believe those standards, so far as sexual partnership is concerned, are marriage or celibate singleness.

We wish to advise the Commission that there are high levels of concern and conviction among our constituencies about this issue and that a radical departure from the tradition of the church at this point could be very divisive and potentially schismatic.[25]

By the end of 1996 AFFIRM had achieved many preliminary objectives but they had a long journey ahead of them. And ARMNZ still had its own mission to fulfil.

---

25. A Submission to the Tikanga Pakeha Commission on Sexuality, AFFIRM, 8 May 1996, para 7.4, AFFIRM and Sexuality Commission file, Battley papers.

The ARMNZ Review

Following the 1992 ARMNZ tenth birthday event the Council commissioned a review of the ARMNZ ministry.[26] We applied for and were granted $2000 from the St John's College Trust Board to fund it and confirmed the review team of Bishop David Moxon, journalist Julia Stuart and Capt Peter Lloyd of the Church Army.[27] Julia and Peter met with the Council on 15 March 1994 to discuss their proposed process[28] and in November 1994 the review team presented their report to the Council.[29] It was a very professional and basically affirming review.

Their principle findings were that the image of the renewal and ARMNZ was quite positive around the church and that, 'If ARMNZ did not exist, the Church would be the poorer in people, in resources and in ministry'.[30] They recommended that Council needed to prioritise its stated objectives (even though all fifteen were valid); to consider appointing regional coordinators to share the load and strengthen clergy support systems; to consider the significance of all five aspects of mission (some of which seemed to be absent from ARMNZ concerns); to be more intentional in tackling bi-cultural aspects of the church and resource sharing; to get closer to church resource and training centres with our resources; to be aware of how financial limits were constraining our work and to seek additional income; and to continue strengthening relationships with similar voluntary societies and church structures.

---

26. Council Minutes, 22 October 1992, item 13, ANG 076/2/1.
27. Council Minutes, 22-24 November 1993, item 15, op. cit.
28. Council Minutes, 14-16 March 1994, item 26, op. cit.
29. Council Minutes, 7-9 November 1994, item 5, op. cit.
30. The Anglican Renewal Ministries NZ Review Report, October 1994, 34, Battley papers

Of particular significance to us was Bishop David's report-back of a discussion he had with the bishops. They stated to us:

- The Bishops see ARMNZ as loyal to the Anglican Communion and to the Anglican Church in ANZ&P. 'We affirm and celebrate this.' Many see ARMNZ as a voluntary society which makes a significant contribution to this church...
- Regional diocesan based expressions of ARMNZ are very much appreciated in a number of dioceses. Perhaps there is a need to find a more secure place within diocesan structures in some places ... There needs to be promotion, participation and accountability.
- The Bishops felt that the notion of renewal is a broad, rich concept of which ARMNZ is a very important aspect. But ARMNZ is not seen as the only source or means of renewal. The Director of ARMNZ ministry was affirmed, especially ... as he has helped it restructure and seek accountability and credibility across the Church.
- Any sense of isolation or marginalisation that may be felt at times by ARMNZ was not intentional. The Bishops noted that other groups feel marginalised at times...
- The Bishops welcome ARMNZ as an important part of the life of the Church seeking renewal...
- The Bishops affirm ARMNZ for inviting a self-review, and acknowledge that the questions that ARMNZ is asking itself is in itself a sign of maturity and honesty. They see a challenge for ARMNZ to recognise the diversity of the Church, and to see themselves as part of that diversity.[31]

---

31. Review Report, 26-27, op. cit.

All very fair and affirming comment, which reflects the changes which had developed not only in the renewal but also in the episcopate with the passage of time. We had gained more friends and understanding than we had realised.

Council discussed issues of the review at their November 1994 and March 1995 meetings. We revisited our fundamental values which were summed up as 'Restore radical dependence on God the Holy Spirit; Rely on the Holy Spirit for empowering; Encourage the gifts of the Spirit; Sacrificial service.'[32] Further discussion led us to ideas of mobility: that we need to move out like a wagon train; not to be circled or in a settler mode but to be wagons on the move. Paul Williamson said:

> Renewal within the Anglican Church has come to the end of defensive posturing. God is calling us to leave behind defensiveness and go again. The driver (is) feeling the impetus to go forward – to rage off into the sunrise. That is going to mean that there will be things we've come to expect will be more chaotic and free-wheeling and less able to be stopped and counted and 'anglicanised' … Wagon trains (have been) the leading edge of civilisation. The church as a whole has come up closer and so the wagon train needs to move on…

How prescient was the insight that things were going to become a wild ride!

We noted that renewal itself was ageing – that we needed new thrusts towards youth and children and families, and that the vision needed to be not for six months but for six years (to the millennium) and beyond. For staffing we envisioned making the administrator position full-time and progressively achieving three part-time

---

32. Minutes 8-9 November 1994, item 9, op. cit.

regional coordinators.¹ Waikato ARM promptly appointed the Rev. John Marquet, vicar of Hamilton West, as part-time regional coordinator for the Waikato diocese in which they were strongly supported by their bishop, David Moxon.² We supplied a report to the bishops in 1994 and David Moxon told us 'it was recognised as being professional, humble and not triumphalist'.

My report to Council for that year ended with:

> There are positive signs of a thawing in the Church towards the renewal movement. Anglican Renewal Ministries seems to be increasingly respected for the quality of its ministries and its tenacity of purpose. I am heartened by the growth of the 'branches' and anticipate that they may need to provide much of the action in the middle of next year.³

By that time the new things had already come upon us and were going to take all our energies and gifts to cope.

1. Minutes, 6-8 March 1995, item 4, 5.
2. National Coordinator's Report 30 September 1994, ANG 076/2/5.
3. Ibid.

– 15 –

Beside the Lake
The Birth of Summer Wine

The Birth of 'Summer Wine' – a Galilee Experience

In January 1994 a special guest speaker visited us with quite unexpected consequences. At Jean Martyn's initiative we invited Andrew Maries to visit from the UK to conduct schools in music on worship. Andrew was a talented musician (he played the oboe, always a challenging instrument) and led a church music ministry in the UK and composed renewal-style music. He arrived in January 1994 and conducted a residential music school at Lake Taupo Christian Camp located at Mission Bay, on Lake Taupo. The school enriched many musicians for their worship ministries and Andrew subsequently conducted parish-based seminars at Papatoetoe and Hillsborough concluding with a celebration event in Holy Trinity Cathedral. Jean reported to the Council that:

> attendances totalled over 3000 and we have had very enthusiastic reports of people and groups being challenged and enlivened and given new vision for music in worship. Responses have come from a wide range of people – from the very 'lively' to the really 'trad'. Interesting that the 'Bridging the Gap' theme spoke to so many.[4]

4. Administrator's Report 14 March 1994, ANG 076/2/5.

But the surprise outcome of Andrew's tour was that as the Taupo camp ended, standing on the verandah overlooking the site, I said to Jean, 'What do you think would happen if we ran a summer camp here?'

She immediately said, 'It would be full.'

'Right,' I said, 'I'll see if we can book it.'

The managers of the camp re-organised their bookings to give us the Auckland anniversary weekend in 1995 and so was born ARMNZ's most influential ministry – the summer all-age camps named 'Summer Wine'.

The Lake Taupo Christian Camp (LTCC) became for us a very special place of blessing and joy. One of the many Christian conference locations around the country, LTCC sits above New Zealand's largest lake with panoramic views across the water, a glistening scene of creation and beauty. The camp had a conference room, kitchens, chalets and dormitories and spacious land for camping and the management was not shy about the charismatic dimension. We were welcomed most lovingly and supported with great endeavour by their staff.

I was intrigued as to why the adjacent beach was called Mission Bay when it was known that the renowned missionary to the Taupo area, T. S. Grace, had been based at Pukawa across the lake. A search of the local history showed that the first missionary there had actually been Rev. Seymour Spencer who had been located at what was still called Mission Bay before he was moved after only a year to the Tarawera Mission.

This intrigued me all the more as many years before when I had experienced sites of renewal in the UK they seemed to be based on or near to ancient sites of Christian spiritual power (e.g. St Michael-le-Belfrey was in the shadow of York Minster, and the famed Taizé community was very close to the medieval renewal centre of Cluny).

Observing that, I had said to the Lord, 'I see you are renewing your church on the ancient foundations. But where are there ancient foundations in New Zealand?'

He replied, 'Keep your eyes on where the early missionaries stood – there I will renew my church.'

In the course of time I have seen vigorous renewal at Kaitaia, the Bay of Islands (where Bill Subritzky's farm hosted the Summer Harvest camps alongside Oihi Bay where the first missionaries settled), Tauranga, Matamata, Rotorua, Gisborne, Whanganui, Waikanae and Nelson – all of them original Anglican missionary sites. And this was another.

There was a further feature to LTCC which also touched my heart – Lake Taupo is very similar to the Sea of Galilee. It is about the same size and shape; rivers flow in and out in a similar configuration; Turangi equates to Capernaum and Taupo to Tiberias; and LTCC is where? – pretty much corresponding to Genneseret and Tabgha where Jesus' feeding with the loaves and fishes occurred. What better place to revisit the Word of God and experience Jesus in our midst?

In approaching the idea of a summer camp I was convinced it had to cater for all ages. Where the early CAM Summer Schools – so effective in their time – had been for adults only, the times had changed. Families had to be catered for and all ages needed to be ministered to in the power of the Holy Spirit who is no respecter of age. 'For the promise is for you and your children' Peter had announced in his Pentecost address.[5] We took that seriously but with little idea how to minister to children.

We set about running a summer ministry with four streams in parallel – adults, youth, school-age children and pre-school. It was a considerable challenge to assemble the necessary teams for so

---

5. Acts 2:39.

much ministry but our networks produced many capable workers. The camp could not provide covered spaces for all four, so they arranged to hire a marquee for the adults ministry and we hired large tents for other ministries and workshops. So we suddenly hit the saw-dust revival trail!

'The First of the Summer Wine' camps was held over 27 to 30 January 1995. Around 250 people arrived with children, youth, caravans and boats. They were accommodated in bunkrooms, cabins, tents and caravans and some people lived off-site using holiday homes – such are the advantages of a holiday location. Keynote speakers were all New Zealanders including Brian and Trish Jenkins, who spoke on spiritual revival and its history, and Cecilie Graham who had a well-known healing ministry. Ministry in the youth tent was provided by youth leader Kristen Williams and a team from St John's Bucklands Beach, and children's ministry by Frankton parish. The afternoons were left free for people to enjoy the beaches and lake, so it became a summer holiday as well as a spiritual growth experience. People's response to the whole programme was enthusiastic.[6]

A number of developments in renewal came together at Summer Wine. A strong one for adults was the development that came to be known as the Toronto Blessing. Prayer ministry under the marquee became a high-impact experience for many, with people falling under the Spirit, shaking or weeping.

A second was a bold development in ministering to children in the blessing of the Spirit which came to us through Captain Alan Price of the UK Church Army and the teams he had trained for the UK New Wine. A third was the breakthrough in youth

---

6. Three quarters of the evaluation replies said that the camp had either 'exceeded their expectations' or been 'all I had hoped for'. Evaluation of Summer Wine 1995, ANG 076/5/17.

ministry that had developed in some churches, especially at the Co-operating Parish of Bucklands Beach, which was led by the very gifted youth pastor Kristen Williams.

In the background was the existence of a much larger version of Summer Wine in the UK known as New Wine. The New Wine camps had grown from the impact of the Toronto Blessing, the Vineyard movement and the wider charismatic movement on St Andrew's Church, Chorleywood which had developed the New Wine Conference in Somerset which drew around 14,000 people a time.

Our model was the same – a summertime camp; use of marquees and tenting; dynamic teaching and revivalism in the adult ministries; Holy Spirit-empowered ministry in the youth sector, and ministry that introduced children to the Holy Spirit – a potent mix to move whole families into renewal. Indeed, a background insight was that it was not good to move one member of a marriage into renewal without the other, or to leave the youth or children behind. Families reported going home from Summer Wine transformed by their shared experiences.

On the final morning of each camp the ministries were brought together for a shared celebration in the main marquee where the younger ones testified and performed what they had learned and it all ended with a massed Communion service, often led by a local bishop. In 1995 Bishop David Moxon of Waikato diocese was our very willing celebrant.

By the end of the first Summer Wine we were able to announce that the next year there would two camps offered back-to-back at LTCC and another one would be launched in the South Island. Captain Alan Price would be coming with a team from the UK to lead the children's ministry, and youth pastor Kristen Williams and his team from Bucklands Beach would lead the youth ministry as 'a camp within a camp'. It was recorded:

The importance of maintaining a charismatic form of spirituality at the camps with no compromise. If non-charismatics wish to come they are very welcome but the programme will not be arranged to suit them.[7]

Just getting Summer Wine and all its necessary ministry teams together had been an epic challenge but the ARMNZ people had responded with great willingness and ability. And then AFFIRM had also been birthed, along with 'Church Alive!' We had entered a period of peak endeavour.

---

7. ARMNZ Council Minutes 6-8 March 1995, item 9.

– 16 –

Cascades from Toronto
The 'Toronto Blessing'

The 'Toronto Blessing'

In January 1994 a Vineyard church in Canada began experiencing exciting but rather extreme manifestations of spiritual behaviour which quickly spread around parts of the renewal movement and was named by some the 'Toronto Blessing' (TB). But was it really from God? Or even justified by scripture?

The experiences began at an event with South African evangelist Rodney Howard-Brown in Tulsa, moved through Vineyard pastor Randy Clark to a regional meeting of midwestern Vineyard churches where 'a powerful demonstration of God's power broke out at the meeting', then on to John Arnott, pastor of the Toronto Airport Vineyard (TAV) where Randy Clark ministered in January 1994.

This encounter gave rise to a continuous repetition of the experiences which lasted for some years and were repeated in many churches in the US and Canada.[1] The manifestations included increased falling and resting in the Spirit; people being shaken when the Holy Spirit fell on them; appearances of 'drunkenness' in

---

1. Bill Jackson 'What in the World is Happening to Us? A Biblical perspective on Renewal', Vineyard document, Urbana Illinois, July 1994, Vineyard file, Battley papers.

the Spirit; crying; widespread and seemingly spontaneous laughing; roaring like lions; and increased prophetic revelations to the leaders of worship meetings.

Initially Vineyard leaders declared it to be a 'renewal' or 'refreshing' rather than a revival.[2] TAV commenced offering worship and ministry services every night except Mondays and thousands of people visited to 'catch the fire' of what was soon being claimed as 'revival' on the basis of the extreme manifestations being seen, the crowds attending and the reported spiritual blessings to so many. A spate of books quickly advanced the idea that a significant God-initiated revival was occurring.[3]

The June 1994 newspaper of London's Holy Trinity Brompton reported the arrival of the blessing to that influential church on 24 May and they declared, 'This is Revival,' and the vicar Sandy Miller wrote that, having visited TAV, 'It is all so excitingly reminiscent of accounts of early revivals' adding:

> I think it is important that we should stay close to the Lord and be grateful for every sign of his grace upon us. Don't let's get too caught up with the symptoms of his Spirit but more with him and his love for us.[4]

In August 1994 John Mullis of CAM led a team of six Kiwis to TAV who reported back to the CAM leadership:

---

2. 'The meetings have been dubbed a "renewal" rather than a "revival" by psychiatrist and author John White and by John Wimber', op. cit., 1.

3. Including in 1994, *The Toronto Blessing* Dave Roberts, *Signs of Revival* Patrick Dixon, *Catch the Fire: The Toronto Blessing* Guy Chevreau, *A Breath of Fresh Air* Mike Fearon and in 1995, *Keep the Fire* John Arnott, 'The Impact of Toronto' extracts from *Renewal* magazine, and many others.

4. Holy Trinity Brompton's Newspaper June 12, 1994, Toronto file, Battley papers.

What was important was not the external manifestations, but what was happening through the ministry of the Holy Spirit internally, within people. They constantly exhorted us to keep our eyes off the manifestations which are only an indication of something happening within a person. Their concern is with what happens in a person's life and through a person's life... They were very candid that some of what we would see/hear/experience would be of the flesh, some of the devil and much of the Holy Spirit. They trusted the Holy Spirit to minister and control – (warning that) once before the pastor had condemned this, discouraged that, and the whole thing died.[5]

An Auckland Anglican from that team, after describing their experiences at TAV and comparing what they had seen with the seriously declining statistics of the diocese of Auckland, said this 'may be the beginning of the long awaited and desperately needed revival that will 'fill the earth with the knowledge of the glory of God as the waters cover the sea.'[6]

In September I reported to the ARMNZ Council:

The 'new wave' flowing from Toronto is of interest and seems to fit a pattern that the Lord sends a wave of renewal about every ten years at about the centre-point of each decade: 1965-6; 1975-6; 1985-; 1995?? Let's be open to that, and seek to be responsible and bold at the same time.[7]

---

5. Mullis Report, paras 9 & 11, op. cit.
6. Habbakuk 2:14, Mullis Report, op. cit.
7. National Coordinator's Report 30 September 1994, ANG 076/2/5.

No Way Back

At the Toronto Airport Vineyard

It was in that spirit of openness that we had invited Brian and Trish Jenkins as our lead speakers at the first 'Summer Wine' to speak on the blessing and revival. Interest in the Toronto Blessing remained high during 1995. In March Eleanor and I commenced a five-month study leave with Eleanor leaving first to do a counselling course at Selwyn Hughes' Waverley Christian Training Centre. She visited the TAV on the way, but did not seem overly impressed. I left at the end of March, attended a clergy training course at ERM's Evergreen Conference Centre and then visited the TAV.

The TAV presented seminars during the day which included prayer ministry. As they prayed for us at a meeting for pastors, I saw very strong works of the Spirit everywhere and as I rested in the Spirit the pain and tears of a lot of hurt came free for which I was very thankful. I knew this was the necessary starting point. Whenever I tried to sit up, a sense of heaviness pulled me down again. Clearly it was a soaking time and I was pleased to rest and receive. I was also ministered to at the two evening ministries. Of the first time I recorded:

> When I finally rested I was under a great weight; I staggered up to try to leave, sat and rested against a pillar and felt this extraordinary loving weight on my chest, upper legs and arms. I was sure it was the 'kabod' – the glory weight of the Spirit.
>
> As I lay back again I had this distinct impression of being embraced by the Father – held, loved, secured, and then I got a stern but loving talking to about directions and priorities and concerns which had distracted and diminished my ministry – all in a combination of firmness and love which is very hard to describe. This time I really knew the Father's

love! and I know I have known it, and with no sentimentality but some firm marching orders.[8]

After the ministry time on the second evening, I wrote:

> I ... went to the back to line up – was prayed for twice, the second time with a strong inrushing of breath and a time on the carpet when some spiritual sins surfaced in powerful conviction and repentance. There was no doubt about the reality and depth of experience before God – had rarely ever known such unexpected or deep repentance. For some time unable to rise; then rose to dance slowly to the music; prayed for again, rested in peace ... Went forward to observe and learn but after a time felt 'Let's reach out for more' – began to dance quietly again and suddenly an experienced pastor was in front of me. This time I told him of my role and the needs of my nation ... He called for a power anointing sufficient for my coming ministry and I had an extraordinary gasping intake and breath, some coughing, more infilling, fire in the hands... . They continued the prayer for some time till I could stand no longer.
>
> As I rested, waves of energy passed over me, then my fists began to beat slowly and firmly on the carpet. I had not seen this action but knew exactly what it was. I had seen a vision of a hammer on an anvil the previous day ... The hammering would go for a while, then rest, then start again. Finally the power lifted; I rested, sat up to look around me. Around me was a pandemonium I had been aware of but not troubled by. My own events were real, deep and very significant, but around me were some in hysterical laughter, seeming to

8. D. H. Battley 'Reflections on my visit to the TAV 28-31 March 1995', 3.

No Way Back

be egged on by the people ministering to them; five men roaring on the platform roared louder whenever the leading pastor called for 'More, Lord', and beyond us two groups either laughed uproariously or ministered to two screaming women. Not really my cup of tea!

By now it was well after midnight ... but the power waves continued. I remained deeply satisfied and untroubled by my own experiences but the environment taxed my pastoral perceptions without alienating me. I felt whole and not at all involved in hysteria, manipulation or anything sinister. I had been met all the way exactly as I knew I needed to be, and so had hundreds of others as far as I could tell.

Finally the roaring men fell silent and curled up together peacefully in each others' arms. Only the next day did I recall pictures of lion cubs snuggled up to each other... I was invited into one of the laughing groups and felt the infection of it and left soon. Earlier I had heard the Lord say 'I do not want you to contaminate your ministry' and had therefore been selective, yet open, in what I gave myself to... Nevertheless, I feel very whole, sound, light and joyous – have not really been like this since I was baptised in the Spirit in 1974.[9]

One evening I took with me Professor David Reed of Wycliffe College in Toronto. David was a former Pentecostal now an Anglican priest and a specialist in charismatic movements. When I asked him what he thought he replied, 'Feel the expectation!' David seemed very at ease with it all both theologically and with the manifestations. David had previously said to me that he saw many signs of the coming collapse of some liberal power centres

---

9. Ibid.

in the Anglican Church in Canada and rising evangelical strength. When the liberal church caves in, it will be the evangelicals and charismatics who will have the strength to reclaim the church, though he questioned whether the charismatics have the theological maturity to do the task.[10]

From Toronto I journeyed on to a range of experiences in London and the UK, visiting Bruce Collins in Harrow parish, Chorleywood with David Pytches and Barry Kissell (who were moving very strongly in the TB); then to Skegness to 'Spring Harvest' – a more evangelically-based ministry which skilfully used three speakers from different streams in Christianity to present any topic – a good example of balancing the image and interpretation; then to Wycliffe Hall at Oxford for a month's study with Alister McGrath during which time we worshipped at St Aldate's in Oxford and Holy Trinity Brompton (HTB). The former seemed to be emphasising a re-iteration of early charismatic teaching; while HTB was modelling the Wimber and Toronto additions.

After a month's personal holiday we joined a team led by Michael Green in a 'Springboard' Mission to Eastbourne; then we attended the Hensol retreat[11] held at Chorleywood followed by 'New Wine' in Somerset. I was astonished to see how similar the UK New Wine was to Summer Wine – except that it was 14,000 strong! We had been led to the same model at the same time.

It was clear that not only the TB but also the Wimber Conferences and role-modelling from previous years had affected many renewal churches in the UK.[12] Yet responses seemed to be

---

10. D. H. Battley, 'Reflections on my Visit to the TAV 28-31 March 1995', 3, Toronto file, Battley papers.

11. The Hensol retreat was a charismatic-style week-long retreat offered in a house named Hensol in Chorleywood.

12. John Arnott claimed in 1995 that 'out of 50,000 churches (in the UK)

No Way Back

mixed; some were stepping back to a greater emphasis on biblical teaching; some were surging ahead into the increased experiences of the Blessing; some, especially Holy Trinity Brompton, seemed to be working a fine synthesis of the earlier renewal, plus sound biblical teaching, continuing Anglican culture (liturgy in a magnificent building), some Vineyard style of prayer ministry and a cautious openness to the TB experiences. We had seen much that would be relevant to the ministry of ARMNZ and the development of renewal in New Zealand. But what were we to make of the Toronto 'revival' style?

Assessing the Blessing

On our return in August I reported to the Council:

> This (Toronto) blessing arrived in strength while we were away[13] and some clergy and parishes in the Auckland area are already experiencing much new empowering. I believe this move has much potential to quicken people's flagging spirits and to make 'renewal' accessible to others. There are some signs that people left behind or out of previous moves of renewal may be blessed by this new move. I certainly believe that a focus for ARMNZ for the next year must be to spread this blessing widely throughout this church, to interpret it all, and to provide times of training for leaders and ministry for all comers.[14]

at least 7,000 are flowing in the renewal'. D H Battley, 'Reflections', 2, op. cit.
13. Rodney Howard Browne had ministered in New Zealand while we were away and caused quite some controversy.
14. National Coordinator's Report, September 1995, ANG 076/2/5.

But the Toronto Blessing phenomenon did not go unchallenged. During 1995 it became the focus of much re-assessment and some tough criticism. Anglican renewal groups each had to assess it: ARM in England published a series of balanced articles in their magazine *Anglicans for Renewal*;[15] ARM South Africa published three articles on the Blessing in its June/July newsletter under the heading 'Toronto, HTB, SA – So What's Next?',[16] ARM Australia's *Spirit Life* newsletter reported their positive responses in August, quoting SOMA Director John Wyndham's comment:

> I sense (God) is wanting to renew Renewal and also to empower the whole Church for a great offensive in evangelism during the next five years. 'Renewal' and many of its leaders have become weary.[17]

Wholeness magazine editor Chris Lethbridge reported having twenty-one magazines with articles on the so-called Toronto Blessing on his dining room table as he wrote.[18]

In October the Evangelical Fellowship of NZ presented two open forums on the TB which presented both critiques and advocacy. In a carefully balanced statement the leadership group presented 'An Evangelical Declaration on "The Toronto Blessing"' which, while reiterating classical evangelical convictions, affirmed the role of revivals in Christian history and the fact that 'there has often been an increase in the frequency of physical phenomena

---

15. *Anglicans for Renewal*, Vols 59 and 60.
16. Anglican Renewal Ministries SA, Newsletter June/July 1995, Toronto file, Battley papers.
17. *Spirit Life*, Number 48, August 1995, ARM Australia, Toronto file, ibid.
18. *Wholeness: A World Digest of Christian Healing*, No. 150, 1 August 1995, ibid.

associated with repentance and conversion and also with the joy of new and abundant life in Christ but that these are secondary'. They strongly cautioned against 'polemical arguments that denigrate one another within the body of Christ'. They declared that 'we do not believe that the church in New Zealand is presently experiencing revival'.[19]

The resolution of the debate came unexpectedly from the Vineyard movement itself. On 13 December 1995 a statement came from Bob Fulton, the International Coordinator of the Vineyard Churches, that a letter had been presented to the leaders of the TAV advising them that if they did not conform their practices to the policies of renewal authorised by the Vineyard movement the TAV could not continue under the name of the Vineyard movement. Apparently John Wimber and others had been expressing their concerns to the TAV leadership for some time.

John Wimber's concern was that 'this whole thing has redefined renewal for the Vineyard'. Stated concerns included that: the approach to ministry was putting the idea that falling down was an important issue; that the phenomena were being put up on stage in front of everyone; and that prophetic meaning was being given to phenomena, especially sounds people were making. They thought it was important in modelling renewal that 'it's important to use models that do not highlight the phenomena'.[20]

In an open letter John Wimber stated even more clearly:

> We cannot at any time endorse, encourage, offer theological justification or biblical proof-texting for any exotic practices

---

19. An Evangelical Statement on 'The Toronto Blessing', Evangelical Fellowship of NZ, October 1995, Toronto file, ibid.
20. Letter, Bob Fulton, International Coordinator, Association of Vineyard Churches, 13 December 1995, ibid.

that are extra-biblical – whether in Toronto or elsewhere. Neither can these practices be presented as criteria for true spirituality or as a mark of true renewal… it is our conviction that these manifestations should not be promoted, placed on stage, nor used as the basis for theologising that leads to new teaching.[21]

The TAV accepted the decision of the Vineyard association and their disassociation and acknowledged that 'some of what is happening in Toronto is outside the Vineyard model'.[22] The TAV renamed itself Toronto Airport Christian Fellowship and founded Partners in Harvest, a group of churches that shared similar beliefs. The church was renamed Catch the Fire – Toronto in 2010.[23] John and Carol Arnott continued to minister world-wide to people who shared their approach.

Immediately following the December announcements, John Mullis of CAM sent out a prayer letter entitled 'Forget Toronto!' in which he sought to lead people's attention back to 'renewal on a scale that's beginning to dwarf its predecessors the Pentecostal and Charismatic Renewals'.[24] The National Chairman of the NZ Catholic Charismatic Renewal Service Group commented, 'What we witness is the birth of another Protestant stream.'[25]

Wimber and his leadership team rightly saw the issue as one of

---

21. John Wimber, Open Letter 13 December 1995, Association of Vineyard Churches, ibid.

22. Letter John Arnott, 5 December 1995, ibid.

23. Wikipedia article, 'Catch the Fire World', accessed 8 October 2018.

24. John Mullis, Prayer Letter from the Director's Desk, November/December 1995, CAM.

25. Frits Bergman, Chairman, C.C.R. National Service Group, *Tongues of Fire*, Vol 9 No 1, February 1996, 4.

what models of renewal were fitting and biblical. They drew the line at the emphasis on manifestations at TAV and set limits on what was, for them, Christian renewal on a biblical basis. Yet much of what occurred at the TAV appeared to be based on emphases John Wimber had himself promoted, especially the emphasis on experiences of power in mission. His core books and conferences had featured an emphasis on spiritual power – 'Power Evangelism' and 'Power Healing' had been core ideas of his books and conferences.[26] There had been an explicit emphasis on what he called 'Signs and Wonders'.[27] With such expectations raised, how could he be surprised when it gathered pace?

The emphasis on spiritual power had not gone unchallenged. One telling critique, amongst many, had been the book 'Power Religion. The Selling Out of the Evangelical Church?' written in 1992 by a panel of prestigious evangelical writers.[28] John Wimber had already been removed from the teaching faculty at Fuller Theological Seminary California for over-emphasising signs and wonders in his teaching.[29] Now the chickens had come home to roost. John Wimber died in 1998 after a battle with cancer. In a tribute to John, Bishop David Pytches wrote:

---

26. John Wimber with Kevin Springer, *Power Evangelism*, 1985; and *Power Healing*, Hodder 1986. John White, *When the Spirit Comes With Power – Signs and Wonders Among God's People*, Hodder 1988.

27. John Wimber, *Signs and Wonders and Church Growth*, Conference Manual, Vineyard Ministries International, Placenta, CA USA, 1984. *Power Healing. Signs and Wonders and Church Growth Part 2*, Conference Manual, Mercy Publishing, 1987.

28. Michael Horton, ed. *Power Religion. The Selling Out of the Evangelical Church?* Moody Bible Press, 1992.

29. C. Peter Wagner, *Signs & Wonders Today, The Remarkable Story of the Experimental Course MC510-Signs, Wonders and Church Growth at Fuller Seminary.* Publ. Christian Life Magazine, Wheaton, 1983.

A well-known leader in the US recently described John as one of the ten most influential Christian leaders of the last twenty-five years. I think there is much truth in that... There were not many who could call a conference, time and again all round the world, and 5,000 would turn up.[30]

By the beginning of 1996 the charismatic movement in the NZA had been subjected to a sequence of new emphases and continuing changes to worship and ministry styles. In the thirty years since Dennis Bennett's high impact visit we had seen anglo-catholic modelling of renewal worship in a high mass; healing ministries in a quiet, peaceful mode; exciting Life in the Spirit Seminars; large conferences featuring gifted overseas speakers; clear biblical teaching from mainly evangelical speakers; the promise of 'More, Lord' from Chorleywood, John Wimber and the Vineyard people; and now this Blessing with extreme manifestations.

Each step seemed to push the renewal movement further from its Anglican context (with its historic principle of 'all things decently and in order'). Each minister and parish affected by these differing models then had to adapt them back to their own often quite modest settings. How do you take an experience at a conference of 2,000 or more people back to a congregation of perhaps fewer than 100 people? Even if you explain it and try to use it, will it last? The issues of application of models from the UK and USA were never easy and often led to disappointment.

The Alpha Course

A resource of lasting impact came from Holy Trinity Church at

---

30. David Pytches, 'Tribute to John Wimber', New Wine Magazine, Issue 5 Spring 1998, 1.

Brompton in London. HTB had a long evangelical and renewal history based on a stable ministry by John Collins and then his successor Sandy Millar. Sandy and Nicky Gumbel had developed an introductory course to Christianity and the gift of the Holy Spirit which they named 'Alpha' (for 'starting point').

It managed to combine the function of the Life in the Spirit Seminars and the UK equivalent Saints Alive! with a more contemporary use of video presentations by the eloquent teacher Nicky Gumbel. The first known use of Alpha in New Zealand was by British priest Ken Boullier in Kaitaia parish in 1994 who had been familiar with it in Chorleywood and brought it with him. While Ray Muller was on study leave in the UK that year he met with Nicky Gumbel (Ray happened to visit the staff at HTB the day the Toronto Blessing fell on the staff team). In May 1994 he attended their Alpha Conference and was impressed with it and thought Alpha would work in New Zealand. Ray booked the Alpha team for an Alpha Conference in New Zealand.

By January 1995 Ray and colleague Alistair Davis had decided to promote Alpha in New Zealand. Ray did some introductory seminars around New Zealand and published information about it in his Church Growth Report. By November 1996, seventy churches were running Alpha in New Zealand using the newly produced videos. The first New Zealand Alpha Conference was launched in Auckland's Holy Trinity Cathedral and around eight hundred attended. The team from HTB included Sandy and Annette Millar, Nicky and Pippa Gumbel, Emmy Wilson and Simon Jones for Youth Alpha.[31] Alpha swept the field and the use of LiSS ceased and there was little use of Saints Alive! thereafter.

I was a little miffed at the time that Alpha was running separately from ARMNZ but it soon became apparent that this was a

---

31. Email R. J. Muller to D. H. Battley, 25 October 2018, Battley papers.

resource for many denominations which needed its own supporting organisation. Ray ran the Alpha network very ably for many years and Alpha was still in regular use twenty years later.

– 17 –

Spreading Waters
Beside Two Lakes

Summer Wine developed exponentially from 1996 reflecting the hunger amongst charismatics and the suitability of the all-age summer camp model. It filled the gap left by the ending of the CAM Summer Schools, picked up on some of the expectation aroused by the Toronto Blessing and went deeply into ministry in the Spirit to children and youth. In both those areas we had leading-edge ministry from people who were bold and confident in ministering spiritual experience to their age sector.

Summer Wine Expansion

The 1996 Summer Wine camps were held at LTCC over 19-22 and 23-26 January. For our children's ministry 'KidZone', Captain Alan Price, a UK children's evangelist who led the children's ministries at New Wine UK, brought a team of five others with him to model their ministry style for the children. The team were Capt. Tony Maidment (CA), Keith Barratt, Joy Martin, Alisdair Campbell and Sandy Schukins.

Observing them in private I noticed how they all had very active 'playing child' behaviours – although competently adult, they enjoyed the pranks, jokes and 'high-jinks' usually seen amongst children. I'm sure this was why they were so effective in children's work. Features of their approach were a delightful range of original songs designed for children; the use of puppetry and crafts; and, in prayer-ministry time, they invited the children to receive the Holy Spirit and to pray for each other using 'drain-piping', that is, one arm up to God and one arm out to the person being prayed for.

This was a new and bold approach to bringing children into the work of the Holy Spirit – until then we had treated children as Sunday school recipients but not active participants in God's work. Children were blessed and inspired by what they experienced. For this KidsZone ministry we needed a ratio of one adult to eight children and for the first camp had to find twenty volunteers.

The youth ministry was even more radical. It was led by evangelist/youth pastor Kristen Williams from St John's Co-operating Parish Bucklands Beach and he brought with him a remarkable team of twelve late teens and young adults. They also had their own original music. Their pre-camp promo said, 'The ministry will be loud and spiritually challenging.'[1] We put the youth tent at the far end of the camp site and let them go for it. A number of late teens with strong church backgrounds said afterwards, 'The Youth Tent saved my faith.' Some are now in full-time ministry.

In the adult marquee we focussed on revival and the Blessing under the theme 'Times of Refreshing', the main speakers being myself, Lorraine and Peter Lloyd (of Church Army), Laidlaw bible scholar Tim Meadowcroft, Archdeacon Max Scott and, at Camp 2, Cecilie Graham.

At these camps we achieved a long-standing ARMNZ goal of getting New Zealand speakers up front to show that we did not always need to sit at the feet of big-name overseas speakers. All ministry locations experienced blessed times of worship, word and reception of God's grace in prayer ministries. Manifestations were not extreme but were certainly present. At the final morning's

---

1. Summer Wine 1996 files, ANG 076/5/18.

worship all the age-groups joined together and shared what God had been teaching them. It was a great time of celebration and enthusiasm.

The two camps at Taupo drew 650 people while around 200 attended the first 'Southern Wine' at Geraldine.[2] People's responses were ecstatic: 'It was great to experience full on worship, profound teaching and plenty of time to rest in the Spirit and to let God do his work in me.' 'I came as a Vicar on "empty"; I left a Vicar on "full". Thank you God for loving me that much!' 'I'm speechless with what God in Trinity has done in my life. All Glory to Jesus.'[3] At last we had reached a point where we as New Zealanders could present substantial ministries that met people's spiritual needs, including their families. It was a grace-filled time.

Summer Wine in 1997 reached even further, offering three camps at Taupo, the middle one being a training camp in children's ministry led by Alan Price and a team, youth evangelism led by Kristen Williams and his team, and contemporary music in worship led by Brent Chambers. At Taupo, despite the threat of cyclonic winds, almost 500 attended the first camp, 180 the training camp and 425 the third camp. Yet even then Lake Taupo Christian Camp seldom felt crowded.[4]

Alan Price's team was strengthened by people who came with him to settle and minister in New Zealand, Church Army officers David and Nicky Rees, and Keith Barrett, a UK teacher. They served afterwards in Masterton and Papatoetoe parishes respectively. All three gave many years of service in children's ministry. 'Southern Wine' was offered at Geraldine and drew 150 participants.

2. *NETWORK* newsletter No. 29, 1.
3. Ibid, 5.
4. *NETWORK* newsletter No 32, 2-3.

Beside Another Lake – Rwanda visit

While Summer Wine burgeoned as a new and much appreciated ministry, ARMNZ carried on with its established ministries: ministry tours by the National Coordinator couple; regional ministries organised by the local groups; annual Church Alive! schools; and tours by overseas speakers. In 1996 Jean Martyn retired as administrator and was replaced by Sue Thomson, another former parishioner from Pakuranga days, and Alan McLean served as treasurer/accountant. Then something totally unexpected arrived: SOMA-UK was invited to send an international team to minister in the Anglican Church in Rwanda in response to the 1994 genocide. SOMA-NZ director Gradon Harvey was unable to go and I was invited to go in his stead.

The Anglican charismatic movement, led by the Rev. Michael Harper, had been reaching around the widespread Anglican Communion especially through his agency SOMA (Sharing Of Ministries Abroad). Strong relationships had been developed by Michael and other leaders he had trained with the many formerly 'missionary churches' in the developing world. These newly self-governing Anglican churches frequently showed dynamic, confident faith derived from the missionary heritage that had founded them, yet many of their countries had severe problems of political instability, poor leadership and weak economies.

Two of the most vulnerable were the tiny nations of Rwanda and Burundi in central East Africa. Former Belgian colonies, they had been poorly prepared for self-government and inherited severe tribal tensions between politically dominant Tutsis and numerically dominant Hutus. A number of times these countries had slipped into genocides which caused large numbers to flee to neighbouring countries, creating further difficulties of whether they would be allowed to return to what are the most densely populated agrarian countries in the world.

The worst such event happened in Rwanda in 1994 when around 800,000 Rwandans were killed. The small Anglican church in Rwanda suffered gravely during this slaughter and lost many of its bishops and clergy while inheriting huge problems of care of orphans and traumatised people. A new multi-tribal government was stabilising the country but much help was needed for the country and the churches.

SOMA had already visited Rwanda and was invited to send an international SOMA team to teach and pray with the Anglican survivors. I chose to take a Maori priest, Bert Karaka, with me to represent New Zealand's approach to multi-racialism. Bert was funded by the Maori bishopric Te Pihopatanga and a lasting relationship between Te Pihopatanga and the Anglican Church in Rwanda resulted.

So on 30th June 1996 Bert Karaka and I flew from Auckland via Singapore and Mumbai to Nairobi for our first experiences of Africa. It was an extremely challenging experience. The bus trip from Nairobi to Kampala was the scariest ride of my life (they think nothing of passing on blind corners) and shelled-out buildings from a previous civil war in Uganda greeted us at the border. The team from about eight countries stayed and were oriented at the Kampala University.

A well-educated Anglican chaplain there said to me one day, 'I have been an African nationalist all my life but now I have to admit that we Africans have failed ourselves. In all but South Africa and Tanzania, where the founding fathers are still alive, we have had civil wars and violent transitions of power. If the West does not come to save us, we will perish.' A sobering preface to our entry to devastated Rwanda.

The SOMA team of over twenty people was taken into Rwanda in mini-buses sometimes passing the detritus of the civil war that had precipitated the genocide. When we gathered in the grounds of the cathedral in Kigali we were told there had been no killings there – until we saw the bullet holes in the steps where the Tutsi dean had been shot down, betrayed by his gardener.

The bishops who greeted us were fine, strong men facing huge challenges. To get around their dioceses some of them had to travel in armoured vehicles for their safety.

Images of the devastation were very visible – the concrete slabs of former Catholic churches which could no longer be used because such terrible things had been done in them; an Anglican church standing empty as a memorial to a congregation that had been hand-grenaded because they would not yield up their Tutsi members; a large secondary school, never used as a school, now filled with bodies laid out so surviving family members, if any were left, could identify their loved ones. The associated stories were appalling. What things we humans can do when law and morality are overtaken by fear and hatred.

The teams were sent out to different dioceses and Bert and I, led by a Kenyan deaconess, were sent to the most southerly diocese of Cyangugu where only one priest had survived the killings and the diocesan bishop was in the Congo suffering from post-traumatic stress disorder. Its location alongside a lovely lake that looked quite like Lake Taupo was a confronting contrast. Before I left New Zealand the Lord had given me a picture of an African man standing paddling a long canoe. I saw the very picture on arrival beside Lake Kivu.

The diocese was being led and reconstructed by an Englishman who had been consecrated as their non-stipendiary assistant bishop, the Rt Rev. Ken Barham, the son of the first bishop of Rwanda-Burundi. Bishop Ken had recruited six young men from the six areas of the diocese, trained them with the help of one aged Tutsi priest and then ordained them as deacons after three months' training to send them back to the villages to heal the people and rebuild the congregations. He had promised them that he would pay for the roofs and windows of any church they built the walls of – and found them outrunning his resources in new church planting.

It was to these courageous young men and their wives that we found ourselves bringing our soft Western ideas, across translation from English to Swahili to Kinyarwanda. How inadequate we felt. I don't know if we did much good but felt that the important thing was that we went, spent time with them and prayed with them. Our accommodation was in a guest-house alongside the border with the Congo. Soon after we left a mortar round came through the roof.

The mission ended with a mighty service of praise in the cathedral. I slept in the van most of the drive back to Kampala from sheer exhaustion. It is pleasing that Rwanda seems to have done quite well, with much outside aid, even while there has been major civil war across the border in the Congo and instability in Burundi. Ken and Jill Barham were able to come to our next Summer Wine and broaden our world vision. They had such love for the Rwandan people. 'Christ is Africa's only hope,' Ken said to me.

The life of ARMNZ kept growing: in-parish ministries; regional renewal events; a steady stream of AFFIRM meetings, regular Church Alives, and a range of overseas speakers from the USA (Mike Flynn and a team), Ireland (Niall and Gerry Griffin), the UK (Joyce and John Hugget) and Canada (Prof. David and Carlyn Reed). Summer Wine grew year by year with an extra one being tried at Blenheim. I asked Council, 'How big will it grow?' and denominationally, 'How much wider should we go?'[5] – questions that would become pressing in the future.

I was able to report that as a result of a review of the Church Alive! programme ARMNZ had been granted $6,000 by the St John's College Trust. By September 1996 Eleanor and I had minis-

---

5. National Coordinator's Report to Council March 1996, ANG 076/2/5.

tered in twenty-five parishes that year, and I was serving on General Synod, the St John's College Board of Governors, the Auckland Evangelism Council and the Common Life Hui on Evangelism.

Into an Ecumenical Stream

I reported I was fatigued and wondering how much longer Eleanor and I could sustain such a mobile life-style.[6] A year later I reported a less rewarding year and signalled a need to retire from the position. My assessment of the renewal was pessimistic:

> Sadly, I conclude that the renewal scene is faring little better than the rest of the Church when it comes to aging, shrinking, and trying to repeat the past… There are times that I feel gravely concerned about not only the Anglican Church but also the state of Christianity in New Zealand, and of the New Zealand culture. I sense that the culture has become callous, deceitful, debased ('coarsified' one pastor called it last week), spiritually hostile to the Christian faith in particular, and increasingly demonised.[7]

By then I was exhausted and feeling the need to stay in one place. I was approaching sixty and had led the ARMNZ ministry for almost twenty years.

When I became the National Coordinator, Cecil Marshall, who had been General Secretary for CAM for a time, told me that I would be able to survive five years in the role but that would be it. I had done nine by then. I was also sensing that the situation in

---

6. National Coordinator's Report to Council, Year to 30 September 1996, ibid.
7. National Coordinator's Report to Council November 1997, 1-2, ibid.

parishes had changed in ways I did not quite comprehend. I felt it was time for younger leadership, with current parish experience.

I began to consider how I could spend my last stipendiary years, and for a while was interested in the role of Bishop's Chaplain for Development in Auckland but the position went to a close friend.

I became aware of the situation developing in the Co-operating Parish of Bucklands Beach, alongside Pakuranga. It had a long association with the renewal movement having had its first LiSS in 1975 under the Rev. Graham Drummond and then five renewal years with Anglican priest Max Scott. It had then been led for ten high-impact years by a Presbyterian minister. The Toronto experience had strongly affected it, and their youth ministry – now substantially a talented young-adult ministry – was very dynamic as we saw each summer at Summer Wine. I waited to see how the changeover might take place and whether it might come our way. It happened – badly.

– 18 –

Where the Rivers Divide
Millennium Transitions

The possibility of the charismatic movement splitting from the mainline[1] churches had long concerned me. In 1986 I had been invited to supply an article on the subject for *The Ecumenical Review* of the World Council of Churches which by then had a 'charismatic desk' in its system. In that article I had said:

> The liberal-modernists have all too often treated the charismatics with rudeness and disdain, though the poor relating has been from both sides. Charismatics fear that in the cut and thrust of engagement they, and the truth they perceive, will be the continual losers... There is in fact a deep cleavage which is now becoming increasingly evident in the churches and it represents, if not a new ecumenical frontier, at least a reactivated ecumenical issue.

---

1. 'Mainline' is an American term which stems from the expansion of the railroads across that country. Wherever a railroad established a town, the existing denominations established churches 'along the main line' – i.e. the Methodist, Episcopalian, Presbyterian, Catholic and Baptist churches, and maybe others. The term thus has come to mean the major American churches of the nineteenth century.

Rival Currents

I referenced the comment of a British observer that the leadership of the CofE was unwilling to face the fact that many of the younger leaders of the church 'had already decided that there is no future in modernist liberal Protestantism and were already going in the direction of full-blooded apostolic Christianity'.[2] I continued:

> Here is the sound of a battle that could dominate the life of the Church for a generation. Its potentiality to drive Christian liberalism into the defensive use of ecclesiastical power is very great. The casualties on each side could be many but the steel has been forged on both sides in many furnaces. It could be a critically important fight if fought openly and well, but if 'won' badly by either side the results for the Church of the twenty-first century could be disastrous.[3]

I stated that the loss of the new conservatives was the more likely outcome and that this was a truly ecumenical issue in three senses: first, it would be a fight within the ecumenical churches; secondly, it had the potential to sunder churches; and thirdly, it would be truly worldwide. I hoped for a better way to avoid separation, observing that:

---

2. David Holloway, *The Church of England. Where Is It Going?*, Eastbourne: Kingsway, 1985, 78.
3. D. H. Battley, 'Charismatic Renewal: A View From the Inside', *The Ecumenical Review*, Vol.38, Issue 1, January 1986, 48-56. At the same time two articles of mine were blended by the WCC to provide an article for *The International Review of Mission*, 'The Holy Spirit: Energy of God for Mission', *The International Review of Mission*, Vol. 75, Issue 298, April 1986, 152-157.

It is ironic that those sub-communities of Christians who have, by and large, not taken the issues of racial and sexual discrimination and disempowerment seriously have themselves experienced the bitter taste of discrimination from those most committed to its elimination.[4]

I lived with this anxiety from then on and it lay behind our formation of AFFIRM to uphold orthodox faith and to monitor the coming sexuality conflict. The leaders of ARMNZ were particularly committed to nurturing the charismatic movement so it remained able to function positively within the Anglican context. Quite a few of the newer bishops of the NZA responded to work constructively with us. When AFFIRM sponsored a South Island conference in July 1996 entitled 'The Way Ahead', Archbishop Brian Davis spoke on 'Dynamic Orthodoxy' and Bishop Derek Eaton spoke on 'The Disciple's Personal Life'. Brian Davis' position on orthodoxy was clearly stated in his book *The Way Ahead*. In a section headed 'A Return to Classical Orthodoxy' he wrote:

> There is an increasing recognition within the church that the theological way ahead is neither the way of narrow anti-intellectual fundamentalism, nor the way of liberal accommodation with the values and assumptions of secular modernism, but a new critical and creative engagement with classical orthodoxy.[5]

He instanced other signs of a shift away from the theological liberalism of the 1970s and 80s in the NZA which included

---

4. Ibid.
5. Brian Davis, *The Way Ahead; Anglican Change and Prospect in New Zealand*, Caxton, 1995, 120.

a change in the theological emphasis at our major residential theological college at St John's, the birth of the Affirm movement, a coalition of Anglican Evangelicals and charismatic groups committed to calling the church back to its biblical roots, (and) a new breed of theologically well-equipped, mainly evangelical clergy.[6]

We were saddened when Brian Davis had to resign as bishop in 1997 due to serious ill health and died soon after. He was a good friend and a firm supporter of orthodox Anglicanism. Despite such episcopal encouragement, by the late 1990s tensions over doctrinal and ethical changes were becoming very apparent in the NZA.

Despite Brian Davis' optimism about St John's College, AFFIRM Council gave time to examining the possibility of forming an alternative theological training facility in New Zealand.[7] This idea was taken up by the diocese of Nelson who in time developed their Bishopdale College into an evangelically-based theological college offering courses in orthodox Christianity in partnership with Laidlaw College, Auckland.

AFFIRM and the Sexuality Issue

The AFFIRM Council continued to meet twice yearly, bonding the leaders of the societies together in joint planning, and continued to publish the AFFIRM magazine. They ran an AFFIRM camp at Levin in 1996 entitled 'Standing Firm in Christ' which was

---

6. Ibid., 121.
7. Letter John Meadowcroft to Don Battley, Derek Eaton, Bob Robinson, Brian Jenkins and Les Brighton, 22 September 1994. Thoughts about Creating an Alternative Theological College file, Battley papers.

attended by over seventy-five people.[8] AFFIRM's work increased from 1997 onwards with the sexuality issue developing rapidly in the Anglican Communion. At its March meeting concern was expressed about comments from members of the recently formed Tikanga Pakeha Commission on Sexuality and it was agreed to prepare a response.[9] The response became an open letter written by biblical scholar Francis Foulkes and co-signed by biblical scholars Peter Carrell, Tim Meadowcroft and Les Brighton, which stated:

> It is very clear that the church is not in a position to make a united decision about homosexual relationships, and any attempt to press for a decision or recommendation on the issue would be divisive. It is not just a matter of homophobia over against homophilia, but a deep cleavage of conviction in theology and in interpretation of the Bible.[10]

They urged the commission to place its main focus on heterosexual relationships 'where there is such a strong distinction between the Christian ideals of sexual relationships, of marriage and the family, and the practices that are prevalent in our society, practices that are causing great suffering and distress'. The Sexuality Commission was only one item out of twenty-three on the Council's agenda at its August 1997 meeting.[11] At the AGM in March I had stated that

---

8. AFFIRM North Island Conference 1996 file, Battley papers.
9. AFFIRM Council Minutes, 10-12 March 1997, item 3/97.20, AFFIRM Council meetings 1997 file, Battley papers.
10. Francis Foulkes et al. 'An Open Letter to the Tikanga Pakeha Commission on Sexuality', (undated), AFFIRM Meetings 1997 file, Battley papers.
11. AFFIRM Council Minutes, 18-20 August 1997, AFFIRM Meetings file, op.cit.

although Presbyterian and Methodist AFFIRMs were focussing strongly on the sexuality conflicts in their churches, 'our concerns are wider and we will not focus on that one issue, unless this church chooses to make it a critical issue'. Our concern was more on the attacks on orthodox beliefs and I observed that:

> We believed, and believe still, that such advocates of radical reconstruction of Christian beliefs are a small minority and do not really speak for the central core of this Church.[12]

At AFFIRM's AGM in February 1998 as outgoing chairman I stated our position quite clearly:

> The origins of this AFFIRM ... lie in the perceived need for the voluntary societies in this church to set in place some formal relationships that would enable them to support each other ... and to enable them to envision courses of action that might be better undertaken together rather than apart... However, no sooner had we begun to meet than two issues landed in our lap: first, our own experiences of the pain and departure of significant numbers of evangelical Anglicans from this church. All our societies had documentary evidence of this sad reality. Most of the departures were occasioned by falling confidence in the faith and/or mission competence of this church. At much the same time a visit by a post-modernist American bishop alerted us to the threat to the soundness of Christianity posed by the post-modern decline of reason and (loss) of respect for the learnings of past generations. We found ourselves being drawn to address areas that we had too long ignored.

12. Chairman's Address to AFFIRM AGM, 11 March 1997, op.cit.

On the sexuality issue I reported:

> AFFIRM finds itself inevitably drawn into this church's struggle with the complex issue of the place of homosexuals[13] in the church's ministry. We have absolutely no wish to be drawn into controversy in this delicate area. When General Synod set up a commission to examine issues of sexuality we sought to cooperate with their decision to try to process these questions privately, out of the eye of the media. We have made a number of submissions to the commission, both biblical, pastoral and theological... The AFFIRM Council has no wish to get into any conflict or contradiction with any group in this church. However we are very concerned about the possibilities for division that may arise in this church if the question of sexual discipline amongst the clergy is handled in other than a traditional manner.
>
> The (Council) has today ... resolved unanimously *'that the Council recognises the extreme seriousness of the issue of the ordination of practising homosexuals and of the numerous related issues, and commits itself to serious study of the questions with the aim of publicly stating and defending its convictions'.* We will await the findings of the Sexuality Commission with much interest and concern and may then have to speak on behalf of our constituencies.[14]

In a working paper for the Council I predicted that the sexuality

---

13. The more inclusive terms gay and lesbian or LGBT had not come into general use at the time.

14. Chairman's address to AFFIRM AGM 25 Feb 1998, AFFIRM Council 1998 file, Battley papers. The chair-person role had been rotated between leaders of the societies. It was my turn at the time.

commission would find that there were two views in the church that could not be reconciled and would be alienated if the other view was enforced, and that it might propose that each congregation, i.e. parish, be granted the freedom to choose whether it would accept a partnered homosexual as its priest, and that some would see that as 'a wise and accepting way ahead'. I predicted that the coming Lambeth Conference would set up an international commission and that the matter might be delayed for years.[15]

When the 1988 Lambeth Conference of the bishops of the Anglican Communion addressed the question of church policy for gay and lesbian people it came out with a firmly traditional statement, which was agreed to by a vote of 536 in favour with seventy against and 40 abstained. It is rare for any Lambeth Conference resolution to be by a divided vote. The resolution affirmed marriage or abstinence as the scriptural standard and, while affirming care for and listening to persons of homosexual orientation, stated that it 'cannot advise the legitimising or blessing of such unions'.[16] At the same time, a pastoral statement was issued by 145 mainly Western bishops expressing their regret that the needs of gay and lesbian people had not been heard and pledging their continuing commitment to achieve full inclusion for them. They called on the entire Communion for prayerful, respectful conversation on the issue of homosexuality.[17] Almost all New Zealand bishops signed the statement.

AFFIRM Council responded in September with a statement that welcomed the clear decisions in the Lambeth Resolution 1.10

---

15. Notes re AFFIRM, General Synod and the Homosexuality Question, AFFIRM Council 1998 file, Battley papers.
16. Text of Lambeth Conference Resolution 1.10 on Sexuality, acnslist, 6 August 1998.
17. A Pastoral Statement to Lesbian and Gay Anglicans from Some Member Bishops of the Lambeth Conference, August 8, 1998.

and committed itself to continuing study and creative listening to all who are involved in ministries with people struggling with issues of sexuality, and called on the bishops of NZA to abide by and uphold the plain meaning of the resolution 'in the light of the clear position and moral authority of that Resolution'.[18] Latimer published an Occasional Paper by Bishop Brian Carrell, 'The Ongoing Dialogue: Revisiting the Sexuality Commissions Report in the Light of Lambeth'. In a careful analysis of the process and wording of the resolution Brian Carrell observed,

> The weight of Anglican opinion in this area revealed in the voting patterns of Lambeth cannot afford to be overlooked as ongoing dialogue is entered into in the light of the Lambeth Conference response.[19]

The conservative statement from the Lambeth Conference was a reassurance to AFFIRM members but it was evident that a long journey lay ahead for Communion. By early 1999 I reported from AFFIRM to ARMNZ that 'things had gone strangely quiet since a few statements after bishops returned from Lambeth'.[20] It did not remain so. Twenty years later, at the time of writing, the contest of wills continued, with AFFIRM and General Synod negotiating a 'two-integrities' policy in an attempt to allow both the liberal and conservative policies to co-exist in good conscience in the one church.

AFFIRM continued to pursue its policy of promoting orthodox

18. AFFIRM Council: Lambeth Resolution on Human Sexuality, 25 September 1998, AFFIRM September 1998 file, Battley papers.

19. Brian Carrell, 'The Ongoing Dialogue: Revisiting the Sexuality Commissions Report in the Light of Lambeth', Latimer Occasional Paper, No. 3, September 1998, 4.

20. Report of AFFIRM Council meeting 8-9 March 1999, AFFIRM Council 1999-2001 file, Battley papers.

faith and theology in the NZA. For its 1999 national conference they invited Dr Tom Wright, then Dean of Litchfield, Professor Gerald Pillay from Otago University and Rev. Peter Corney of the Australian Institute for Contemporary Leadership as keynote speakers. Tom Wright spent nineteen days in the country, attended and spoke at the AFFIRM Conference (27-30 July) and spoke also in Wellington, Christchurch, Dunedin, Hamilton and Auckland.

Two years later AFFIRM conducted a consultation with its core constituency, sixty-two of whom attended a three-day consultation at Waikanae Christian Holiday Park. Rather than feature big-name speakers the consultation provided nine workshops in which participants contributed to collective statements compiled during the process. The focus was mainly practical issues such as 'Leading a Church Today', 'Ministering to the under 30s', 'Winning and Losing on Sunday' and 'Christians in the Workplace'.[21] The overall process was facilitated by Brethren Pastor Brian Hathaway of Laidlaw College. Learnings achieved flowed forward into AFFIRM's on-going life.

The St John's Bucklands Beach Schism

My own up-close encounter with schism was with a different set of issues in the Co-operating Parish of Bucklands Beach.

Hearing from my ARMNZ staff, who were members of the parish, of what was developing there, I felt I needed to at least warn my bishop, by then Bishop John Paterson, that trouble was brewing. The Minister at the time was a Presbyterian so the parish was under the oversight of that denomination but would soon become an Anglican responsibility when the next minister had to be appointed. (According to the Cooperating Venture (CV) process, the ministers and denominational oversight alternated). The difficulty facing the

---

21. AFFIRM Consultation 18-21 November 2001, Battley papers.

minister was that after ten years of service – the maximum allowable period – there was a strong type of revival occurring amongst the younger adults and teens and he felt called to stay with this once-in-a-lifetime opportunity. But under the clear rules of CVs, he had to resign and move on.

A group of parish leaders who did not like the revival behaviours petitioned the CV management to apply the rules. They agreed and told the minister he had to go. The revivalists objected and they moved out with the minister and youth pastor going with them.[22] Half the parish and its income left to form a new church and half remained, feeling shell-shocked and betrayed.

The bishop, being aware of my concern for the parish, asked me if, as someone who would understand the spiritual dynamics, I would be willing to take care of the parish during the interim until an Anglican priest could be appointed. At first I declined, then relented and suggested to the bishop that he appoint me and Eleanor as joint interim ministers. He liked that idea greatly. And so we took up the temporary pastorate of a wounded church, stipend-sharing while I continued with ARMNZ half-time. Eleanor was thrilled to be in a designated pastoral role, even as a lay pastor. 'I'm doing what I most like,' she exclaimed 'and I'm being paid to do it!'

There were still keen renewal people in the parish and we hoped that they would soon heal and find a new way ahead but it was a challenging task. Pastoring a wounded church is known to be one of the costliest tasks a minister can take on. I found it hard going but Eleanor and I soon saw that we should stay with the parish and accept the position of joint ministers and the parish nominators agreed. We had a short study leave overseas and in August 1998

---

22. The youth pastor, Kristin Williams, assured me that he had in no way encouraged the split but finally felt he had to go with the people he had discipled. I believed him.

were appointed joint ministers of the parish and co-archdeacons of Manukau archdeaconry. Eleanor was astonished to find herself an archdeacon when she was not even ordained, although there had been a few other lay archdeacons in New Zealand. She was probably the first lay woman archdeacon in the Anglican Communion.[23] Her supervisor had to encourage her to just 'keep on and learn as she went'. We soon allocated the roles so that I did the administrative things and she did the pastoral care roles.

I carried on as part-time National Coordinator with ARMNZ but could soon see I was not doing the job justice and stood down a year later. I handed the leadership on to the Rev. Paul Williamson, then co-vicar of Hataitai, which caused the ARMNZ office to move to Wellington. I asked only that I could lead one more Summer Wine in January 2000 as my millennium farewell.

St John's Bucklands Beach carried on as a warm and lively church but its average age was by then high and they grieved for the loss of the younger people into whose evangelisation they had invested much ministry and money. We were joined by a Pentecostal couple, Susan and Graeme Howarth, who had come from a wounding experience in their previous church and needed a safe haven and were a little surprised to find it in a mainline church. Susan soon showed high talent as an evangelist and families' pastor while Graeme was studying for a masters degree in theology. They brought new hope with their ability to attract younger families, but it was hard work for all. The half-parish we had inherited consolidated and grew a little over the next six years. We were all much appreciated.[24]

---

23. When we attended the pre-Lambeth Conference on Renewal in Kent in 1998 the British organisers were non-plussed as to whether to issue her a white or green name badge – was she lay or clergy?

24. Susan and Graeme returned after a time to their home area of Nelson and were ultimately both ordained.

Meanwhile the new church, which had called itself 'The River', set up in rented premises, held together and evangelised a mainly younger age-group, and has continued.

But whatever optimistic spin can be placed on the split, it was a big loss for St John's and a salutary warning to the sponsoring denominations. While the charismatic movement and Toronto revivalism could be seen as being responsible for the schism, the real fault lay in the design of co-operating ventures. In the early design of this useful ecumenical structure the designers had tried to prevent any one denomination taking over the CV by its minister staying for a very long time, so – drawing on the Methodist practice of moving their ministers on a rotational basis – they designed a policy of an initial five-year term, plus a permissible extension of three years plus a final extension of two more with an absolute maximum of ten years.

The weakness in this rigid policy was that, in both the Anglican and Presbyterian traditions, a minister once appointed is free to stay for as long as they feel called to do so, and some ministers do long pastorates very effectively. The minister at the time was only asking for what would have been his by right in his own denomination.

The CV governing group have since changed the policy but its effect on St John's was very harmful (except for those who wanted the revivalism stopped). So St John's became a casualty of both a structural fault and the over-the-top energies of Toronto revivalism.

But for me the experience was very salutary. Whatever the specific causes of the Bucklands Beach schism, I was living through the damage that splitting a church can cause to a church long-term. The survivors can become cautious about taking adventurous action and their memories of betrayal can last for a generation. Despite the rally that Susan's gifted ministry created, the rejuvenation did not last beyond her time as families' pastor. St John's remains an ageing church faced with the challenge of rapidly changing local demographics.[25] And it is sceptical about the benefits of charismatic spirituality.

What I did find fulfilling was the experience of being an archdeacon under Bishop John Paterson. By the late 1990s the tide had turned and the passage of time and election of bishops with renewal experience brought many charismatic clergy into the archdeacon role: Graham Langley in Southland, Mike Hawke in Christchurch, Richard Ellena in Marlborough (subsequently bishop of Nelson); Ray Muller and Dale Williamson in Wellington, John Marquet in Manawatu, John Anderson in Whanganui and many others. In Auckland we included Bruce Moore (subsequently assistant bishop), Brian Jenkins, Max Cranch, Max Scott, Murray Spackman, Harvey Smith, Eleanor and myself. (Apologies to any missed!) Any sense of exclusion had been overcome. Bishops who were open to the renewal included Penny Jamieson (Dunedin), Derek Eaton (Nelson), Brian Davis (Waikato and Wellington), David Moxon (Waikato), Ross Bay (Auckland) and Andrew Hedge (Waiapu).

Eleanor and I shared the oversight of thirteen parishes across the city of Manukau, a quite diverse area ranging from wealth to low income and industrial to rural. Most of them had experienced charismatic renewal to various stages although some had faded since the 1980s.

Only St Elizabeth's Clendon showed an impressive expression of renewal, managing to combine anglo-catholic worship with vibrant Pentecostal passion and bold social justice action. This was the product of the dedicated and intelligent ministry for many years of the Rev. Fr Mark Beale, a dear and admired friend.[26] A number of

---

25. The area is now significantly Asian and the church has had to develop partnerships with new Asian congregations.

26. See Mark Beale, *Full of Surprises. The Story of St Elizabeth's Anglican Church, Clendon, Aotearoa,* Pic Quick, Manukau, 2008.

other parishes drew on some of the energies bequeathed to parishes by the renewal, especially Papatoetoe and Papakura.

Millennium Transitions

An Auckland team of Summer Wine leaders and I continued to organise Summer Wine for two more summers – 1999 and the millennium year of 2000. The two camps at LTCC in 1999 drew over 700 attendees and the speakers were all Kiwis, including the ministry directors from Presbyterian Renewal Ministries, Ian Wood and Margaret Waight. A South Island Summer Wine was also held at Geraldine.

In January 2000 we had to combine the two Taupo camps into one and ministered to over 700 people at LTCC, with about 200 attendees living off-site. Guest speakers were Bishop Moses and Cynthia Tay from the diocese of Singapore, a diocese that was possibly the leading diocese in renewal in the Anglican Communion. Summer Wine Taupo had grown into a $75,000 operation.[27] By then ARMNZ had decided to split the Taupo event into a southern camp nearer to Wellington and a 'top half' further north, which went to Living Springs at Matamata. The millennium camp was a triumphant joy (with some emphasis on blowing of trumpets and a ram's horn) but we left Lake Taupo with real sadness. It had been a place of Galilee-type encounter with God. One major church told us that if we left Taupo for a land-bound site they would not be back. The scenic venue had a closeness to the God of nature that was hard to replace.

But my time was done, and now in our early sixties and with a parish to lead, Eleanor and I needed more restful summers to

---

27. Don Battley, 'A Report on Taupo Summer Wine Camp, with suggestions for 2001', Summer Wine 2000 file, Battley Collection.

recover in. It was four years before I had the energy or desire to attend another Summer Wine, arriving just in time to dissuade the Matamata camp leadership from closing it down, using the biblical line of Luke 13:8 ('dig around it and fertilise it for one more year. If it bears fruit next year, fine!'). It continued for many more years.[28] The Summer Wine camps remain ARMNZ's greatest and most enduring achievement.

A further millennium project was for us to lead a pilgrimage to Israel, Turkey and Europe. Forty others joined us on a tour which began in Athens and went on to Israel where we were guided by long-time friend the Rev. Dr Calum Gilmour, who had been a tutor and tour guide with the Anglican college at St George's Cathedral, Jerusalem. Calum's knowledge of classical and Israelite history was voluminous and passionate. The impressions and experiences are too many to detail.

During the journey I wrote spontaneous poems almost every day – a new literary development – and subsequently self-published them.[29] From Israel we toured Turkey including Gallipoli – another fascinating country – and then visited Taizé in France ending at Canterbury and London – an impressive tour of Christian origins.

Gathered Pilgrims
(in the queue at Calvary)

From every nation now we come
and speak in many diverséd tongue,

---

28. In time it was moved to Warkworth where it continued until 2018. The 2019 camp had to be cancelled due to lack of teams to staff it. New Wine NZ email 23/10/2018, 'New Wine's Warkworth festival 2019 is cancelled.'

29. Don Battley, *Poems and Prayers of Pilgrimage 2000,* Polygraphia: Auckland, 2001, Battley Collection.

> the agéd and still-growing young,
> we cluster to your place of shame,
> > of triumph, and of strangest gain.
>
> Jesus, did you know deep in your holy heart,
> > that this would be?
> Or did you walk to Calvary
> > in cold-steeled faith?
> – that from your gentle obedience
> > the God you served,
> > whose Name you knew,
> > > would work his strange purpose
> > > > just partly glimpsed?
>
> Obedience that trusts the God-will in scriptures shown
> > and from that daring act
> > > has raised up eternal pilgrimage
> > > in common lives lived patiently;
> > > > before a thousand candles
> > > > making richness
> > > > > from their silvered lights.[30]

Eleanor's Ordination

An unexpected consequence of Eleanor becoming a stipended pastor was that she then experienced the call to ordination.[31] Over the years I had suggested to her that she should consider being ordained and she had always responded with a forthright statement

---

30. Ibid. 7.
31. Over the years, I had seen this happen many times: put a person in the ministry role and they often then experience the Holy Spirit's call.

that she felt called to minister in the strength of her baptism and not to move beyond that.

I always accepted her decision, albeit with a little disappointment. Numerous clergy spouses had become ordained and it seemed to me to be a fruitful development which I thought would be good for us. But she had a point – if all the ministry-motivated people became ordained, what was the message being given? That only ordination was real ministry? – the very opposite of the priesthood of all believers. I supported her decision to seek ordination as, amongst other factors, I thought it would be good to preserve her ministry gifts into our coming retirement. I had seen a number of older women giving excellent ordained service in their later years and could see that being fulfilling for her.

Eleanor was already studying for a post-graduate diploma in theology and, excellent learner that she was, was loving it. When she went before the bishop's examining chaplains, who assess whether a person should be trained for ordination, they were split fifty-fifty. Half of them believed her work and role-modelling as a lay person was so valuable it would be a loss to the church to lose it! It fell to the bishop to decide and he encouraged her to proceed to ordination. Eleanor was ordained deacon in 2001 and priest in 2002.

I felt immensely proud of her and only wished it had happened decades earlier, though what she had achieved in those years was superb anyway. Bucklands Beach parish loved her being an ordained priest for our final few years with them. In 2004 she added a Graduate Diploma in Theology to her previous qualifications.[32] In 2006, following our retirement from Bucklands Beach parish, she served an interim ministry at Papakura and did it very well, and we shared an interim ministry at Hillsborough in 2008.

---

32. B.A. in French and Dip. Ed. with a thesis on St Stephen's School, Bombay.

It was a great privilege and joy to be Eleanor's husband and partner in life and ministry. She had a remarkable character filled with grace, intelligence, patience and wisdom. Her faith was strong and uncomplicated, but well-informed. She had been a product of the Student Christian Movement at university and gained an early diploma in theology. A natural and skilled teacher, she had innate authority yet was never domineering – she treated everyone with kindness and respect. As a Christian counsellor she spent endless hours with troubled people some of whom I felt were wasting her time, but she never lacked patience with them.

As her husband I probably benefitted from her patient nature many, many times as, unlike her, I was prone to stress and exasperation if fatigued. But we were a good pair, balancing each other and well-partnered spiritually, culturally, educationally and vocationally.

I think she always wanted to be a minister's wife, having been nurtured by the humble Rev. Bill Garraway and his wife at St Columba, Grey Lynn. Babysitting for a vicarage couple had left her with no illusions about the simplicity of the lifestyle and, coming from a wage-earning household, her financial expectations were modest. In fact, our prosperity as the years went by gave her opportunities she would never have imagined when young – but so it was for so many of our generation. Born just before the Second World War into a Western nation, we were the most privileged generation the world had ever seen and we travelled widely in ways never available to our parents.

Life in ministry was an unusual contrast between the doggedness of parish work and exciting occasions of international travel. I estimate that Eleanor travelled out of the country at least twenty-two times, most of them on ministry-related travel.

Eleanor's search for a deeper spirituality certainly drew me into the charismatic movement and she seemed to be a natural at it. One of her strengths was that her deeply stable and well-educated personality meant she never slipped into the uncritical emotionalism of some charismatics but remained a remarkably reliable bringer of prophetic words and pictures. I never heard her deliver an erroneous word and every picture she had was unique. She thus became a very trusted exponent of prophecy. She told me that very early in renewal she said to the Lord, 'Anything you want me to speak, I will speak for you,' and she did. It helped her that she was not in awe of the vicar! She was in so many ways a pure and deeply obedient vessel.

It was a tragedy when at 71 she began to manifest cognitive impairment (as had her mother before her) and she spent her seventies sliding into dementia – a great loss to her, to me and to her loved family and so many friends. Eleanor had the type of dementia where they know what is happening to them and she found it very painful until her self-knowledge disappeared.

I have had to come to terms with the reality of aging, mortality and of irreversible illness. As our then bishop, Ross Bay – a protegé from our Papatoetoe years – caringly observed, 'Life is messy – life doesn't always play by the rules.' She had lived a responsible, loving Christian life all her days and did not deserve this tragic loss of cognition.

– 19 –

The Ebbing Tide?

Eleanor and I retired from full-time stipendiary ministry one day after my 65th birthday – I was weary and unaware that I had developed a heart condition. Bishop John Paterson invited us to continue as co-archdeacons of Manukau which we agreed to do. We each did half-time locums in 2016, Eleanor at Papakura and me at Massey.

At the same time I did a short spell as acting Bishop's Chaplain for Development which produced a research document on the need for parish expansion in many areas of Auckland.[1] I predicted that the metropolitan urban limits would be breached quite soon, which is what has happened. I managed to get Synod to agree to make three million dollars available to assist six parish church builds that were urgently needed.[2]

This late-life burst of activity pushed me into a modest heart attack which persuaded us to retire properly. We had had a great run in Anglican ministry. I began work on family history and doing a diploma in historiography with historian Peter Lineham at Massey University.

1. D. H. Battley, 'Prospects of Development. A Report to the Bishop and Diocesan Council of the Diocese of Auckland, June 2006', Battley papers.
2. The churches were St Chad's, Meadowbank, St Elizabeth's, Clendon, The Cedar Centre, Birkdale-Beachhaven, St Stephen's, Whangaparaoa Peninsula, St Paul's, Botany and the Church of the Good Shepherd, Massey. The first four had been completed by 2019.

ARMNZ becomes New Wine

After I stepped away from ARMNZ they carried on with the Rev. Paul Williamson as half-time National Coordinator. They continued the Summer Wine camps, establishing them at Rathkeale College near Masterton and Totara Springs Conference Centre at Matamata as well as continuing at Geraldine. New leadership, mainly by lay people, emerged and the camps grew.[3]

It became apparent that the ARM ministries in other countries were declining or closing and that the era of denominational agencies was dying out. Presbyterian Renewal Ministries NZ closed; the Methodist Aldersgate Fellowship merged with the newly formed Wesleyan Methodist Church and Catholic Charismatic Renewal services, while continuing, was much reduced.

The ARMNZ Council spent about three years discussing ARMNZ's future and whether to bond to and become New Wine which was clearly the prime expression of charismatic renewal in the UK. The culture and spirituality of ARMNZ was similar to New Wine UK, whereas ARM UK had gone in a very liturgical direction which was not where New Wine, with its strongly Wimber and Toronto-style culture, was going. And the ARMNZ Summer Wine camps were being strongly fed by speakers and children's ministries from New Wine.

Discussions developed between ARMNZ and the UK New Wine leaders; both were open to closer relations but the ARMNZ leaders were cautious about losing their role within the NZA while New Wine did not want to get enmeshed in the sexuality conflict developing in New Zealand. ARMNZ wrote a new constitution for themselves which included the statement that 'we have a special, though not exclusive, concern for the Anglican Church and other

---

3. Interview with the Revs Paul and Dale Williamson, 2 January 2019, 1.

traditional churches'.[4] According to Paul Williamson the document 'still had the spirit of ARMNZ'.[5]

They adopted New Wine policy documents and renamed themselves New Wine NZ Trust in 2004.[6] John Marquet stated that,

> ARMNZ didn't want to trade off our heritage, and were not quite into absorbing all that was New Wine ... they did want to draw on New Wine resources but they didn't just 'follow mother'. An example – we had a lay woman leader. That was hard for the Brits to accept.[7]

Paul Williamson considered that 'the Brits did not understand what ARMNZ would lose by this change'.[8]

Subsequently a policy crisis occurred about how interdenominational New Wine NZ was to be. According to the Williamsons the New Wine NZ Council decided in May 2007 to stay clearly Anglican but when the camp managers came into the meeting they tipped it over and New Wine NZ was 'de-anglicanised'. Dale and Paul Williamson and Eric Etwell resigned.[9] Paul recognised that by then he was 'completely out of touch with the new generation' and the Rev. Learne McGrath became chairperson.

With New Wine becoming interdenominational, a supportive bishop like bishop of Wellington Tom Brown, who had really

---

4. P. Williamson, Letter 'New Direction for Anglican Renewal Ministries New Zealand', 31 May 2002, Summer Wine 2002 file.

5. Interview P. and D. Williamson, op cit., 2.

6. Deed of Variation of Charitable Trust: New Wine New Zealand Trust, 14 October 2003, 1, Summer Wine 2004 file.

7. Interview with the Rev. John Marquet, 24 January 2019, 1.

8. Williamson interview, 2.

9. Dale tendered her resignation, 11 Sept 2006, Letter in her computer.

enjoyed presiding at the final eucharists, was disappointed to be advised he could no longer preside at the communion as the New Wine camp was no longer Anglican.[10] Some of the communion services became distinctly Baptist.[11] By this time around 1,500 people were attending the three summer camps. Dale Williamson commented that 'New Wine lost a voice in the NZA at that time'.[12]

New Wine NZ continued with a lay person, Lydia Reed, as the employed leader based in Palmerston North. They maintained the summer festivals; brought in touring speakers, mainly from the New Wine UK network; presented seminars for ministers and for worship leaders, drawing attendees from many denominations.

By 2019 the South Island summer camp was independent of New Wine; the camp at Warkworth north of Auckland could not be conducted due to difficulties with getting adequate teams, but the New Wine Festival at Kapiti drew 1,600 attendances. The largest groups were from Wellington-area Anglican parishes, with 160 churches in total attending from fourteen denominations.

I attended the 2019 festival and was delighted by many features of it. Not only had the model of ministering to all ages and providing on-site camping continued but the content of the teaching ministry was of high standard with four of the presentations addressing the history of missions, philanthropy and the Treaty of Waitangi with frequent use of Te Reo [Maori] in both songs and addresses. The local Anglican bishop, Justin Duckworth, gave full support to it and was a keynote speaker. Around forty-five Wellington Anglican clergy attended. Undoubtedly the quality operation of New Wine NZ in the lower North Island has strengthened the renewal movement there.[13]

---

10. Marquet interview, 2; Williamson interview, 2.
11. My personal experience at Matamata.
12. Williamson interview, 2.
13. Notes of New Wine at Kapiti College, January 2019, Battley papers.

Views differ on whether New Wine is delivering to Anglicans all that ARMNZ was set up to do. Some renewal clergy miss the 'Church Alive!' ministers' training four-day residential events ARMNZ offered, but John Marquet believes that the one-day events New Wine offer cover that need. Resourcing in the area of church growth studies seems to have declined.[14]

It appears that the renewal has gone through distinct stages of organisational resourcing: the initial interdenominational launch period from 1966 to 1980 with CAM; the period of denominational agencies from 1980 to the early 2000s; and now a return to cross-denominational work with a strong Anglican-Vineyard partnership shaping the ministry style.

A New Current – St Paul's Symonds Street reborn and St Augustine's Mission

In 2003 a remarkable church planting project occurred at St Paul's in Auckland. After the high period of 1970-84 under Fathers Prebble and David Balfour, St Paul's gradually declined until by the early 2000s its congregations were quite small.

A number of Kiwis who had been evangelised by Vineyard-influenced parishes in London asked a London parish, St Mary's Bryanston Square, whether they could create a new church in Auckland to provide them with the type of church they had known in London. The diocese managed to steer this request towards St Paul's and in 2003 a team of thirty arrived from London to revitalise

---

14. 'We have lost the Church Alive! course (where) we got people together for about four days and they bonded and drew strength from each other, and met as Anglicans and addressed Anglican parish stuff. Some of the Church Growth stuff is missing – a whole lot is missing, actually.' Interview, Ray Muller 20 January 2019, 1.

St Paul's.[15] The Bishop's Chaplain for Development, Harvey Smith, acted as vicar-facilitator for the transition over 2003-4 and the leader of the team, the Rev. Mike Norris, became vicar in 2004.

The effect of this bold move was electrifying. Armed with vision and talents from London, Mike's team effected a rapid re-growth of St Paul's until after ten years its membership topped 1000. The churchmanship was totally different from the previous anglo-catholicism and in time this compelled the previous congregants to disperse elsewhere, but St Paul's grew by transfer growth from other churches, Anglican and non-Anglican, and from conversion growth. Mike Norris served as vicar for over ten years before returning to England and was followed by the Rev. Jonny Grant, the son of well-known evangelical couple Ian and Mary Grant.

This transformation at St Paul's raises many questions: why could the Brits achieve what the Kiwis had failed to do? What was so effective about their ministry style and team skills that enabled them to compete effectively with the highly-talented nearby Pentecostal churches? What were the features of their faith and theology that were working with so many younger adults? What really is the key to this HTB/Wimber/Anglican-Vineyard/London mix that can work so effectively? These questions need to be addressed and clarified. In 2017 a group moved out of St Paul's to form a new Anglican mission named St Augustine's (how Anglican is that?). They rapidly outgrew St Columba's Church, Grey Lynn, and a year later moved to worship at Auckland Girls Grammar School.[16] What is the key to such inner-city growth?

Clearly the charismatic renewal has generated resources that can, with the right leadership, transform churches. And these are not

---

15. Reportedly the team, which included one priest, brought with them £100,000 to bank-roll the venture.

16. Sourced www.saintaugustines.org/about, accessed 6 June 2019.

the only examples – Auckland diocese has a number of strong suburban churches which are based on charismatic models and others persist around the country.

AFFIRM – Trying to Keep the Streams Together

AFFIRM entered a period of prolonged difficulty and challenge with increasing polarisation throughout the Anglican Communion over pastoral policy towards gay, lesbian and transgender people. The decadal meeting of bishops known as the Lambeth Conference struggled to achieve an agreed policy and from 1988 onwards the Anglican Communion was splintering between its conservative and liberal streams. Early on it was my conviction that this issue would not pass around the NZA – it would pass through it.

The AFFIRM leadership found itself between a rock and a hard place: its objective was to sustain and strengthen orthodox and creedal faith in the NZA and it did not wish to become seen as a single issue movement. Yet the steady advance of the LGBT objectives within the church and the strengthening of the international resistance movement known as GAFCON[17] and the formation of a breakaway Anglican movement in the North American Anglican churches known as the Anglican Church in North America (ACNA) caused conservative New Zealand Anglicans to firm up their commitment to traditional biblical and ethical positions and to develop political strategies to protect their convictions.

The details of AFFIRM's journey need to be told by someone who lived it but by May 2014 the General Synod had agreed a way forward which affirmed covenantal marriage but also sought to provide a liturgical recognition of committed same-sex partnerships. On 15 May at an Auckland AFFIRM meeting I witnessed

---

17. GAFCON is based on the words Global Anglican Futures Conference.

one colleague resign his ministry and in time he took forty-four parishioners with him as he exited. I recorded the moment in a paper entitled 'Devolution Begins' and concluded:

> So the melt-down that I have been warning about since 1986 has begun. The grapevine already suggests that there are others who will take the same course. The really interesting thing will be whether they have done enough forward planning to already have a contingency plan to form an alternative Anglican-type church in this country and to find episcopal covering for it. If they have, then devolution is upon us.[18]

Another vicar departed in the Waikato diocese with most of his parish in July 2014.[19]

AFFIRM responded to General Synod's decision by circulating a petition affirming the traditional position on same-sex activity which was signed by 2,015 people. This led the leaders of General Synod to accept that there were in the NZA 'two integrities' regarding Christianity and same-sex relationships.[20]

By 2018 General Synod had accepted a proposal from AFFIRM and the Fellowship of Confessing Anglicans (FCA) leaders[21] that if General Synod were to approve same-sex blessings and ordination of people in same-sex relationships there should be established a safe place within the NZA for those parishes which wished to stand to the traditional policy. It was agreed that parishes could choose

---

18. Don Battley paper, 'Devolution Begins', 15 May 2014, Battley papers, 4.
19. Letter from the Bishops of Waikato to the Parishioners of the Anglican Parish of West Hamilton, 20 July 2014, Battley 21C papers.
20. Williamson interview, 5.
21. The petition was signed by seventy-one clergy and was championed by Jay Behan, leader of the FCA in New Zealand.

(by a two-thirds majority) to affiliate with an association called 'The Community' which would still be within the NZA but could stand aside from the new LGBT policies.[22]

Difficult choices now face parishes with a significant conservative element. While some may achieve the two-thirds vote to join The Community, others may find themselves with 60/40 or even 50/50 votes. Damage, departures and division of parishes may then ensue as people choose to move elsewhere in response to their convictions. This sorting out process might take some years,

The appeal of the GAFCON movement and its subsidiary the FCA has become so strong that some parishes and clergy have already chosen to disaffiliate from the NZA with the intention of forming an alternative Anglican church in New Zealand.[23] It is reported that by April 2019 at least ten faith communities of this disaffiliated new Anglican structure already exist[24] and on 17 May 2019 they elected a bishop for themselves.[25] It looks as if the offer

---

22. Conversation with Peter and Lorraine Lloyd on AFFIRM, 28 March 2019. Lorraine was executive officer and Peter network coordinator for AFFIRM.

23. 'A Dunedin church opposed to the blessing of same-sex civil marriages has withdrawn from the Anglican diocese ... (Bishop) Benford said: "It is with a heavy heart that we have heard the decision of a portion of St Matthew's parish to disaffiliate from the Anglican Church."' 'Church exits over same-sex marriage'. *New Zealand Herald*, Saturday, 17 November 2018, A3.

24. 'Members of six ministry units ... from three dioceses, have formally voted to disaffiliate from the Province. Another six clergy have resigned to start church plants.' Dave Clancy, 'A new Anglican structure in 2019', Latimer Focus Issue 44, Autumn 2019, 21. Four of the disaffiliating Christchurch parishes represent twenty percent of that diocese's worshipping Anglicans. Lloyd's report to Council for AFFIRM ministry units and Associate members, 2 October 2018, Battley AFFIRM papers.

25. 'Jay Behan to be first bishop of new diocese of Confessing Anglicans in New Zealand', Gafcon Australia, email 17 May 2019.

of The Community within the NZA may be a case of too little too late, especially as it is less than the requested alternative episcopal jurisdiction that AFFIRM and the FCA had requested.[26]

It is observable that those choosing to move out are mainly classical evangelicals, who may or may not have some charismatic element in their ministries, while those who have been working for The Community option have been long-term charismatic leaders. A motivating factor here is that the charismatics, of whatever Anglican background – catholic, evangelical, liberal, centrist – have worked to a vision of renewing the Anglican Church's life and mission from within. They remain opposed to walking out and would prefer to remain engaged with a muddled church than to step out into a 'pure' church.

Time will tell how these options work out. What is certain is that the damage I foresaw in the 1980s is now upon us, and the NZA will, over all, be numerically weaker as a result. Whether it will be morally and spiritually better or worse depends upon how one sees the current issue – whether acceptance of same-sex unions is seen as a serious and damaging compromise of biblical values, or a compassionate and Jesus-like response to the needs of Christians who have been poorly treated by Christianity for a very long time.

An Ebbing or a Rising Tide?

Where I live on the Whangaparaoa Peninsula I am daily reminded of the ceaseless rise and fall of the tide, each stage of it beautiful in its own way. And in every season of the year people swim in it.

So it is with 'life in the Spirit'. The ocean of God's graceful activity in and through creation never ceases and the church in

---

26. 'It was the failure of General Synod to provide alternative episcopal oversight that pushed the FCA people out.' Interview with Peter and Lorraine Lloyd, 8 February 2019.

particular is a special sea of God's activity. So to the question, 'Is the charismatic movement over?' one has to answer confidently, 'No. Of course not!' for the church itself *is* the charismatic movement. It is created and sustained by the active presence of God who has declared, 'I will never leave you or forsake you.' The Holy Spirit forever breathes within and upon the church of God, whether the Spirit's presence is recognised or not. The very survival of the Christian church through twenty centuries of change and turmoil is evidence of God's faithful presence within it.

The charismatic renewal in the NZA has dispersed widely through the church and often it is no longer possible to identify who are 'the charismatics' and who are not. It appears that a majority of those being ordained have had active experience in renewal, Alpha, healing ministries, New Wine, and renewal-type parishes. Some clergy remain explicitly 'charismatic' in theology and style, but many appropriate other strands of contemporary Anglican thought and values and thereby model integrated belief and practice.[27] The future health of the Anglican Way may come from them.

Nevertheless, division and actual schism is also at hand. Those who desire to step out of the NZA to form an alternative Confessing Anglican Church in New Zealand will face a hard road,[28] but will get support from overseas and may show high energy and creativity. My concern is whether their theology and practice will be reactive and overly conservative. The future will see societies experiencing rapid transition. Will the new Anglican reality be reactionary, or a new missionary force?

---

27. For example, most of the lecturing staff at St John's College have had hands-on charismatic experience. Something that was unimaginable thirty years ago is acceptable now.

28. For instance, they have to leave their buildings and other assets behind and start again.

Other charismatic parishes will be allowed to designate themselves as 'non-blessing' parishes and, if they so wish, to join The Community and be able to hold their position with integrity while remaining full members of their respective dioceses. This act of accommodation is a very Anglican response to a clash of convictions. It remains to be seen how many parishes will choose this option and how its mission-life will develop.

Some charismatic-evangelical parishes have already chosen to stay in the main diocesan stream and see no need to step sideways into The Community. If this trend increases, The Community may become a defensive side-show. The future may lie with those renewed parishes which are confident enough to live openly in the main stream of diocesan life, participating confidently in the broad dynamics of the Anglican Way.

The charismatic movement in the NZA can thus be perceived to be dividing into three streams: one that is dispersed confidently within the mainstream of Anglicanism; one that will be to one side yet still within the historic NZA; and a third trying to start a separate church. Is this a failure of the renewal to reach its full potential, or an understandable response to the diverse and complex nature of Christianity itself in an increasingly diverse society? As the river of renewal spreads out into a widening delta, it is worth recalling that river deltas can be places of great fertility.

What is striking about the last two decades is the number of adult children of Anglican charismatics who are now committed and talented mission leaders themselves. Very many seeds have been planted through the charismatic movement and its ministries. The full fruit may yet be about to flower. While my generation of leaders is concerned at what looks like an ebbing tide, at New Wine 2019 the younger generation of leaders confidently sang, 'The Tide is Rising, The Tide is Rising.' May their hopes be fulfilled.

An Epilogue

In re-reading this work I am aware that personally I have moved on theologically, not in a way that disowns what so inspired my life in ministry but in reassessing where faith and reflection have now taken me.

In the narrative of this book I have sought to express what we thought and decided at the time while negotiating the rushing river of life in ministry from the 1960s until 2004. We were swept by the fourth aspect of Wesley's Quadrilateral – 'experience' being added to scripture, tradition and reason (the Anglican three-legged stool). We discovered so much that was clear in scripture, belonged in the tradition and that reason told us would make faith available to many people. For that, 'I regret nothing' (a comment I owe to my learned colleague Peter Stuart).

But perhaps we were not always wise or balanced, and we sometimes fought against others in the church who saw other needs and worked as passionately for them as we did for ours. If I, or 'we the charismatics' offended them, I regret that. In my retirement I am finding that many of my 'liberal' friends pray more and believe as much as I have ever done. I respect you. And I forgive you for any of the hurts this book reports. We are brothers and sisters in the one 'body of the Spirit of Jesus'.

For myself, my faith and reading have moved me into such mature thinkers as N. T. Wright, Keith Ward, John Polkinghorne and many others and, in post-evangelicalism, Brian Mclaren, Brad

No Way Back

Jersak, John Walton and Peter Enns. In the same-sex matter, David P. Gushee shows a pathway ahead for us all.[1] May we follow more closely the Spirit who led Jesus and the early church across so many cultural and religious boundaries in their times. May we do no less in ours.

My thanks to so many friends and encouragers, to the archivists at Kinder and Auckland Anglican Archives, to my mentor Peter Lineham, publishing manager Andrew Killick and publishers Castle Publishing. If it takes a village to raise a child, it takes a community to write a book.

Don Battley
August 2019

---

1. David P. Gushee, *Changing our Mind, 3rd Edition of the Landmark Call for Inclusion of LGBTQ Christians with Response to Critics,* Read the Spirit Books, Canton, Michigan, 2017.

Glossary of Abbreviations

ACCG	Anglican Charismatic Core Group
ACNA	The Anglican Church in North America
ACRG	Auckland Charismatic Renewal Group (interdenominational)
AFFIRM	Anglicans For Faith Intercession Renewal and Mission
ANZ&P	Aotearoa New Zealand and Polynesia
ARMA	Anglican Renewal Ministries Auckland
ARMNZ	Anglican Renewal Ministries New Zealand
ARM UK	Anglican Renewal Ministries in England
CA	Church Army
CAM	Christian Advance Ministries
CHARM	Christchurch Anglican Renewal Ministries
CMS	Church Missionary Society
CofE	Church of England
CPE	Clinical Pastoral Education
CR	Charismatic Renewal
CV	Co-operating Ventures
D Min	Doctor of Ministry degree
ECF	Episcopal Charismatic Fellowship
ERM	Episcopal Renewal Ministries
FCA	Fellowship of Confessing Anglicans
FGBMFI	Full Gospel Businessmen's Fellowship International

GAFCON	Global Anglican Futures Conference
GS	General Synod
HTB	Holy Trinity Brompton Church, London
IDC	Inter-Diocesan Conference
LGBT	Lesbian, Gay, Bi-sexual, Transgender
LiSS	The Life in the Spirit Seminars
LTCC	Lake Taupo Christian Camp
NZA	The Anglican Church in Aotearoa, New Zealand and Polynesia
OE	Overseas Experience – the equivalent of the modern gap year
SAMS	South American Missionary Society
SERF	Scottish Episcopal Renewal Fellowship
SFTS	San Francisco Theological Seminary
SOAR	Southland Otago Anglican Renewal
SOMA	Sharing Of Ministries Abroad
SOMA-NZ	SOMA New Zealand
TAV	The Toronto Airport Vineyard Church
TB	The 'Toronto Blessing'
TEC	The Episcopal Church (USA)
TEE	Theological Education by Extension
WARM	Waikato Anglican Renewal Ministries

Index of Topics

Alpha Course, The 258-259, 301
Anglican Renewal Ministries NZ (ARMNZ)
    Formation of 160-163, 162
    NETWORK Magazine 175
    National Coordinator 188, 191, 192, *209*
    'Church Alive!' Course 191, 203-204, 264, 267, 295
    Tenth Birthday 205-208, *209*
    Summer Wine *210, 211,* 241-244, 251, 261-263, 267,
        282, 285-286, 292
    Becomes New Wine 292-295
Anglicans For Faith Intercession Renewal and Mission (AFFIRM)
    Formation of *215,* 220-221, 273, 274
    AFFIRM Covenant *214, 215,* 221, 224-226
    A Confessing Movement 222-229
    AFFIRM Magazine 226, 227
    Alister McGrath 230, 232
    Sexuality Issue 274-280
    AFFIRM Consultation 2001 280
    Keeping it Together 297-300
'Anglicans In Aotearoa' 155
Auckland Charismatic Core Group 136, 147, 151
    Becomes ARM Auckland 176, 200
Auckland Commission on CR 84-86

Baptism in the Spirit 29, 37, 43, 45, 49, 80, 94, 98, 143, 208
Baptismal Crises 148-9
Bishop Gowing 'Call to Renewal' 48
Bishops' 'Call to Renewal' 1977 139
Bishopdale College 274
Bucklands Beach Co-operating Parish
    Summer Wine Youth Tent 243, 262, 269
    Schism 280-283
    Battleys as Co-Ministers 269, 281-284

Canterbury Cathedral 26, 140
Catholic Charismatic Renewal 68-69, 73, 74, 143, 154, 197, 202, 255, 292
Christ Church Parish, Whanganui 178-180, 181-183, 188
'Church Alive!' Course 191, 203-205
Church and People 83, 84, 85
Church Army NZ 21, 30, 91, 218, 225, 228
Church Missionary Society of NZ 219, 225, 228
Christian Advance Ministries 71-72, 295
    Summer Schools 73, 79, 81, 83, *110,* 135, 138, 180, 183, 241, 261
    And Vineyard Movement 184, 255
Clinical Pastoral Education 93, 95
Conferences on Renewal
    1978 Canterbury Conference 140-144
    Tawa Anglican Conference 145-149
    First National Consultation 151-155
    Second National Consultation 157-160
    Third National Consultation 160-163
    'Disciples in Mission' 188-189
    1988 Canterbury Conference 189-191
    1988 ARMNZ Conference 189, 191-192

Index of Topics

1991 Partners in Renewal 201
Congress on World Evangelisation 199

Death of God Controversy 32, 82
Decade of Evangelism 197-199, 206
Diocesan Liaison Priests
    Proposed 154
    Declined 158

Elderships 120-123, 168, 171
    Thesis 185-6
Episcopal Church of the USA 228, 229
Episcopal Renewal Ministries 141, 142, 144, 174,174, 201, 203
Evangelical Fellowship of NZ 253

Fountain Trust, The 67, 68, 71

GAFCON and FCA 297-299
General Synod Commission on CR 86

Holy Trinity Church, Brompton 246, 251, 257, 296

Kaitaia Parish and George Carey 130, 187
Kohimarama Parish and LiSS 93

Lake Taupo Christian Camp 239-241, 261, 285
Lambeth Conference '68 50
Lambeth Conference '88 278
Latimer Fellowship of NZ 217-219, 225-227
Life in the Spirit Seminars 11
    Creation of and arrival 69-70
    St Pauls and Pakuranga 77, 92, 96

Spread of 93, 127-130, 257, 258
Lincoln University, CAM 73
Lynfield Community Church 82-3

Maori Spirituality 62, 82-83
Massey University, Palmerston North 45, 67
    CAM 73, 138, 146
Methodist AFFIRM 227, 276

Nuclear Threat 16, 22

Pakuranga *see St Peters Pakuranga*
Pentecostalism 12, 29, 35, 50, 60, 97, 147
Pihopatanga O Aotearoa 157, 158
Priests/Spouses Retreat F MacNutt 146-147, 150 (n12), 178
Polynesia, Diocese of 69, 160, 178, 189, 191, 197, 198-9, *212*
Presbyterian AFFIRM 226-227, 276

Revival 113, 243, 254, 281 *see also Toronto Blessing*
Ruawai Parish 29, 32, 129
Rwanda SOMA Mission *213,* 264-267

Sexuality Issue 207, 227, 229, 232, 273, 274-279, 292, 297-300, 304
Sharing of Ministries Abroad 142, 160-161, 177, 190, 264
Singing in the Spirit 64, 100, 155
St Aidan's, Remuera 16-23, *103*
St Elizabeth's, Clendon 284
St John's College, Auckland 27, 45, 51, 136, 157, 197, 220, 232, 233-234, 235, 267-268, 274
St George's, Papatoetoe 169-172, 178-180, 285
St Margaret's, Hillsborough 57-63, 128

St Martin's, Mt Roskill 80-82, 128, 133
St Matthew's, Auckland 41-43
St Paul's, Symonds Street 37, 47, 53-57, 77-78, *109*, 218, 295
    St Paul's Singers 77, 118
St Peter's, Pakuranga 89-102
    Life in the Spirit Seminar 92-102
    Vicarage prayer meeting 100-102
    Worship changes 114-119
    Shared leadership 120-123
    Enlarging the building 124-125
St Peter's, Takapuna 30, 45
St Thomas', New Lynn 79-82, 128
Synod Debate, Auckland Diocese 84

'The Community' 299-300, 302
Tongues, The Gift of 11, 30, 37, 38, 39, 40, 43, 44, 49, 64, 81, 97, 98, 102
Toronto Blessing, The 245-257, 258, 261, 269, 283
'The Changing Church' UK 190
'The Servants of Christ the King' 28, 31

Vineyard Movement 183-185, 254-255, 296
    A 'Third Wave'? 184

World Council of Churches 135, 271

Index of Names

Allfrey, Peter, Capt. CA 91, 100

Balfour, David, Rev. 68, 78, *109,* 114, 131, 132, 143, 159, 172
Barham, Ken, Bishop 266
Barton, Terry, Canon 98
Battley, Don, Rev. Dr
    Childhood 15-17, *103*
    Confirmation 18
    University 20, *104*
    Overseas Experience 24-26
    St John's College 27-30, *105*
    Curacies 30-32
    Ruawai 32-35
    Pakuranga 89-102, *107, 108,* 111-126, 167-168
    Doctor of Ministry 167, 185
    Papatoetoe 169-172
    ARMNZ 172-178, 186-193, 195-208, 235-244, 261-268, 285-286
    Whanganui 178-180, 181-183
    National Coordinator 195-208
    Bucklands Beach 280-285
    Pilgrimage 2000 286-287
    Retirement *216,* 291

Index of Names

Battley, Eleanor, Rev. (neé Nelson)
    Courting 25, 27, 31, *105*
    Marriage & Parents 31, 32, 35, *106*
    Pakuranga 90, 91, *107, 108*
    Life in the Spirit 94, 97, 101-102
    In worship 115, *106*
    1978 travel 140
    Papatoetoe 169
    Whanganui 183
    Canterbury '88 189
    ARMNZ ministry 195
    Singapore Congress 199
    ERM Evergreen 201
    Study Leave '95 248
    Archdeacons 281
    Ordination *216,* 287
    Tribute *216,* 289-290
Battley, Mark, Dr 31, 140, 180
Battley, Christopher 32, 140, 180
Battley, Philip, Dr 35, 140, 180
Batts, Derek 38, 92, 96, 98, 127, 134
Bay, Ross, Bishop 284, 290
Beale, Mark, Rev. 284
Beere, Lionel, Ven. 23, 24, 50
Bennett, Dennis, Rev. 37, 67, 150, 257
Boniface, Herbert, Ven. 43, 49, 57, 84, 131, 134, 136
Boyd-Bell, Harry, Rev. 31, *106*
Bridge, Martin, Rev. Dr 129, 172, 180, 203
Brokenshire, John, Rev. 93 (n8), 94, 129, 131, 136
Brokenshire, Sheila 94, 146
Brooker, Stephen, Rev. 156
Brown, Colin, Rev. 174

Buchanan, Colin, Bishop 177
Buck, Lee 203-204
Buckle, Ted, Bishop 35, 85, 140, 180
Burnett, Bill, Archbishop
    Mission Auckland 135-136
    Canterbury '78 142

Cameron, Manga, Canon 82, 84, 85
Carey, George, Archbishop 178, 186-187, 189
Charles, Austin, Canon 19, 21, 23
Cullen, Lloyd, Rev. 127

Dallaway, Joan, Rev. 93 (n7), 100, 122
Davidson, Paul, Rev. 178, 182
Davis, Brian, Archbishop
    McNutt Retreat 147
    Waikato ARM 177
    Episcopal Advisor 191, 192, 284
    AFFIRM 224
    John Spong 231
    Orthodoxy 273-274

Eaton, Derek, Bishop 75 (n24), 196, 205, 207, 273, 284

Foster, Raymond, Rev. Dr 28, 34, 52
Foulkes, Francis, Rev. 205, 207, 231, 233, 275
Fountain, Wyn 38-39, 41, 43, 94, 129, 134

Gerritsen, Tony, Canon 182
Gilberd, Bruce, Bishop 19, 21, 89, 90, *105*
Gilmour, Calum, Rev. Dr 286
Ginever, Geoff, Rev. 137

Index of Names

Glennon, Jim, Canon 56, 61
Gowing, Eric, Bishop 23, 43, 59
    Call to Renewal 48, 50
    On CR 84
    Bill Burnett Mission 135
Graham, Billy, Dr 21-22
Graham, Cecily 242, 262
Gravelle, Paul, Rev. 42, 79
Green, Michael & Rosemary 195, 201, 208, 251
Greenwood, Harry, Rev. 63, 81
Grundy, Roger and June 100
Guthrie, David, Rev. 51, 79

Hall, Keven, Rev. Dr 71, 83, 85
Hare, Trevor & Laurel 133
Harper, David, Rev. 28, 29, 74, *110,* 147, 159, 183
Harper, Michael, Canon 49, 50, 54, 67, 135, 140, 141, 142, 157, 160, 173, 177, 184, 198, 228, 264
Howarth, Susan & Graeme 282, 283

Irish, Chuck, Rev. 144, 174, 178

Jamieson, Penny, Bishop 163, 284
Jenkins, Brian Rev. & Trish 70, 80, 114, 129, 131, 164, 224, 242, 134, 136, 151, 159, 172, 192, 21, 248, 284

Karaka, Bert, Canon *213,* 265
King, Gordon, Rev. 30, 31
Kissell, Barry, Rev. 183, 186, 195, 251

Legge, Ron 192, 219
Lightbourne, Derek, Rev. 155

315

Lineham, Peter, Professor 11-12, 291, 304
Lloyd, Peter, CA & Lorraine, Rev. 129, 130, 203, 224, 235, 262

MacNutt, Francis, Rev. Fr 68, 146, 150
Maries, Andrew, musician 239
Marquet, John, Rev. 238, 284, 293, 295
Marriott, Wallace, Rev. 86, 162
Marsden, Maori, Rev. 62
Marshall Cecil, Rev. 46, 68, 71, 74, 137, 140, 157, 159, 192, 268
Martyn, Jean, administrator 172, 205, 239, 264
McGrath, Alister, Rev. Dr 230, 232, 251
McGregor, David, Rev. 56, 71, 182
Minns, John, Rev. 196
Moore, Bruce, Bishop 89, 284
Morton, John, Professor 83, 85, 205, 207
Moxon, David, Archbishop 190, 203, 235, 236, 238, 243, 284
Mullane, John, Rev. 48
Muller, Ray, Ven. Dr
    Visit of D Bennett 39, 46
    Palmerston North 41, 46, 67,
    Forms CAM 71, 143
    New Lynn 79
    General Synod Commission 86
    Tawa Conference 142, 145
    ARMNZ 173, 193, 205, *209*
    PIM 220-221
    Parish Ministry Consultant 191, 203
    Church Growth Resources 219, 258
    Archdeacon 284
    Alpha 258-259

Neil, Allen, Rev. 53 (n1), 57, 62, 73, 83, 86

Index of Names

Nelson, Mick 100
Norman, Edward, Bishop 173

Paterson, John, Bishop *216,* 280-281, 284, 288, 291
Pelly, Raymond, Canon Dr 157
Philip, Peter, Rev. 143, 157
Prebble, Kenneth, Ven. 37-43, 47, 49, 68, 69, 78, 84, 134, 143
Price, Alan, Capt. CA *210,* 242, 243, 261, 263
Pulkingham, Graham, Rev. 55, 56, 57, 77, 122
Pytches, David, Bishop 195, 251, 256-257

Read, David, Prof. 250, 267
Rees, David and Nicky CA 263
Reeves, Frank and Florence 90
Reeves, Paul, Archbishop
    Waiapu and Renewal 138, 147
    Renewal Consultations 148-154, 157-160, 163
Robertson, Murray, Rev. 46, 146
Robinson, Bob, Rev. Dr 224
Rutherford, Joan 93 (n7), 96 (n9), 100

Scott, Max, Rev. 262, 269, 284
Simkin, John, Bishop 18
Smith, Bill, Rev. 29, 31, 37, 42, 43, 46, 129
Smith, Harvey, Ven. 41, 46, 138, 284, 296
Spackman, Murray, Ven. 43, 62, 63, 128, 284
Spong, John, Bishop 229-231, 276
Stuart, Peter, Canon 147, 159, 161, 303
Stuart, Julia 235
Subramaniam, Edward, Ven. 69, 178, 189, 198
Subritszky, Bill and Pat 64-65, 70, 80, 85, 129, 131-132, 205, 207

Tamahori, John, Canon 157

Vaughan, Roger, Rev. 190, 203

Waldegrave, Charles, Rev. 74
Watson, David, Rev. 77, 142
Welch, Malcolm, Ven. 161, 192, 284
Williams, Kristin, Pastor *214,* 243, 262
Williamson, Dale, Rev. Dr 86, 151, 153, 156, 165, 284, 294
Williamson, Paul, Rev. 203, 221, 237, 282, 292, 293
Wilson, Godfrey, Bishop 148, 157, 163-165
Wimber, John, Pastor 183, 184, 186, 254-257, 296
Wright, Tom, Bishop 280

www.ingramcontent.com/pod-product-compliance
Lightning Source LLC
Chambersburg PA
CBHW071344290426
44108CB00014B/1433